THE COLLECTED POEMS

of

JOHN CIARDI

THE
COLLECTED
POEMS

of

JOHN
CIARDI

Compiled and
Edited by
Edward M. Cifelli

The University
of Arkansas Press

Fayetteville
—•—
1997

01   00   99   98   97   5   4   3   2   1

Designed by Liz Lester

⊗   The paper used in this publication meets the minimum requirements of the American National Standard for Permanence of Paper for Printed Library Materials Z39.48-1984.

Library of Congress Cataloging-in-Publication Data

Ciardi, John, 1916–
          [Poems]
          The collected poems of John Ciardi / compiled and edited by
     Edward M. Cifelli.
                    p.   cm.
          Includes index.
          ISBN 1-55728-449-0 (cloth : alk. paper). — ISBN 1-55728-450-4
     (pbk. : alk. paper)
          I. Cifelli, Edward M.   II. Title.
     PS3505.I27A17   1997
     811'.52—dc21   96-46331
                                                               CIP

To Judith

Some of the best people everywhere
Are waiting always
For less than happens
Every time you smile.

Acknowledgments

I would like to express my gratitude to a small band of students who gave me plenty to think about when I asked which poems they thought should be included in this book: Jennifer Anna, Kelly Backer, Cheryl Bergeron, Jeffrey Ciesla, Christopher Gervasi, Charlene Hennesey, Laura Howe, Ruth Otterburn, Keith Washington, and Patricia Wecht. Thanks again. You did a good job. Special thanks go to the famous Mrs. Quigley for an exceptional job of typing under pressure.

Permission to reprint poems from *For Instance* has been granted by W. W. Norton and Company, Inc.

Contents

from *Homeward to America* (1940)

from *New Poets* (1941)
Anthology with thirteen Ciardi poems.

from *Other Skies* (1947)

from *Live Another Day* (1949)

from *Mid-Century American Poets* (1950)
Anthology with eleven Ciardi poems.

from *From Time to Time* (1951)

from *As If: Poems New and Selected* (1955)

from *I Marry You* (1958)

from *39 Poems* (1959)

from *In the Stoneworks* (1961)

from *In Fact* (1962)

from *Person to Person* (1964)

from *This Strangest Everything* (1966)

from *An Alphabestiary* (1967)

from *A Genesis* (1967)
[a portfolio book of 15 previously published poems by John Ciardi and 15 original etchings by Gabor Peterdi]

from *Lives of X* (1971)

from *The Little That Is All* (1974)

from *For Instance* (1979)

from *The Birds of Pompeii* (1985)

from *Poems of Love and Marriage* (1988)
Posthumously published

from *Echoes* (1989)
Posthumously published

from *Stations of the Air* (1993)
Posthumously published

Foreword

Reprinted here are 450 poems by John Ciardi, over 62 percent of the verse that originally appeared in twenty individual volumes published between 1940 and 1993. To show Ciardi's rich variety of style, subject, and form, at least half of each earlier book appears in this new collection—with the exception of *Lives of X*, Ciardi's autobiography, which is represented here by four long verse chapters. Ciardi's children's poems are not included in this book because it has seemed unwise as well as unconventional to mix what Ciardi liked to call his "juvenile" poems with his "senile" ones. One might note in passing, however, that Ciardi wrote some of his best poems for children and that although one collection of his fifteen books of children's poetry has already been published (*Blabberhead, Bobble-Bud & Spade*, Middlesex County [New Jersey] Cultural and Heritage Commission, 1988), a much more inclusive one is needed.

For those wishing to read the entire *Lives of X* (thirteen sections), it is available in Ciardi's *Selected Poems* (University of Arkansas Press, 1984), which remains a useful book of 136 poems arranged by Ciardi himself according to subject. *The Collected Poems of John Ciardi* is different from *Selected* in two important ways. First, it is much more generous in its sampling of Ciardi poems; and second, by virtue of its chronological organization it will be more helpful to general readers as well as literary historians and critics who try to trace Ciardi's art over the decades. Only the complete poems, a book not currently being considered for publication, will be more valuable as a way of gauging Ciardi's contribution to mid-twentieth-century American poetry.

Old Ciardi hands will know what to expect in these poems, but for the benefit of new readers, a few observations may be helpful. For example, expect extraordinary range, not just in subject but in technique and tone as well. Be prepared for Ciardi's sometimes painful honesty, his unflinching gaze into the real world and its people. Listen for the tenderness he was capable of as well as his characteristic sense of irony and the sharp wit that could descend into sarcasm and occasional coarseness. Notice the full range of his emotions and how deftly he avoids the sentimental and all poetic affectations and pretensions. (He refused to prettify poems because, as he liked to say, "The pretty is never the beautiful.") Watch for the many technical masterpieces that appear throughout this book, for Ciardi could be a virtuoso performer working within tight structures whenever he was so inclined. Be prepared for Ciardi's struggle with what he saw as the impossibility of a traditional belief in God—and his courageous exploration of all the earthbound human possibilities that are left. Look for a world populated by characters who are weak because they are human, which is the very same reason, he tells us again and again, they deserve mercy and forgiveness. Observe the movement of subjects, too, from the big ideas on war and peace and man's inhumanity to the commonplace thoughts about everyday life that produced what Ciardi came to call the Unimportant Poem. And don't miss the happy marriage of language and dance that characterizes so much of his work.

In the end, it is good to be in John Ciardi's company as he writes his way in verse through a lifetime of careful observation. And it is good to be with him as he manages the poet's craft, 450 acts of language that show not only *what* one of the better poets of our age was wrangling with in his poems, but *how*.

Edward M. Cifelli
County College of Morris
Randolph, NJ

Introduction
by John Ciardi

Every good poet writes one poem more than his index shows and that is the total poem of all the others put together. In the total poem, every enduring poet leaves not only his words, his images, his rhythms, and his forms but a voice that speaks him as an individual, his personality. That personality, however, is a created thing. It is not in the life of the man, it is nowhere but in his poems.

> —John Ciardi,
> *Saturday Review,*
> 5 January 1963

Poetry and Personal Definitions*

Poets are forever being given odd introspective assignments. Sir Philip Sidney's command to his confused spirit was simply, "Look in thy heart and write." Today the new exhortation seems to be from the critic and it is more likely to read, "Look into your psyche and explain yourself." It has become an article of the True Faith that the introspection of poets will finally reveal a mystery called The Creative Source.

I have myself toiled in that abbey. In 1950 I published an anthology titled *Mid-Century American Poets,* a collection designed to introduce the work of fifteen poets of the Forties, and as the editor-abbot I spent months in exhorting the poets to prayer and meditation that each might produce a prose "Statement of Intent" as a preface to his poems.

Now William Martz of Ripon College, a good man and a gentle abbot, is preparing an anthology to be called *The Distinctive Voice* and he is after me, in some sort of return justice, to introduce (or to introspeculate) on "the poetic voice." He says: "I am including in the head notes for each poet his comment (if he'll give it to me, which most have done or promised) on what he thinks, as of 1965, the voice of the poet is, or what he aims to be as a poetic voice. The accent is on personal definition."

As it happens, I like vague personal questions and pray only that no man will ask precise ones about my character. Within that character, whatever it is, and with the accent on personal definition, I do have some strong feelings about the nature of the poetic voice, and I think my feelings run counter to what most teachers are telling the young, and what most poets are practicing.

It was, I believe, Andre Malraux in, I believe, *Museum Without Walls,* who observed that Van Gogh had carried personal style to the point at which he could paint (as he did) a simple chair with such individuality that he made of it as much a signature as an object represented. I am moved to generalize further that one mark of every artist we call "modern" may be found in his impulse to achieve not "style" but "a style." By "style" I mean the way the medium is used to forward what used to be called "the subject" and is now generally called "the esthetic experience." By "a style" I mean the way the medium is used to forward the author's individuality. Nor need it be understood that one of these impulses can exist in a work of art without the other: I am after a matter of emphasis. "Style" is, at root, representational (whether of outward appearances or of inner response-to), whereas "a style" is signatory.

So in poetry with "voice" and "a voice." Many contemporary poets, it seems to me, are a bit drunken in their compulsion to emphasize the signatory way of writing, and even a number of good poets are self-limited by that compulsion. Robert Lowell, for example, is a good poet. Yet any given line of his is more likely to sound like Robert Lowell speaking than like a line reaching out to the nature of the thing spoken. Consider the following:

A brackish reach of shoal off Madaket—
Here the jack hammer jabs into the ocean
Bringing the landed promise and the faith
Once more where braced pig iron dragons grip
And crush the crab these Quaker sailors lost.

The lines are Lowell's but only as a pastiche from five different poems jammed together by a few syntactical violences intended to give the passage a spurious unity. A dirty trick, and for it I owe Lowell an apology and offer it honestly. I mean no malice. I mean only to show that such a pastiche has, in addition to the spurious unity I have imposed upon it, the true unity of "a voice," the lines being always signatory to themselves.

Such a signatory voice is not necessarily bad and every good writer will inevitably identify himself by using some of his own habituated tonalities. Yet is it worth asking if contemporary taste has not gone too far in enshrining "a voice" at the expense of "voice." For when the impulse is first to achieve a unique way of speaking and then to find the world, the danger is that not enough world will be found.

For myself, and even at the risk of not believing everything I say, I still dream that "style" is potentially a better instrument than "a style." Since I am invited to personal definition, let me confess that I do not know enough about who I am to settle for "a style." Or perhaps I am merely formless and want them all—one for bird, one for bee, and one for Hell and the roaring sea. Let me dream that a willing reader might perhaps cull from the sum of my failures a few poems, each in its own voice, and with no two voices co-signatory, but with each formed to the subject-experience rather than to one habituated way of speaking.

I am dreaming, that is, of an act of language so entirely responsive to the poetic experience that my habituated way of speaking will be shattered and leave only the essential language called into being by the esthetic experience itself. The dream is, finally, that the poem may seem to declare not "X spoke these words" but rather "man spoke these words of himself."

Impossible? Probably so. Yet small steps may go toward unreach-able distance. My dream will in any case identify my pleasure in some observations made by William Dickey in reviewing my *Person to Person* in *The Hudson Review*, Winter 1964–65:

> The quality that I find most notable in Mr. Ciardi is that of observation: he sees things with an intensity and accuracy that no conventional language can wholly contain. The effect of a convention is to smooth out the differences between things; it expects, having established a form of language, that all objects will be equally amenable to its ministrations. But Mr. Ciardi's objects break these bounds; his sight is defined by the object itself, and he accepts and uses the object's own recalcitrance toward language that will soften it. "Hunchback bees in pirate pants," for example, is a phrase wholly determined by what its object looks like, rather than by a kind of language that is felt to be appropriate to the discussion of objects in general. Mr. Ciardi is often sententious or sentimental in his attitude toward things he discusses, but these attitudes never prevent him from seeing what is before him. This ability to see is neither easy nor usual, and it represents one of the most important ways in which the floating world of poetic language can be given a per-sistent human relevance, a persistent reference back to the solidities of existence.

Since the passage, in isolation, sounds highly laudatory, and since I am after definition rather than self-advertisement, let me underline Mr. Dickey's notes on my faults (which the reader can see for himself) and let me point out (as the reader cannot see for himself) that Mr. Dickey was writing a round-up review and that he moved from my book to others he liked better. I was not the star of his show, but I shall settle happily if the ideas he identifies can be so taken. As Archibald MacLeish might have said, though he didn't, "A poem should not say but be."

*Originally published in *Saturday Review*, 9 October 1965.

Homeward
to America

⁓•⁓

(1940)

Letter to Mother

It was good. You found your America. It was worth all
The coming: the fading figures in the never-again doorway,
The rankness of steerage, the landing in fog.
Yes, and the tenement, the reek and the shouting in the streets
All that night and the terror. It was good, it was all good.
It is important only that you came.

And it is good to remember that this blood, in another body,
    your body, arrived.
There is dynastic example in a single generation of this blood,
    and the example good,
But, Mother, I can promise you nothing.

This traveling is across the sprung longitudes of the mind
And the blood's latitudes. I have made a sextant of heart
And nailed my bearings to sun, but from the look-out
There is no hailing yet of the hoped-for land.
Only the enormous, wheeling, imperative sea,
And the high example of this earlier coming—

But there will be no Americas discovered by analogy.

The Foolish Wing

Is done now with bright thinness of upper air. Weight
Of body sinks earthward: good capture. Probing of wing's
Torn muscle under the raised and eager feathers
Points obvious and necessary truth. Time grows too late
For the torn ligament to attempt heaven. There is
Nothing either in rememberings.

Through thin and remote heavens the broken arc
Turned earthward at point of rupture. It was past peak

Of the far height the wing failed. Clearly
As pomade of sun on flashing porpoise, mark
The inevitable. We have invented nothing: when we speak
It is Time's journalism only: we are reporting merely.

Winter Music

November and trees blown bare and leaves stippling
The autumn-stripping wind and trees futilely fingering
Lee-wind after down-streaming foliage . . .

The bright birds are gone and their small and excellent music,
Their nests unleafed and visible to ridicule of sparrows and pigeons. . . .

Now turn. From no feathered throat shall be this winter's music.
Nor from memories of music in deserted nests.
Now turn to wind's cry in the bent trees and the granite gaps,
And in the city clattering the billboards together,
And furious between houses flinging the snow against frosted windows.

Turn here to this extravagance for voice and music.
Open imagination to the clash of gigantic air.
For wisdom, there is the sunlight falling unbent across such fury.

To Westward

Westward I had expected reminders: somewhere in the Dakotas' carpet
A milestone, by the cottonwoods a cross
Marking trail's-end below the obscuring grasses,
Pointing the miles of added footprints. Facing West.

And names would be remembered: Bloody River, Denver, Utah, Dry Gulch—
Salty on the tongue like your own sweat at the woodpile.
And names of men: Clarke, Custer, Pike, Johnny Appleseed—
The imagined faces color of dark blood from sun, the eyes important.

Day after day of parched earth was the answer, barnyards heaped high
With rusted iron, and wherever two routes met, a town
Rotting in the sun. Or a city: one green street north of the tracks,
The rest slum and gray factory. A bit of grass also by the City Hall.

The names read: Eureka Dishpan Inc., Carbonula, Hi-Jinx Novelty Co.
Many lumber mills, smelteries, much soot. On the streets
Gray-muscled men loitering. Drifting into clusters and breaking apart—
Routine as a minuet, only unrhythmical—nothing to say, waiting.

Fascinated by the boarded windows, the padlock on the door.
The limousine bearing the boss away to Europe or Hawaii
Or Palm Beach. Clarke, Custer, Pike, Johnny Appleseed
Loitering against the wall, kicking their heels, slow beat.

Caught voices were western: half burr, half drawl, the r's prominent.
Blue haze sun headed for was the Rockies, barely visible.
Drone above was the air-mail roaring to the Pacific,
Flying high, almost there—six hours, four maybe—west over continent.

Sun, distance, mountain line, voices: burr and drawl—
These were as imagined. What broke the mind
Like the interrupted poem was lost direction:
Men going nowhere, hands pocketed, heels kicking the wall.

Night Freight, Michigan

Punctual to the midnight—lurch, ruck and chime—
The fast freight breaks from the night and under
The sooted bridges stamps earth and away east. . . .

Windows rattle in their putty and the house shakes
And across the trembling of the dollar alarm clock on the dresser,
Heart, with the certainty of resolved analogy, discovers
The quivering of secret elm root about rock,
The trembling of river bank and the shuttering lip of water,
And on the hillside the running and sifting down of soil
Through dark and silent mazes of hay stubble.

Earth, indigenous engine, robot to all physic,
Answers to all force and it is good.
Great meter of the footfalls of men and the tug of stars,
Calibrating, in the shifting of an elm's clutch on sunken boulder,
The shaking of putty in the pane and river from bank, the settling
Of Time across the dial and soil on the hills;
The passage of one trainload of tires, refrigerators, and hobos
From Kalamazoo to the Junction.

Letter for Those
Who Grew Up Together

Who remembers now the backyards of our innocence
And the ready pretense? The long afternoons
At Cowboys and Indians when a cocked thumb
Was a six-gun for slaughter and many Indians died?

It is far off now and no one tramples the crocuses
Galloping round the house to scout the enemy.
The ruin of beauty by our violent illusions
Was the first discovery. Later

We turned to plays in the damp cellar and stabbed Caesar—
More with our jagged memorizations than the rubber daggers—
And we settled who should recite "Friends, Romans, countrymen"
By all shouting it out together, thrilled by our own noise.

And later there were girls that we kissed by the riverbank.
Stretched in the tall grasses we watched the stars—
Too innocent for more—and talked in murmurs
Of great plans. And watched the stars. And pretended.

Over the first cigarettes we played at cynics,
Warmed by new-discovery of the world's obvious pretense,
And made dramas of our scorn, not guessing
It was only one more act in the plot of our innocence.

And where you are now, into what cities you disappeared
In moving vans and with suitcases, or you who remained—
Polite faces met on the visits home,
Asking the usual questions, betraying nothing—how is it now?

Are we free yet of the empty gesture, the dramas
Between the houses, the cocked thumb?
Number is everything in the serious maneuver.
Are we ready yet? Is the pretense ended? May we advance now?

Letter Homeward

Noon breaks to thunder and the iron hawk
Flings from the earth eastward into wind
And upward, circles once, and is gone
Over the tiny lakes and the rutted valleys
And high over the Hudson churning
The loosened pastures of cloud under
The triumphant propeller, hurdling the Blue Hills under,
Gliding down the Mohawk, and at last above the sea
For the final swoop over whitecaps to the known field. . . .

Through the taken sky the three-mile-a-minute miracle
Shatters all high dreams of poets past
Bearing the simple letter to your hand,
Saying: Nothing has changed. It has been many days
And a great distance but here it narrows.
I wait impatiently my turn across these clouds.

To a Young American
the Day after the Fall of Barcelona

Boy with honor in your heart,
The world is not the world you dream:
Recall the history of the Jews,
Hate screaming in the *Evening News,*
Eyes that beg, eyes that refuse,
Eyes that watch and scheme.

You, who fed on the pure stream
Of Aeschylean fire, have seen
Oedipus blinded, and the sun
Gleaming on Promethean spleen,
And learned to love the tragic day,
Burn your books and come away.

Throw away your little coin
Of childhood, boy, go down, go down
With whetted wits and treachery
And all resource of infamy
Against the enemy known.

Or cling to your bright innocence.
Reduce love to a virginal
Small passion pure beyond all use,
Or to a dream of Grecian sun,
And leave your world to be undone.

Biography

He will not answer now. He will go down
The middle highway through the heart of town
And will not answer when the children call
And the girls, and the dried old women, the men, and all
Who come out doors to sit on the curb toward night
And hope for one last breeze to set right—
Somehow—the day's heat. He will not answer now,
Will not turn to the pavement. He will go
Mid-road between the tenements and down
To the suburban end of time and town,
And through the fields, fade in the final wood,
And not come back. And too well understood,
Parries necessity with a muttered "Later—"

But will not answer now and will not answer.

To One "Investigated" by the
Last Senate Committee, or the Next

And though the walls have ears
and spies are on the street,
 (the shadow that disappears
 when you turn about on the stair,
 but one corner of the eye
 knowing the treachery there . . .)

Shall you for any fear
gag in heart's quickened beat
in danger and become discreet—
the liar's euphemism—and retreat?

Rather hire harlots in your house
and turn procurer
to the lesser passions
of any man with a dollar.
No, keep your honor clean:
run to the sea
and wash your fear in waves:
be murdered whole
if courage fails you
to see honor through.

Or now the net is out
and the thug waits,
be steel against his spring, be stout.
No blade of ignorance may find you out,
nor any lurking thing but fear within
work a disaster near enough to the heart
to make a craven safety
count for honor's part.

Reply to S. K.

Yes, Barcelona is three thousand miles
From where I write and I have not been there
To count the swollen dead and the jagged aisles
Cut by machine guns in the grain. Here
No motors brawl their anger overhead.
I have not seen the roof split to reveal,
For that one moment when the quick and dead
Are congruent, the bomb's bright cap of steel.

All I remember is the newspaper maps,
Boundaries estimated, casualties estimated, thunder
Of headlines fading away to lower caps—
Print, erroneous and glib. Or from under
The blue-buzzing tube the voice of the announcer,
Modulated, distant, saying: *It is done.*
Careful syllables reciting danger
In a lost land.

                    At home there was sun—
Unmenaced bright high noon. The starlings fought
Small skirmishes with sparrows in the oak.
Robins bobbed on the lawn. I caught
A cardinal's whistle and spied him out in the crook
Of the lowest branch, bright red against the green.
The young nephews tumbling on the grass
Came racing out to meet me with a scream
And beg a pick-back ride into the house.

Inside, the world went well: mother had lunch
Spread on the broad white table, in my room
The books were warm bright colors, and a bunch
Of some new-cut and fragrant unknown bloom

From mother's garden-puttering stood in water.
Letters arrived and welcome from far friends
Made diagrams of white on the desk blotter.
Inside the world went well, but there it ends.

Outside the house and off beyond that noon
Spain sent disaster smoking toward the sun
Or took disaster downward in the flown
Bombs shaped like tears that glisten as they come.
Or was it night in Spain? Or could there be
Day again on such ruin? Dared the light
To show . . . But the hyperbole is a lie:
Assuredly and indifferently there would be light.

The ingenuity of physical day
Would even contrive some beauty from the wreck:
A neat spiral of smoke, a rainbow gay
With spring, a bit of shadow work
On a ruined wall, or some one tower
Of all that would not take its bomb and fall—
A silhouette of some what-is-it power
Stones have and men?—You cannot break them all.

But O once let indifference close the will
Into the swivel chair and make the desk,
The immediate papers, the day's work, terminal
To the heart—nothing may save us from the wreck
Of stone and stake and every human wish.
Not one word on another shall survive
To teach the improbable sons what and how much
We meant of honor when we walked alive.

Beauty? What is it? By the river bank
Our younger bodies dreamed among the grass
Or by the back fence or the schoolyard oak
Of bright exorbitant perils we might pass
To win—to win—what? The romance is dead,

Childhood gone under. Time is the offense:
What work we do against the shriveling head
Of years is done in self-defense.

What are we sure of but the stated purpose,
The hope to make it real and the long fear
That time may stamp it VOID, and close
A canceled journal for our meaning here?
Will it be right? Will words count what we meant
In simple prose of sense marked black and sure
Across the scattering fact of incident
Chaotic as blown papers on the floor?

Seal windows tight and see your doors are shut—
No wind will scatter what you learned to say,
And what you dreamed and with long labor wrote
To mark the depth of night, the breadth of day.
You will be safe. But past your shaded light
The stars are deeper than you know, the sun
More violent than you dreamed, and day and night
Crossed wide with danger where the armed men run.

Oedipus Tyrannus

For my teachers

Catharsis builds across the dreadful air
From rostrum to the door. Pity and fear
Swell with adrenalin of imagination
Into the blood. Almost, the hesitation
Breaks in heroic furies. Almost freed,
Passion recoils across the thing unsaid.

Heroics are anyway incongruous
With conservative tweeds. Togas are far more imperious,
And the homeward trolley inevitably disenchanting.
But tell us, because the fear is haunting
That if we miscount we are lost. Tell us because
We hung upon your words—when was it?—once
Before the day was split by the broken faces
And eyes that burned holes through the classic theses.

Tell us by what loophole the characters
Of the mob scene are permitted access
To the stage. Construct for us the philosophy
Of the supernumerary. By what mercy
They have the wings to stare from while the sun
Is turned—exclusive spotlight—on the high tragedian.

Cathedral

One by one the bells have broken their music,
The steeples fall, the leaden roofs bend in.
The rain beats through the vaulting raising puddles
About the feet of Mary Magdalen.

One by one the words have passed to silence.
The dead are incurably dead: look, there ghosts appear.
Silence and the rain beat down together.
One more death awaits the doing here:

The ghosts to lay and the unraveled bones
To straighten in their sepulchres before
One by one the silences yield music
And sun beats down beyond the broken door.

Boy or Girl

White rows of suburbs alternate with trees
Below the summer night. The boy and girl
Endlessly repeated in every shadow
Have seen the windows darken one by one
And stir toward their good-nights: the final cigarette
Arcs brightly outward, doors creak,
Heels fade along the walk, and lights come on
Higher between the shadows of the trees.

What fills your mind, alone in the quiet room
That spills its light into the friendly trees
While sleep grows on the house?
What moon-stirred sweet tooth hungers into pulse
Or jars with memory and will not rest?—

Turn off your light and take the nighttime in.

Elaine

Elaine, the counter-girl from the hat department,
Flaxen and fair as any Lancelot met,
Ends the day's work, returns to the apartment
She shares with the dark lady of a single sonnet
Reciting itself forever in the head
Of the shy clerk—a less heroic Hamlet
Weighing "To ask or not to ask."

Elaine awaits the evening. One by one
The dreams of all that must be done
Emerge across the dresser, while last sun
Shimmers an ancient gold into the curtain,
And loudly purple clouds prepare a scene:
Fabulous landscapes wait the riding in
Of Lancelot
             who will appear in armor
Bright as a gilt cupola, or better—
That they may dance more readily—in silks.

Cloths of gold and jewelled slippers
Make embroidery of young imagination.
Elaine awaits before the mirror.
The clock strikes from the railroad station.

The bell rings. The lady of the one sonnet
Greets Prince Hamlet
And with last sunset
They go down to supper on a loud exit.

    Leaving Elaine alone with Lancelot.
    For whether he come or whether not,
    The cloths of gold are not torn,
    Nor the toes of the silver slippers worn.

Spring Song [I]

Wake early to the early robin,
And pack the picnic basket, and quick
Say to the boy in the next house
Or the next or to the first presentable boy wherever
"Come," and in the field behind the airdrome
Where the silver hawks glint in the sun
Reckon for the almost last time
Or perhaps the last, how spring works.

For the seasons of innocence are numbered
And vegetable roots shall grow carnivorous on the blood
Of the boy in the next house and the next
And of the least of the least presentable boys wherever,
And the trusting robins fall gassed to the lawns
In the torn season.

         Wake,
Wake early to the early robin
And rise laughing to the window before
It breaks inward shattering at your bare feet
The unavoidable barbs.
                And hurry, hurry, girl,
It is spring.

Spring Song [II]

Do you remember by morning when the sun
Pries open the private lids of your eyes in sleep
And you wake and it is day and even perhaps a robin
Hops on the telephone wires and you keep
Deep in your heart the silent amazement that it is spring
And how last night you walked in the river valley
Under the sprouting trees and said "I love you" or some such thing
To the girl who did not believe it but was happy
Nonetheless to hear it said, and accepted . . .

                             Do you remember
How your thought insisted: this is good fighting country:
From the top of that pine a sniper
Might clean the hilltops, and where we lie
A machine gun would bottle the pass, and a patrol
By the river . . .

                 And suddenly how you asked: "Did you
                       believe me? What I said?"
And how she smiled "No" and climbed the knoll
Where sandbags might be placed and a trench furrowed.
And said no more, but the wind was marching men
And tugged her hair as it passed to a yellow wing,
And you cursed yourself for a fool, and then
Thunder's artillery named the name of this spring.

New Poets

—·—

(1941)

George Washington Bridge

The buttresses of morning lift the sun
Across an arc of steel and flying piers.
The twin cadenzas of the cables run
Like landless gulls across the hemispheres.

Out of a step of mist the caisson root
Spires from the consonant rock to the vowel of sky,
The highway rings the morning underfoot
Scoring the traffic for a symphony.

And arc and piers and highway soar from steel
Into a swinging web of flying sound.
A gull's geometry, a flashing keel,
A flowering ceremony of the ground.

The men who climbed like birds to trap that wire,
Like birds were born to know what song and flight meant:
The tempo of an arc, curve of a choir,
The eye's adagio and the blood's excitement.

Time Is the Late Train into Albany

Time is the late train into Albany
Keokuk, Wichita, Mobile.

The drummer in the pullman
Is progress on the wheel.

The ash-blonde in the day coach
Looks up each time you pass.

The dining car is blazing
In silver plated brass.

And hours due everywhere,
Days, years back to climb.

Distance multiplied by need
Of being there is time.

Time is lights and places with no names
Flashing from dark spaces.

Time is the blonde will have a pullman soon
To get down to cases.

Spring in Statue Square

Spring is open windows and Molly Picardo
Laughing across the wash to Mrs. Fink.
And Margie O'Ryan leaning on the fire-escape
Vacant and wondering.

Spring is forty-seven kids unrolling
On a square of concrete and sixteen feet of grass
Between the statue and the wooden benches
And the iron fence, alas.

Spring is people loitering on the sidewalk
Slowed down for something none of them will catch.
And the girls giggling all the more.
And the boys needing to stretch.

Elegy: For You, Father

Father, under the stone, accept your ruin.
Seconded by no fashionables of Heaven
Nor harridans of Hell, undo your flesh
And leave your skeleton to drought. Given
Such piercing illustration how the myth
Works in the literal earth this long dark morning,
Fold your hard hands upon the stony desk
O model patient scholar, but unlearning.

Forgive it, Father, if your remembered counsel
Finds the hard earth upon it in denial.
Your words that aimed at Heaven came apart
Unflying, and rock is palpable
Upon your tongue. Take honor to your bones,
Contrive to understand the echoing word
That would cry down to you but cannot reach.
Father, we break the cross for simple wood.

O white enduring skull believe
We loved you well. Our ritual difference
Is all in how the sky was drained of actors
After the telescopes cracked firmaments
Into a clumsy scattering of fireballs
Colliding in the dark for no known reason.
Apocalypse broke downward from that solstice
And left us nothing toward another season.

Now we have need of even dead men's blessings.
Out of the rock we will not yet explore
Offer the truth of dark to keep us whole.
Father, deliver us one ruin more
From all your ruined stuff: heave back the clay
Until the white bones break—a drastic birth—
Into the light, that even fools may see
The end of heaven and the need of Earth.

Elegy for the Face at Your Elbow

You know and I know what breeds in the dark
And under it, under it, Buffalo Bill
Is stalking (remember?) and up the will
The redskins charge and the rifles bark.

A thousand warwhoops of mixed memory
Yell for that real skirmish. How they run!
As you ran once, thigh-slapping from the nickelodeon,
Yippee—O, after the show, glittering with bravery.

Well, never mind. Does it matter who sees
How the lush strip-teaser from the Burly-Q
Is making eyes—and it rankles—not at you?
Call the fat bartender down and drink a million whiskies.

Oh it used to be when Buffalo Bill
And wild Comanches fired face to face
That you were young and died with the grace
Of an arrow gliding over a hill.

And it used to be you ran like wonder
Forking a pinto that shook the trail,
And you shot like God and never turned tail
And you shook the doors of Hell with your thunder.

It used to be, but used to be is far and far to find,
And the Burly-Q Queen in flesh and green
Is smiling away and you've seen, you've seen,
And nothing you do or dare or drink will break it out of your mind.

Other Skies

—·—

(1947)

Ode for School Convocation

Mechanically, the academic file
Winds to the platform spreading doctoral hoods
And tassels toward the moderate breeze.
The rows and rows of parents on the lawn
Are starched and honorable with ceremony.
Even the students are serious and hushed
While the hymn flourishes from the electric organ.
And then the final doctor finds his chair.
And then the final stop. The President
Welcomes, remembers, hopes, somewhat despairs—
The world being stranger than it was—finally
Declares determination and a firm belief.
Starched and honorable with ceremony.
The rows and rows of parents on the lawn
Welcome determination and a firm belief,
Shift more securely in the moderate breeze.
Even the students are serious and deep
With historic intentions in the moderate breeze.

Now are the years again. Suddenly all the years
Of intention. These faces rapt with occasion
Stir unanimously serious. Surely a glance can tell
The President's reticent rationed dodging,
The paraded faculty's slight foolishness,
The parents' bluff at understanding, the boys' real bewilderment.
Still their faces stir with intention. The wish
Crosses confused under them, but the wish is real.
As Emerson lifts in quotes above the platform
And dies of distortion halfway to the gate.

Where the real wish died, conforming to its shadow
Under the glare of phosphor towers by day
And neon signs by night. A world's trade.
Discussed more tangibly in hotel rooms

By traveling salesmen. Attempted none the less
By the concluding President and the warm applause.

Between the pliant hedges at the public tea,
The faculty meets the parents, bows,
Suggests the frosted cakes, and prefers lemon.

On Sending Home My Civilian Clothes

Good duds, good-bye. Before I shut
The last lid that will shut you out,
Look back, inanimate, serene,
Tie, shirt, scarf, gloves, and gabardine.
Weathers that never touched my skin
Came down on you, my next of kin.
And though your seat and elbows shone
The glint was mine and mine alone.

Here to mothballs I consign
My civil colors, fit, and line.
By a change of place and Law
I am the stalker whose name is Claw.
In olive drab and three-pound shoes
I trample down the hills of Choose.
And all the transformation done,
My map is Do, my hand, a gun.

Good-bye. Where every sun that rises
Calls us up in new disguises,
I have clamped badges to my coat
And hung a number round my throat
And set an engine on my will
To measure, pity, stalk, and kill.

Already foreign as I guess
The postage to a lost address.

Camptown

The streets that slept all afternoon in sun
Waken in neon. Now the busses run
In brightest bug eyes from the darkening camp,
Sway on the local traffic, stamp
Frantic brakes heart-inches from collision,
Bumble a new start, and by long revision
Kiss the stone curbs on which the doors are thrown
Wide, wider—and a drumbeat stirs the town.

Yellow skirt girl will you kiss me tonight
From the river farm to the marquee light,
The mail order catalogue home on the shelf
Modeling the dream of your dreamy self?
Red blouse girl on the spinning year,
Blue hat, bright hat, here, here, here,
The kiss of your pose across your fright
And the kiss of the wish we wish tonight.

Whirling on the sidewalk, eddying the street,
Damned where the juke box tom-toms beat.
Yellow skirt girl the dust I've seen,
Red blouse girl the days between
Breast and breast of a night in town,
The bugles' tears and the lights turned down,
And the talk of you, the talk of you,
The silence and the center of the tents —of you.

Yellow skirt, red blouse, blue hat, bright,
Quilt the covers of your heart tonight.
Swallow me down the music's beat,
Follow my heart and follow my feet.
Follow my days to the weeks between

Where the land is the dust of a hot machine.
Follow where the drums and the brasses run down
For the same dream brought us both to town.

Over the river and the running ranges,
Over the moon—While the record changes:
Last minute boogie, now, now, now,
In the park, in the doorway, no matter how—
Follow, follow, till the neons drop,
One by one the flash-signs stop,
One by one it's over and done—
And we're late and lost unless we run.

Night Piece for
My Twenty-seventh Birthday

Punctually now, by all we learned at school,
The stars fade down the angles of their rank.
First Venus, then Orion. Rule by rule
The book performs. Law, like a marble bank,
Locks to gleaming tumblers, perfect doors,
The sweep of polished pillars and tile floors.

See, it is so: Astronomer, Man of Law,
Priest, Radio Announcer—all who Know
Have prophesied. And all forecasters saw
The omen that was neither rain nor snow
But a precise arrangement of the spheres
Hung in the sky to label all our years.

Now every night beneath this placid moon
I am assured the ordering of a fact:
The Western sky falls first and always soon
The East calls up in light for men to act.
And always between morning and the door
The Law is written on the barracks floor.

What was the omen that the wise men saw?
The dentist, doctor, and chiropodist?
The technical advisor, the man of straw
Who dressed in wax, a side-show specialist,
And in the dim light of the traveling show
Passed for a medicine man by saying so?

Under the taut and tabulated stars
I stand in barracks shadow like a pool
Apprenticed to a sextant and the wars
Where even murder must be learned at school,
And sky, a shadow to be memorized,
Charts the shadows we had not surmised.

This is my night piece to the placid moon,
Memory, omens, and the Men of Law.
By clock and stars the ritual is soon:
The hour ends on the tiniest chime of awe
And time begins another number here
Punctual to the midnight of the year.

I hear the sounds of sleepers in the dark,
Their uniforms in order for the dawn
On shadowy chairs. Now let one sudden spark
Of daylight in, and see, before the man
Stirs back to flesh the clothes have leaped and gone
Row after row. Should I explore this omen?

There was a shining runner who approached
Bright as a star and armored for delight.
He is not lying dead, his armor breached,
Nor racing on the wind as once he might,
He pauses at the lintel of no mood
Carved to a star's computed altitude.

And all the rest is Law. Beneath what trees
The stars may drop him, or upon what cloud
He will return, there are no proofs but these:
Law will not walk the streets to cry aloud
Its future. Law may murder good.
Law is the last Law to be understood.

Poem for a Soldier's Girl

Whatever your mirrors tell you, morning and evening
Are farther always than your wish for them.
Light years to the nearest star, the atoms of lightning,
A halo about the sun or moon foretelling storm—
These are not matters for reverie or a kiss.
States tremble when the dog star runs amiss.

Your life is labyrinths. Though cloud sky cry
Bird-pace, crow-call, sparrow, sparrow,
The days confuse you ineluctably
With chemical composites in your marrow,
And from the spawning molecules of your blood
Time rages to be understood.

Well then, you have his photos, the misspelled letters,
Promise of love, the school prom souvenirs,
The scrapbook with his clippings from the papers,
And a black headline stamped across your years
That is not football nor the school election,
But history's machine for vivisection.

While I, in an invented laboratory,
Sit in a sunny corner and prescribe
Shall we say nonsense or chronology?
No matter: what your mirrors will describe
When you have faced your wish sufficiently
Is not your image but your history.

Take-off over Kansas

At first the fences are racing under. Horses and men
Are different yet—we see the men look up.
Higher, whole rivers curl: the palmistry
Of the forgotten hills prescribing loop by loop
Whatever you would read in your own hand.
  At what altitude is this another land?

At random with the wind clouds touch and leave us,
Ripped by our passage, funneled back by speed.
Then fall away. And fields fall and become a pattern:
A plaid abstraction that no hand or spade
Touched ever in all the wilderness converted.
  At what altitude is the world deserted?

Precisely by altimeters the voice
Speaks on a wire and we ourselves convert.
By mask and tube we suck our lives from tanks.
And gloves that were our hands touch steel, assert
All of our fallacy that we were men
Before the engines left the world again.

What shall the guns think when a shadow spans
The digits of a sight, and triggers move?
Was any human part in the machine
That left its smoke to show which way it dove?
You only see the first plume and first fall.
You think, "It was not human after all."

Once past the sight of faces, where they fade
Immeasurably back to field and seed,
Only arithmetic and scattered cloud
Stay whole above the thundering of speed.
And someone's voice crackling the interphone,
That later you remember was your own.

Goodmorning with Light

To Tom and Helen Ferril

Civilian for a pause of hours
With books and rooms and window flowers,
My uniform across a chair
And the alarm clock pointing there
To unalarmed and perfect noon
Served up in bed (if ending soon,
Held perfectly, colored like sleep,
And shadowless though moving deep).

Like sleep, moved on a fluent fact
Too deep to need the static act
Of reason and the reasoned rise
Of commas and geometries—
Wakening delights a single thought:
The sun is up and I am not.

Goodmorning, then, with light prepared
Almost a day ago. Light shared
By half the world before it made
This last turn through the window shade,
And, after half a world, involved
John Ciardi in the thing revolved.

Goodmorning till another day
When morning comes another way
And tooled and tallied past all thought
I am up and the sun is not.
Switches thrown and levers dressed

Precisely right, and buttons pressed,
Motors checked and energized,

And then the hangar door surprised—
As if a laminated shim
Took on the aura of a whim,
Or engines begged to be released
And like Moslems face the East—

Machines and morning fixed upon
The starting spectrum of the dawn.

Reverie during Briefing

The simplest memory is books by ferny windows:
When you looked up any one at all might be passing,
And most you knew. The bodies had faces.
You would see them again tomorrow again rehearsing
The same distance from bus line to front doors at the same time.
None of it was important. You could count the lives going
From eight to five and returning wasted, and they died when it came time.

Some earlier or later, but there was always logic on the wreath.
The doors had been waiting always for their blooms,
Swinging and swinging shut by hours of the clock
On the dustless, fussy, changeless, unlivable rooms
Where the rented folding chairs were always last
To sit upon a memory like a pew
While the gilded frames on the walls leaned from the past.

Old Mr. Corwin's derby died that way:
There, after all the Sundays of my life,
It sat on the rack and the solemn neighborhood
Went by on tiptoe. Shiny as a knife,
It skulled how many years from sky to sky
To sit upon the hall rack at the end
And watch the solemn neighbors wait to die?

The simplest memory is at last their faces,
Where day by day they went repeating their years,
Past hedges and cushioned rockers on the porches
To dry themselves on someone's final tears.
Something had been forgotten in the public statues,
The guns were made of stone, and the tears were red.
Their eyes were kind and remembered. They died of their virtues,
And did not know the world they left was dead.

Death of a Bomber

We saw the smoke. The blue skull of the sky
Scarred on the black trail of the running fire.
The world came out of doors and every eye
Turned on the afternoon, while higher and higher
The sirens mounted and the watchers' breath
Drew in and waited to be first with death.

It was choice: to parachute or ride.
It was a race: fire against altitude.
He chose to land. Which way would fire decide,
Lapping the tanks, racing to be renewed
Into the thundering of exploded gas
While the charred midgets cometed to grass?

We stood and watched and each man watched his own
Possible future flaming to arrive.
By never-ending inches she came down
Bringing the living back to stay alive.
Still with a sky unclosed, we saw her shed
The first burnt metal, flaking down and dead.

We counted distances by fractional
Unending seconds till her wheels might touch.
While fire grew wider till it lavished all
The warping wing, and something came to clutch
The circled silence of the afternoon,
And the long smoke rode her like a black dragoon.

First feet, then inches. Still a roof above
The blurring ground, the burning engine spat
Clear from the melted wing and dove
Spilling its flame into the landing mat.
And still the wing held and the sky thinned out
Between her and the ground, and with a shout

We heard the brakes squeal, saw the midgets dive
Like dervishes toward grass and rise and run
Across the sweet returning of their lives.
We counted out the crew and one by one
We saw death leave us, and from roof and wall
The held breath broke, as sudden as a squall.

We stood in circles when they brought them in,
And offered cigarettes and held the match,
Not certain where to let their lives begin
Nor our held breaths after the silent watch.
And then it thawed, and inches past a doom
Were all the spaces of the afternoon.

We turned and waited till the fire reached home
And saw the tanks blow and the monstrous cloud—
Orange and black upon the air's blue room—
Slant up through miles of air, the emptied shroud
Still holding us. And crackling down below
We heard the roasted ammunition go.

It took an hour to burn down and be done.
We watched and memorized it flame by flame,
Our faces mirrored in the afternoon
With death gone by and fire become a game.
And when we left the last fire and last smoke
Someone began a drawn-out bedroom joke.

Port of Aerial Embarkation

There is no widening distance at the shore—
The sea revolving slowly from the piers—
But the one border of our take-off roar
And we are mounted on the hemispheres.

Above the waning moon whose almanac
We wait to finish continents away,
The Northern stars already call us back,
And silence folds like maps on all we say.

Under the sky, a stadium tensed to cry
The ringside savage thrumming of the fights,
We watch our engines, taut and trained for sky,
Arranged on fields of concrete flowered with lights.

Day after day we fondle and repeat
A jeweler's adjustment on a screw,
Or wander past the bulletins to meet
And wander back to watch the sky be blue.

Somehow we see ourselves in photographs
Held in our hands to show us back our pride
When, aging, we recall in epitaphs
The faces just behind and to each side.

The nights keep perfect silence. In the dark
You feel the faces soften into sleep,
Or tense upon the fraught and falling arc
Of fear a boy had buried not too deep.

Finally we stand by and consciously
Measure the double sense of all our talk,
And, everyman his dramatist, anxiously
Corrects his role, his gesture, and his walk.

Where standing by a window or a door
We see ourselves on a burning other sky,
And through the clouds that were the barracks floor
Each man looks down and sees he will not die.

Sea Burial

Through the sea's crust of prisms looking up
Into the run of light above the swell
And down a fathom, down a fathom more
Until the darkness closes like a shell.

Oblique, like fall of leaves down the wet glide
Of season and surrender from the tree
Of life across the windows of a wind
To the final ruined lawn beneath a sea.

Glide, glide and fall. How lightly death goes down
Into the crushing fog, pale and refracted.
Seen dimly and then lost, like jellyfish
Flowering a tide, expanded, then contracted,

Once more expanded, and then closed forever
To make a stain on stone and liquefy
The memory that kissed a mountain girl
And ran on grass as if it could not die.

Saipan

In time like lenses, magnified and calm,
A stained cross-sectional of sea and sky,
We enter like a spirochete's alarm
To infect the silence of the measuring eye.

This is our scene, the island of our days
Where clouds come home from sea to look upon
The native's innocence transformed, alas,
To curiosities of gum and gun.

This pinnacle of our times, green, sweetly fertile,
Skulled with the dead's entire integrity,
Who stood in thorn and cave mouth, mad and futile
Against the tank-treads of necessity—

See how it clouds: a dream left on the sea.
Until the waves awaken and recall
That in their legend of divinity
They and the fish shall rule us after all.

Watch how the sea is souvenired with light
Above the troglodytes in sleeps of shale.
Once in a moony marvel of the night
We found the spangled fountain of a whale.

One other time we spotted marker dye,
Like grass that changed from pasture to the sea
And not a bubble rose from shale to sky
To mark a vestige of mortality.

This single rock in time whose flowers we are
To root in and bind tight against the wear
And swallowing wash of surf, almost a star,
Not quite a hope, a pity, or a fear—

Where underfoot we crackle twigs and bone
Passing to be ourselves in memory
Of where our times have brought us, not alone,
Whose other islands sank into the sea—

This is our sea, our tropic, and our fate.
This waited for us just outdoors from school.
This was the bell that rang when we were late,
The dunce, the dunce-cap, and the corner stool.

This wind blew through the trees of holiday.
These clouds were truant with our naked skins
By autumn ponds. And, in another play,
This was our paycheck and our Saturday sins.

Where cloud rained fire, and we were in the cloud—
Its climate, dark, and deluge. And we spread
Simple as rain, like thunder loud,
To be the following weathers of the dead.

Ritual for Singing Bat

"One part Indian, one part Tennessee,"
He said his first day in. We saw him dive,
His feather dress of flame ceremoniously
Prompt to the ritual of the pyre-borne dove.
"You can't quite kill a man named Singing Bat,"
He said. And would have bet. And lost the bet.

Simply as tomahawks had spelled his tribe,
Or guns snicked out the great-grandmother's clan,
Chance would not take a totem's bribe
To pass the dice on one Tennessee man.
Stones will not break completely, but they break.
And a Tennessee man with a gun, make no mistake,

Will crumble less than any battered stone.
He passed into an orange feather dress
From a white sky to a yellow emperor's town.
Bombs opened back like blossoms in the place
Below the black plumed arrow that he rode
Into the misty forest of a cloud.

He never reappeared. Whether our sight
Fixed to an angle's logic, logically
Lost him, or whether totems plumed and bright
Demanded one last mystery from the sky—
A fluff of cloud closed on him and returned
A legend only for the flesh that burned.

Bat, may your bones be diamonded like dice,
And all your blood be whisky fragrantly
Sloshed in a jug of clay, while on the skies
You rattle naturals through eternity,
And every roll be thunder, bet and faded,
For a Tennessee man who shot the sky—and made it.

Letter from an Island

I gave our difference 10,000 miles.
Land, sea, and air passed under. If we fail,
We pass from sight completely as two moles
Digging the cells of earth that keep their jail.

Remember miles are nothing. I have come
This distance faster than a memory:
Dawn in the cities, noon in the world's dome,
And that night's dark on islands past a sea.

Now on this coral rock behind the world
I pace your image, sleep, feel foolish, eat.
Put back my last near dread and at the word
Climb, sung by engines, to the obsolete

Encounter of two corpses still alive.
Miles into sky we function and grow cold.
The rapid arts of killing, like new love,
Run to new spangles, but the art is old.

We have our reasons and are reconciled,
Until, the target and one ocean past,
Our engines burn the wake the white ships sailed
And land us to our solitudes at last.

Then with our war another day away,
The natural man, stepped down from the machine,
Waits in the desert of his apathy,
Lounges, grows dull, sleeps late, and, half obscene,

Half riven by a hunger deep as flesh,
Beats on the native tropic like a fool,
Eyes the few native women like a fish,
And burns at night, himself the flame and fuel.

I am that natural man and in a haze
I see this tropic down my ancestry.
And with another thought I see our days
Running forever parted on the sea.

What was the poet's simple solving pun,
That pure souls stayed as one though worlds divide?
A dressed and fancy notion out of Donne
That all the seas and separate winds deride.

Shall we dream pure, and I baptize your mind
To name you more than woman past a sea?
I need you fleshed, and sudden as the wind.
I have no appetite for memory.

Oceans that fail between us not by words
Open to close us back where we begin.
Only one wish will keep us across worlds—
Stay hungry with my hunger, and we win.

Elegy Just in Case

Here lie Ciardi's pearly bones
In their ripe organic mess.
Jungle blown, his chromosomes
Breed to a new address.

Was it bullets or a wind
Or a rip cord fouled on chance?
Artifacts the natives find
Decorate them when they dance.

Here lies the sgt.'s mortal wreck
Lily spiked and termite kissed,
Spiders pendant from his neck
And a beetle on his wrist.

Bring the tick and southern flies
Where the land crabs run unmourning
Through a night of jungle skies
To a climeless morning.

And bring the chalked eraser here
Fresh from rubbing out his name.
Burn the crew-board for a bier.
(Also Colonel what's-his-name.)

Let no dice be stored and still.
Let no poker deck be torn.
But pour the smuggled rye until
The barracks threshold is outworn.

File the papers, pack the clothes,
Send the coded word through air—
"We regret and no one knows
Where the sgt. goes from here."

"Missing as of inst. oblige,
Deepest sorrow and remain—"
Shall I grin at persiflage?
Could I have my skin again

Would I choose a business form
Stilted mute as a giraffe,
Or a pinstripe unicorn
On a cashier's epitaph?

Darling, darling, just in case
Rivets fail or engines burn,
I forget the time and place
But your flesh was sweet to learn.

Swift and single as a shark
I have seen you churn my sleep;
Now if beetles hunt my dark
What will beetles find to keep?

Fractured meat and open bone—
Nothing single or surprised.
Fragments of a written stone
Undeciphered but surmised.

Note: The text follows the revised version published in Selected Poems.

Expendability

Thinking too much of death by curves of chance,
Imagination's curse (the nearest ghost)
Sees all too readily the falling dance,
The motion down and lost,
The glide away forever from your touch
To the reduction of all wish, all thought.
All choice of you, all dreams become too much,
All action idled, and all fears outfought.

Dear, was it kisses that we planned to bring
(Your body pliant in the single night)
Or days with reason mad enough to sing,
Choice to abide, to measure, to make right?
See, we are numbered serials of our choice.
(I brood our epitaph.)
Fire is our image, guns our voice,
And where we are stands plotted on a graph.

Nothing we do except to stand and wish
Will serve. Nor ever stop the fear.
All night on islands scrubbed by tidal wash
The planetary whistling shadows near.
Shall I be posed with bravery to wear?
I wish your flesh to wear. I cannot cool
To the machine and metal of a gear,
Not wholly be the pure and selfless tool.

I beg of chance the green and living day.
I wheedle numbers, plot new averages,
Alchemize probabilities (a play
Of superstition tarred by our dark ages—
That numbers have a ghost to give,
Proof is a chart)
Because to dream your flesh is my last live
Near-perfect art,
Concocted from whatever symbols lie
Nearest to hand to prove I will not die.

Elegy

For Kurt Porjescz, Missing in Action, 1 April 1945

Some gone like boys to school wearing their badges,
Some calmly with a look of measuring
While every wind is April in the hedges
On a grotesque of bony birds who sing
A metal note, weathering and weathering.

Here in this good green scene and plate of sea
The April world astonishes my look.
This island rock in space turns flowering endlessly
To peaks of cloud still mounting where you took
Your last high passage and your faltering luck.

The boys are flowers: they strew themselves in seed
And spring again, anonymous and pure,
For the same tears to follow the same deed
Of bending in the wind, and soon and sure
Fold, fall, and fade from what they could not cure.

Ah love has followed them and tears attest
They stood as slim as grass, they moved like fish
Into the silent oceans where they rest
Dark as the squid. Like trees they held their wish
A season on the leaf, and cannot perish.

April is their return in chlorophyl.
Protein and water celebrate their root.
The lavish world's extravagance, they till
The loamy crust, while blindly underfoot
They crush their own unrecognized green shoot.

Clouds had them once, and wreckage mars them now.
And the same wreckage scatters on your fall.
Spring that amazes more than we allow
Of our dark selves to show, sets equally after all
On the blind wreck of gland and rationale.

The East runs like a stain across our mouths,
Our engines cry the faltering dark sun down.
And one default of metal breaks our oaths
To cross on sky above a burning town:
On metal's meeting wish is overthrown.

Now only memory keeps its aftermotion.
Good-bye, where no luck serves, nor any word,
Across a swell of sky and cloudy ocean
While April wind and bony bird
Discuss our futures, and have not concurred.

Poem for My Twenty-ninth Birthday

Once more the predawn throbs on engine sound
Down coral slope, papaya grove, and pine,
Into the sea whose pastures girdle round
The native in his jungle, I in mine,
And you in yours, O gentle stay-at-home:
Your talons, too, have raked the living bone.

We waken, and the cities of our day
Move down a cross-haired bomb sight in the mind.
The thoughtless led, those only in the way,
The powerful by intent, wake there and find
Their jungles closing, each man tangled tight
Into this day that may not last till night.

Now I have named another year of time
Learning to count not mine but a world's age.
And on the morning of no birth I climb
To sign in fire your and my heritage:
The bomb whose metal carcass dressed and bled
Is our day's gift to populate the dead.

See from his living garden, damp with dawn,
The native turn from weeding as we pass
His centuries upon this flowering stone.
Our trucks arrived in clouds of dust and gas
Coat his green jungle till the daily rain.
He sees us past and turns to weed again.

His is the simplest darkness, our grotesque
Of straps and buckles, parachutes and guns,
Our gear of kit and cartridge, helmet, mask,
Life vest, rations, and the elegance
Of all our conscious gestures and our gum,
Darken us further than his guess can come.

We leave his green past. On a metal din
Our gears resolve us from the valley night
To plateaus where the rapt emblazoned fin
Our perfect bomber lifts to the first light
Mounts on the air up which the morning sun
Prophesies Asia and a depth to come.

Already now, my dear, this turning sun
Has been your day, and here returns to me
Where I inherit on a bomber's run
Your image from the sundial of the sea.
I dream you smiling, waking fleshed in grace,
And see, a gun sight photographs your face.

I cannot lose my darkness. Posed and dressed,
I touch the metal womb our day will ride.
We take our places while a switch is pressed,
And sun and engines rise from the hillside—
A single motion and a single fire
To burn, return, and live upon desire.

Look at the sea and learn how malice shines
Bright as a noon come down through colored glass.
We are the soaring madness of our times
Marking our own flown never-ending loss.
The whitecaps strewn like lint on a stone floor
Wait, will swallow, close, and wait once more.

Now, westering, our day has named its course:
Far down in frost and tiny symmetry
Fuji, the magic mountain of what was,
Places our past on the trajectory
Of the co-sined and wind-computed fall
Our bombs descend to save or kill us all.

What has been lost when once the bomb is flown?
(We fire at fighters and await the rose
Blossoming in fire upon the town
Whose living history we have come to close.)
The dead are not our loss. My memory is
Our simplest day was guiltier than this.

Our innocence shall haunt our murderous end
Longer than statues or the tabled walls
Alphabetized to death. Shall we pretend
Destruction moves us or that death appalls?
Are we the proud avengers time returned?
—We dreamed by all the windows while time burned.

Now, our intention bloodied late by need,
We sit our jungles hemispheres apart;
I, blossomed awkwardly from dragon seed,
You, endlessly the pure and gentle heart.
And death run loose like shadows in a wind
On all the reasoned motions of the mind.

And, last, by dark, we have our rock again:
Our wheels touch and our waiting lives return.
Far off the dead are lying in the rain,
And on their dark the ruined cities burn
Our jungles down with light enough to see
The last compassionate necessity.

Note: The As If *version (1955) dropped the three stanzas before the last one.*

Wafflebutt

Reveille rung on telephones awakes
The opening movement of an opening day.
    Alphabets in mosaics,
    Reports and rosters weigh
Some who came through, some pending, some who died,
And some delayed while oceans wait outside.

One minute now, one paperclip to pin
On one regret to tabulate and file
    A finished lifetime in
    (Not mine). One fraction while
The silver bubbles rise, the corpses sink—
In one more minute I will stop and think

What boundary this surf makes at this shore,
What fallen statues soften in the sea,
    And from a bomb-bay door
    What crossed trajectory
Spatters in flak, or checks its breath to dare
The rip cord of a rent fantastic air.

(Our bombs like phallic comets scanned the air
Across the flowerfall of the tumbling chutes
    That bloomed hydrangeas where
    The dead in fancy suits,
All flowered in flame, heaved from the flaming ground,
And settled back like seed pods—black and round.)

The other side this surf, one leap above
The ground, a single day beyond this day,
    Nostalgias not completely love,
    Fear never put away,
Demanded and recalled and churned our sleep
With a lead-gutted terror, dreamed and deep.

To file by rank and name (no longer ours),
Insured in triplicate, indorsed, and signed
    Six days a week in office hours.
    But oh the telephone is mined,
And boredom booby-traps desk, file, and wall
Where day and day destroys us after all.

Improvisation for a Southern Night

The native's myth, as lavish as the night,
Tracks down the centuries of his half-light,
Naming the moving people of the wind
By logics that his waking cannot find.

Lacking a legend, let me improvise:

There was a lady in the moon's round house
Loved by the Sun, who, bound to other skies,
Wooed her as Sultans would, or Khans, or Pshahs,
With couriers and gifts, till her jewel box
Groaned with his trinkets—and her locks.
(She had a woman's instinct for the real.)
Nightly she took his signal and his gift
Reflecting love and light, till on the wheel
Of chiming orbits came at last—the rift:
She looked too long on Mercury or Mars,
He felt his heavenly oats, and, hot with pride,
Came, bristled, threatened, flailed her hair and hide,
And flung aside her jewel box, scattering wide
The shattered shining trinkets of the stars
Lavished forever on the Southern night
When the Sun sulks down and the lady of the light
Speaks to the native children on the sand
Beside the white man's swath burned on the land.

Well, it will do or it will have to do.
I listen, drowned in surf-sound, and recall
Our angers shall outshine us after all.
We have no other prodigy left us now.
And we are planted on a coral walk
Between two surfs, above us and below:
The first extravagantly hurled on rock,
The other droning where the bombers go
Hurling their sound at cloud, themselves at space

In the enormous rift of moon and sun
And threading red light green light on the face
Of a legend improvised by gun and gun.

And as the sun might love his arrogance,
Or moon her light, her darkness, and her loss,
I weaken toward the engines of our madness
And almost think we scatter stars across
The ukase of our bombfall down the air.

. . . Until I need your light and your despair
Across the metal crackle of the rain
To certify a human night again.

v-j Day

On the tallest day in time the dead came back.
Clouds met us in the pastures past a world.
By short wave the releases of a rack
Exploded on the interphone's new word.

Halfway past Iwo we jettisoned to sea
Our gift of bombs like tears and tears like bombs
To spring a frolic fountain daintily
Out of the blue metallic seas of doom.

No fire-shot cloud pursued us going home.
No cities cringed and wallowed in the flame.
Far out to sea a blank millennium
Changed us alive, and left us still the same.

Lightened, we banked like jays, antennae squawking.
The four wild metal halos of our props
Blurred into time. The interphone was talking
Abracadabra to the cumulus tops:

Dreamboat three-one to Yearsend—loud and clear,
Angels one-two, on course at one-six-nine.
Magellan to Balboa. Propwash to Century.
How do you read me? Bombay to Valentine.

Fading and out. And all the dead were homing.
(Wisecrack to Halfmast. Doom to Memory.)
On the tallest day in time we saw them coming,
Wheels jammed and flaming on a metal sea.

Hometown after a War

The river blackens in a frame of snow.
The air is one commotion of more snow falling.
I walk into a day like Christmas cards,
New England winter meeting memory
Snow scene by snow scene to bring back to touch
Wet snowballs on wet mittens, cheeks numb and fired
With all the boisterous cold and noise of growing
Amid the serious businesses of throwing
A snowball faster, further, and—smack—
Between the ear muffs and the Mackinaw collar—
Precisely down McGinty's Irish neck.

I count the snowfall clinging to my sleeves
And think how we used to run, mouths up and open,
To snap a snowflake clean out of the air
That moved here long ago down years of growing
Since last I wore white piping on my ears,
Or carried a gauze shingle on each eye,
Or felt so grateful for my body's heat
Against the winter that could swallow it.

We were mad, busy, imagined, and already
Tired of fights in the schoolyard and after school:
McGinty's blood on my knuckles, mine on his,
And our few memorized obscenities
Waiting for any meeting to hate each other.
We weren't the nicest kids in school,
We smoked too early, swore too well,
And didn't always tip our hats to ladies.
But the snow knew us, we two savages
Who fought the winter back and trampled it.

I think there was too much motion of the air,
Too many patterns falling from the sky
Like snow, to numb and make us loud.
Until we lost a way and found a way.
The strangeness is this echo of returning,

This walking down the same streets where we were
To touch ourselves upon the interim
Between two winters, years and names apart,
And feel ourselves grow secret like the river,
Deepening in the white frame of a thought,
Learning that what we left for lost, was not.

Serenade in a Drugstore

I am my verified and proper self
Mirrored across the laboratory air
Of soda fountains mounting shelf by shelf
On plastics lit by progress where
A cyclotron concocts my morning coffee
In the verified and proper year A.D.

And Mr. Shank in a white interne's coat
Calibrates my nickel in his machine
So to deliver (black, no sugar) hot
From the chrome vats my Byzantine
Wiped marble edifice of morning state,
Fluorescent, air-conditioned, immaculate.

Oh I would travel, love, a furious length
To be your body's bed, and you my bride.
And Mr. Shank has pills to give me strength
And elixirs profoundly certified,
And furniture of marvels, priced and near.
And I will bring you all of these, my dear.

Barbados rum and Pentecostal wines,
Books, bronzes, cordials, incense, aspirin,
Beauty, deodorants, valentines,
Extracts, testosterone, adrenalin—
For Mr. Shank has treasuries to sell,
And home is where the cap comes off the bottle.

Chelsea Naval Hospital

Oceans beyond the nearest war we fought
I found the wounded surplus, cot by cot,
Stretched on the white sheets of no future.

How many thousand miles they brought the wound
Home from an eruption of the ground
To train it here for scalpel, cast, and suture

No map will measure. Pain is not a mile.
Morphine is neither East nor West. The smile
A nurse leaves by the side of the bed,

And the attempted joke that brings no laughter,
Were never anywhere before or after.
For they have slipped through longitudes like the dead.

What is the ceiling saying where you stare?
And when the silence rustles in your ear
Like paper invasion money, no good for spending,

What does it say in these denominations
Of days and weeks? Oh, numb and drugged with patience,
Must even pity have a bankrupt ending?—

Making the gestures of cigarette and match,
Turning the radio on, bringing a batch
Of detective stories, a pinochle deck, clowning around,

Groping through a measured hour to say,
Where are you?—with my pity in the way,
And the barbed fences that defend your wound.

On a Photo of Sgt. Ciardi a Year Later

The sgt. stands so fluently in leather,
So poster-holstered and so newsreel-jawed
As death's costumed and fashionable brother,
My civil memory is overawed.

Behind him see the circuses of doom
Dance a finale chorus on the sun.
He leans on gun sights, doesn't give a damn
For dice or stripes, and waits to see the fun.

The cameraman whose ornate public eye
Invented that fine bravura look of calm
At murderous clocks hung ticking in the sky
Palmed the deception off without a qualm.

Even the camera, focused and exact
To a two dimensional conclusion,
Uttered its formula of physical fact
Only to lend data to illusion.

The camera always lies. By a law of perception
The obvious surface is always an optical ruse.
The leather was living tissue in its own dimension,
The holsters held benzedrine tablets, the guns were no use.

The careful slouch and dangling cigarette
Were always superstitious as Amen.
The shadow under the shadow is never caught:
The camera photographs the cameraman.

Live Another Day

Another Day

—•—

(1949)

To Judith Asleep

My dear, darkened in sleep, turned from the moon
That riots on curtain-stir with every breeze
Leaping in moths of light across your back . . .
Far off, then soft and sudden as petals shower
Down from wired roses—silently, all at once—
You turn, abandoned and naked, all let down
In ferny streams of sleep and petaled thighs
Rippling into my flesh's buzzing garden.

Far and familiar your body's myth-map lights,
Traveled by moon and dapple. Sagas were curved
Like scimitars to your hips. The raiders' ships
All sailed to your one port. And watchfires burned
Your image on the hills. Sweetly you drown
Male centuries in your chiaroscuro tide
Of breast and breath. And all my memory's shores
You frighten perfectly, washed familiar and far.

Ritual wars have climbed your shadowed flank
Where bravos dreaming of fair women tore
Rock out of rock to have your cities down
In loot of hearths and trophies of desire.
And desert monks have fought your image back
In a hysteria of mad skeletons.
Bravo and monk (the heads and tails of love)
I stand, a spinning coin of wish and dread,

Counting our life, our chairs, our books and walls,
Our clock whose radium eye and insect voice
Owns all our light and shade, and your white shell
Spiraled in moonlight on the bed's white beach;
Thinking, I might press you to my ear

And all your coils fall out in sounds of surf
Washing away our chairs, our books and walls,
Our bed and wish, our ticking light and dark.

Child, child, and making legend of my wish
Fastened alive into your naked sprawl—
Stir once to stop my fear and miser's panic
That time shall have you last and legendry
Undress to old bones from its moon brocade.
Yet sleep and keep our prime of time alive
Before that death of legend. My dear of all

Saga and century, sleep in familiar-far.
Time still must tick *this is, I am, we are.*

Morning in the Park

A green morning of indolence one hedge beyond
The rags-to-riches nonsense of traffic
Suns all my mind. A vegetable with eyes,
I fit my coat to greengoods and give back
The drift of cumulus over my head. My sight
Dizzies through heights of light. Higher than all towers
I soar like bubbles into iris air:
Veils of it gather on my shining. An hour
Of this bemusement crazes the practical sense:
A week of it and I would be unemployable
Forever, a character beyond the hedge
Sky-socketed in a ringing skull and cracked
With queer illuminations, secrets I'd know
Of local zeniths where devout pigeons
Flattered me for crumbs with wings, wings,
Loud beating storms of love to my St. Francis
In a multi-million stirring of affluent air,
Adorations of my rich escape.

Three Eggs Up

Three sunset eyes on a white plate
Almanac the day and date.
One for you and two for me:
House, time, and trinity.

Though history pull religion's leg
Here's one more day we will not beg
In the Eurasian garbage can.
I fill my plate and am a man.

The western legend eye to eye
With its native calory
Certifies us man and wife
In an advertised way of life.

When in time the children come
Soldiers need not give them gum.
They shall have chocolate before
We vote to send them off to war.

Their faces shall be spread with jam
Long before the spastic slam
Of metabolic bullets drips
Raspberry blood across their lips.

And Mississippis of their bread
Wash down the Jordans of the dead
When mad-dogs in the midday sun
Eat the dead American.

Chaplains wearing bars of gold
I speak to you: tales have been told
Of mystic globes through which we sight
The heavens of the recondite:
I look through these three eyes and see
The protein of eternity.

Dead Pigeon on South Street

A crumb or maybe a peanut dropped in the suburb
Called it down from the sky. The living bird
Started away too late from the world's wheel;
So spread a map of wings across the gutter.

Death as a map of wings pasted on tar
Had not occurred to any of us before.
Its bloody capitals and dirty rivers
Sullied our white houses and brick walks.

As if a reckless planet soft as pulp
Had splashed our lawns whose pickets said KEEP OFF
To such intrusion: we resented it.
But there it was, its own radical world.

And almost before we knew it, war broke out.
Squadrons of gnats thick as an atmosphere
Swarmed to corrupt battle. The bloody capitals
And dirty rivers burned in the uprising.

Auntie of course had wigwagged indignation
Over the phone to all of City Hall,
But savage children for the price of a thrill
Already poked their sticks into serious war.

The white houses and brick walks shuddered
In the fierce burning of that war in the sun.
Flames of it tainted even the nerveless children.
And somebody, Auntie warned, had best do something.

So finally two men drove up with shovels
And carted the whole business out of the neighborhood—
Death, war, and ominous planet. And that was that:
The lawns had been saved for Auntie and we all felt good.

The Pilot in the Jungle

I

Machine stitched rivets ravel on a tree
Whose name he does not know. Left in the sky,
He dangles from a silken cumulus
(Stork's bundle upside down
On the delivering wind) and sees unborn
Incredible jungles of the lizard's eye:
Dark fern, dark river, a shale coliseum
Mountained above one smudgepot in the trees
That was his surreal rug on metered skies
And slid afire into this fourth dimension
Whose infinite point of meeting parallels
He marks in ultra-space, suspended from
The chords of fifty centuries
Descending to their past—a ripping sound
That snags him limb by limb. He tears and falls
Louder than any fruit dropped from the trees,
And finds himself in mud on hands and knees.

II

The opened buckle frees him from his times.
He walks three paces dressed in dripping fleece
And tears it off. The great bird of his chute
Flaps in the trees: he salvages its hide
And starts a civilization. He has a blade,
Seventeen matches, his sheepskin, and his wits.
Spaceman Crusoe at the wreck of time,

He ponders unseen footprints of his fear.
No-eyes watch his nothing deep in nowhere.

III

He finds the wreck (the embers of himself)
Salvages bits of metal, bakelite, glass—
Dials twisted from himself, his poverty.
Three hours from time still ticking on his wrist
The spinning bobbins of the time machine
Jam on an afternoon of Genesis
And flights of birds blow by like calendars
From void to void. Did worlds die or did he?
He studies twisted props of disbelief
Wondering what ruin to touch. He counts his change
("Steady now, steady . . .") flips heads or tails and sees
The coin fall into roots. An omen? ("Steady . . .")
He laughs (a nerve's slow tangling like a vine)
Speaks to himself, shouts, listens, hears a surf
Of echo rolling back to strand him there
In tide pools of dead time by caves of fear,
And enters to himself, denned in his loss,
Tick-tick, a bloodbeat building on his wrist,
Ratcheting down the dead teeth of a skull
(The fossil of himself) sucked out of sight
Past heads and tails, past vertebrae and gill
To bedrocks out of time, with time to kill.

Letter from a Rubber Raft

Eleven stars and clusters on a flying gun;
"Glug," said the ocean . . .

Is this the man?

This is the man, books, belts, lunchpails, pity.

Twelfth day:

Every sleep is a new confusion of hope.
Every awakening grows simpler . . .

Now at last I have seen myself always
On this uneven record, groove after groove
My dustball gathering before the needle.
Now the recording is ended, the needle
Wobbles on the inner cutting,
The dustball slips and skids.

You may wish to know how it went:
It was mid-sea. A day named high for April
In a sky of apple blossom clouds.
First one engine,
Then another.
Then the third beginning to cough.
The Engineer
Opened a fuel line and found the gas dirty.
Someone's error of untidiness.

We dropped our bombs as if shriving
Our guilty association, circled on a moderate sea,
Braced ourselves for the ditching. To the end
You might have thought it a field spread for us,
So calmly it waited. Then the trough
Opened under us. Its dike met us like stone.
Momentum spattered us like eggs against a wall.
But somewhere the wall opened and I was through

In the drowned silence of oil. One reflex
Lived, inflated my vest. I rose like an insect
Coupled to my bubble of air. The raft
Had been strapped to me. It too opened.
All else closed.

You may wish to know how it stood:
I had the raft and its emergency packet:
Water (one pint), a hacksaw blade,
Quinine, bouillon, fishing cord (eighteen feet),
Two hooks, a bar of chocolate,
Four biscuits.
A vest pocket anthology of life.

. . . What was it I meant to say?
Immense. Immense.
Forgive me fear.

Thirteenth Day:

Last words are a last mercy.
I would like to neglect my death long enough
To find the words of it honestly.
Let me have someone to pity.
Ten sponges staining a ripple pink,
Pulps that were men.
Without transition.
I have their deaths to die for them.

Fourteenth Day:

Nothing in sight.
Nothing ever in sight.
And somewhere there comes upon me
The notion that I am
Man,
That I am Man's bubble

Adrift on the licking universe.
When I break
An age will have been placed in perspective.

But there is no comfort in being a mythology.

Have I said I love you?
How I mock my own sapping under this sun
That lacks even a phallus for your memory in dreams?
How your breasts are eleven deaths needing a memory?
This parched water is you:
Caked upon my dying. Destroying me
With the distances of many departures:
Awakenings left in a room where, turning, we saw a river.
Airfield boom towns drunk and drowned.
Harmonica nights under Byronic palms
Spending ourselves on souvenir nostalgias.

This is the end of something I regret.

Eighteenth Day:

I want you to know that two days ago—
Two or twenty—
I caught a fish. (This is my gift to you:
To labor at living by all devices.)
I remembered skills from a strange training:
Hacksawed my fish, made a tourniquet to compress him,
Squeezed an ounce of water free.
Is this something like ravens?
He fed me and gave me water out of the water
Of my death. Sweet fish,
I made a doggerel for him:

Fish, fish
Is the dead man's dish.
On a platter of sea
Blue plate to me

In the hour of my wish
Came fish.

God, God
Appeared in a cod.
Is that so very odd?
Was it a cod?
But water and food
And very good.

Sea, sea
You've done me shabbily.
One fish from so many
Because I hadn't any.
Is it always to the poor
You say "so much, no more"?
Or is it just that oceans
Lack notions?

Too lay a lay for clerical times? I made another stanza:

Love, love
Is hand in glove,
Bone under skin,
And blood within.
Now I feel
The glove begin to peel,
The bone begin to flow,
The blood begin to go.
Things do not touch
Very much.
Often spill
Beyond our will.
Words we say
Fade away.
Death, death
Is out of breath.

Which day is this?

. . . You are swimming iris depths below the sun's glaze.
Shall I go under
To where you are all colors
And coral castles land-escaped
By waving fronds and veiled transparencies,
Botanical gardens of nerves?

I wish, I wish, I wish, I wish, I wish

Later:

My time has run out
Of numbers. No matter:
I have given up watching horizons
Or waiting for voices of flight above me.
When I have finished, I shall lie here in my shell
And be rocked by you.
That will be better than counting improbable chances:
You will be able to say
My last thoughts were of you. I
Shall lie here and memorize my pity
Dying of someone else's error
The death by untidiness.
Now I have oceans to wash it in
And time for a kind of neatness.
I have scrubbed the stones of eleven pities
And made a path to my absolute conscience:
I could fill the world's room with eleven beds
For love to dishevel.
I envy all those adrift before me
Who expected a further meeting.
It is not hard to let go. I cannot.
I have eaten all my bait but my line is out:
If some foolish fish will bite metal
I may live another day.

Homecoming — Massachusetts

After the satyr's twilight in the park
Where the Greek children burn among the bushes,
And past the Roman wall where icons are
Beside the hospital's white Renaissance,
I stroll across the Indian Burial—
A glacial till on a Mesozoic ledge—
And come again to Mrs. Quinan's hedge.

Everything I have known here is dark.
The fruit we pilfered from her rustling trees
Is gone, and the trees are gone. She will not damn
Our thieving souls again. Her fishwife's tongue
That was a legend and a merriment
Was throttled by a cancer, a cross, a stone
On a darker night than this. I turn alone

Onto the pavement, knowing we grow old
In any thought. My life waits on this street.
I walk it back from memory, a legend
Of mineral, vegetable, fish, fowl, and flesh,
Saurian, savage, satyr, Roman, clerk—
And Mrs. Quinan's imp, who died like her
Leaving a faint distaste, and then, no taste,
On a street of centuries. Good friends, good friends,
Nothing in our beginnings knows our ends.

To My Students

Last Class, Last Words

They are dancing the rain dance in Bali,
Praying in Rome, marrying in Key West.
We have a ceremony of our own.
You can never stop ceremony. This
Is our theological pause before traveling,
The four feathers thrown to the wind at the crossroads
Omening the name bearer, the sign of the cross
Absolving the diver from the high board.

Where have we been? Let us say: Growing.
Growing and Meeting. Learning the local arts:
Prayers for hunting, potencies against drowning,
Control of weather.

              Soup must be drunk silently.
Speak to the hostess when arriving and leaving.
Art must be worn casually: only tools
Are for worship. Education
Is always a corporation.
The unimpassioned travel as far as any.
There is a philosophy for any act,
A moral formula for any equation.

If destiny love you, the feathers may always
Be cast again, till the wind is where you wish it.
Theology, like direction, leads everywhere.
All final reckoning is by institution.

Go out and make a dollar, and God will love you.

Vale

To Irwin Swerdlow

Cambridge, an outdoor library stack of bricks,
Files one more year into the catalogue.
It's the end of a season, trains leaving, sailings,
Visits to airports, tail lights fading away.
Goodbye to psychoanalysis by bourbon
And to all gathering of literary drunks
From every specialized professional century
Thronging in quotes around the seltzer and ice
While empties file like footnotes from the sink—
Goodbye. To janitors, to staff, to proctors,
To all doctors and nearly doctors,
To bumpkins, to lumpkins, to fidgets, to flubs,
To freshmen in the Wursthaus, to seniors in the clubs,
To the solvent, to the arty, to the clerical,
To the materio-revivalist-hysterical,
To the high and low and middle-high inane,
To the eccentric, to the sane and the insane—Goodbye.
And goodbye, Widener and the clever apartments,
And to all heads and assistant heads of departments.
Goodbye. Goodbye. To all the year goodbye.

Iubet vicissum, and now all tickets read
The Sphere of Man. God and the Liberal Arts
Far-fling the seed pearls to the jowls of time,
And all neurosis must go home alone,
Trailing the breath and spirits that awake
(Come the next Fall from grace) in Ashtabula,
Sodding the loamy young with moss from Cambridge
For an outdoor ceremony of the arts.

Goodbye. Goodbye. To time by institution,
To the flowering and deflowering of intent.
Goodbye to all ourselves that were and went,

Sending back penny posts of sentiment.
For we were visited if not quite blessed.
Longinus in pin-stripes, Plato in harris-tweed
Left seals on various gates and various walls,
While bibliogs in pince-nez and French-cuffs
Pumped the divine afflatus leisurely
In suburbs of the Beautiful and True.
And there were some, untidy but nearly beautiful,
Who stood by blackboards doodled with good data
And diagrammed civilization's eccentric charm
In smiles of admirable uncertainty.
Their vistas were always real—and parenthetical.
Then, too, there came the specialist from the sea:
Culture's ambassador to all assistant professors
Presented a British glottal to the press
And swapped a charming competence of manner
For God-knows-what-he-knew and never said,
But went away well honored and well paid.

To all of them on every clock, goodbye.
On every door, goodbye. In clubs, in pubs,
In rooms, in restaurants, in offices,
In taxis, in convertibles, in the subway—
Goodbye in tweed, goodbye in whiskey and beer,
Goodbye in books. And year by year by year
Goodbye. Goodbye. We'll see you in the Fall
In Paris, in Kansas City, or not at all.
All we are sure of is goodbye, goodbye.

Philosophical Poem

The disease of civilization is not tools, citizen.
Ignorance might be closer to it.
Politics closer. But only Money
Will hit the brass tacks everyone wants to get down to
Squarely on the head.

Above all, I have no case against human nature.
Whatever that is, I like it.
I like mechanics with wrenches,
Taxi drivers' photos on licenses,
Drunks lighting cigarettes.
What the hell else is there to like
After you've kissed your wife and gone to sleep?

I like everything but important people being important
And academic people being academic.
What I like least is bookkeepers
Spending their human eyes on accounts receivable,
Interest receivable, payment due, balance on hand.
And columns of soldiers marching.

A Visit to Aunt Francesca

Pigment of wax apples bleeds into
The glass refraction of a little sun
On marble table tops, and light through wine
Purples our fingers toying with the glass.
It was or never was. At Aunt's command
My hands are poles to orbit colored yarn
Flowing away in little strands of light
From Sunday Fauntleroys and good behaviour
In a dark room divided by the sun.

Three black hairs mustachio her lip
And she was beautiful. The Sèvres cup
Is cracked and glued. I think I hated her.
And that changed too. But still we may not smoke.
Color fades from the daguerreotypes
That manteled all our days. A little more
And all the light is gone. The yarn is gone
In baskets for the night. Only that glimpse—
I cannot reach the rest—a pale gray hand,
A dry kiss like an epigram, a door,
And footsteps sounding on our last goodnights.

For My Nephew Going to Bed

It takes a whole house to put a child to bed.
I wonder what he dreams worth all the business
Of washing, inspecting, kissing, and being carried
Pick-a-back for all the aunts to witness
He's one day older and on his way like us all
To being sorry for it. I recall
Times when a smile was its own good moral:
Laugh and the world's half saved,
Be gently thoughtful, wash, comb, eat your cereal,
And God will always know you're well behaved
And must not be aimed at by unemployment, shrapnel,
Eviction, delirium tremens, or sin's black market,
Nor be allowed to grow like your uncle—mad
With measuring our unbalanced etiquette,
Where normally to put one child to bed
Takes more commotion than half the world's corpses get.
While I stand stupid-solemn, a little daft,
Surprised that I have this much pity left.

In the Year of Many Conversions and the Private Soul

A sun gas coughed. A million miles of flame
Leaped half an inch across an instrument
For lens-eyed men to give the trick a name,
And papers Sunday-featured the event
In tabloid metaphors, as: a sidewalk brick
Heated to such a temperature in Peru
Would boil the Caribbean dry, half the Atlantic
And Pacific, and char the Americas through
To whatever continents char to when they char:
Be comforted that things are as they are.

We were not comforted. The belching stars
Kept a sky's distance from us. No seas boiled dry.
Converts were converted. Many wars
Were fought and lost. And temperatures ran high—
Still there was always something left. And still
We were not comforted, and the mind's clay
Baked hotter, flaked, turned powder in the skull,
Blew like volcanic ash, sifted and gray.
And on whatever Sabbath senses had
We looked upon our work, that it was bad.

There wild in space, the sun; here lost in space,
The displaced persons of a dying time,
While the star-hurlers, athletes of grace,
Compete for Gothic mountains souls may climb
To be received by sun-belch on a throne
Of saints and zodiacs in eternal heat
Above the earth-belch in iced meat and bone
Shivering our last image on the street:
The world-offended child, the surplus man,
Picking the horn of plenty's garbage can.

Mule

See what a trick this is: two meeting bloods
Come to a dead stop here: one generation
Of boredom and traction on country roads
Is all his line, a leathery commotion
Bitten by flies, a vicious vigilance
That finally has neither sex nor mind
And was not born but made: a circumstance,
Part of a plow and cartshaft left behind
To be no-passions joke for the price of a stud
On the screaming jackass and the trembling mare
Who shook a jungle bush inside their blood—
By insemination. See him there: exiled
From generation, a round bee in his ear
Buzzing nothing, being dead and reconciled.
Planners of species, pity your useful child.

A Christmas Carol

The stores wore Christmas perfectly
With little bells to ring for sales.
In neon, the Nativity
Proclaimed the spirit never fails.
Accessory to Monsieur's paunch
Madame's embezzled look
Harassed the velvet screen where Punch
(Watched by wide-eyed kids) forsook
Judy. Forced to abdicate
She did a wonderful children's trick
And disappeared in billingsgate
Like a chattering monkey-on-a-stick,
And reappeared (gift-wrapped) to be

The nephew on the itemized list.
Monsieur, impatient, turned to flee,
But Madame had him by the wrist:
"Three more, my dear, and we are done.
Now please be patient." Box by box,
The puppets waited one by one:
Judy next to Goldilocks,
Pluto by Pinocchio,
Mickey next to Jack-be-Quick.
Neon, pink upon the snow,
Made of every flake a wick.
Till the last item itemized
By Madame and the little bells,
Collateral to the surprised
Morning look of boys and girls,
Made carols on the children's air
And brought a smile to Tiny Tim
And to Madame, and to Monsieur,
Making a sudden light in her,
Ten years difference in him,
And so much difference in me,
I'm ready to forgive you all
For what you'll turn around and be,
Starting at nine the usual
Morning after memory.

Christmas Eve

Salvation's angel in a tree
Stared out at Blake and stares at me
From zodiacs of colored bells,
And colored lights, and lighted shells.
A cherub's face above a sheet:
No arms, no torso, and no feet,
But winged and wired against The Fall,
And a paper halo overall—
A nineteen hundred year old doll
In a drying tree. What does it see?
The house is sleeping; there's only me
In the cellophane snow by the lethal toys
That wait all night for the eager boys:
Metal soldiers, an Indian suit,
Raider's tools, and gunner's loot.
I mash my cigarette and goodnight,
Turn off the angel and the light
On a single switch. The children toss
In excited sleep. Alone in the house
I feel the old confusing wind
Shake the dark tree and shake my mind,
Hearing tomorrow rattle and bang
Louder than all the angels sang.
By feel I lower the thermostat
And pick my way through a creaking flat.
The demon children, the angel doll,
Sleep in two darks off one dark hall.
I move through darkness memorized
Feeling for doors. One half-surprised
Wish stays lit inside my head.
I leave it on and go to bed.

New Year's Eve

Snow came with dusk, building itself on windows.
The bare world turned from fallow into white
Around the stone-shine of the ice-rimmed river,
Then turned on separate street-light scenes toward night.

One by one the doorbell summoned in
Our friends in colored scarves and overshoes.
Mary went coy about the mistletoe.
Frank Oliver began with "Where's the booze?"

At seven o'clock in topical excitement
The radio brought London's midnight noise
On Big Ben's chimes. Then for five homeless hours
The New Year drifted west beyond the buoys.

From channels to no channel. Away from light
It met the sailors at nostalgia's rails,
Said nothing whatever to the lipping waves,
Confirmed the Naval Observatory's dials,

And touched land like two glasses clinked in air
Where all our drunken friends around the clock
Posed for their ritual selves, radio timed
In seven seconds to be tick and tock

With holiday like laurel in their hair
And twelve long chimes down from the white church steeple.
Margie ogling Herb, Francesca giggling,
Jane drawling, "You do know the damnedest people."

Drink by drink the radio followed on:
Chicago's noise at one, Denver's at two.
While morning dropped like tabloids on the curb
Steel guitars played *Auld Lang Syne* on Oahu.

And time to gather in the Christmas lights
And tinsel from the tree and burn the boughs
With one last cigarette and the relief
Of being ourselves again in an empty house

With ash trays spilling, glasses on the floor,
Crumbs on the carpet, rubbers left behind,
The year still turning on Pacific palms,
And one more number changed inside the mind.

.22

The legend is bull's eye, part of a local scene,
That boys and guns and alchemy make men.
The fastest gent on the draw, the coolest eye
Left museums by trail-sides. Time and a toy
Still play at death: that boy in every wood
Intent on squirrels, magazine of manhood,
Calibre of a culture, stock of success,
Perfects his legend—never to miss
The sudden flag of chance from any bush.

Though some have yet been stopped by the bright rush
Of rare wings into sun—cardinal, thrush—
Tommy guns have sprayed most plausibly
Among the bird-notes of old history
Behind his practice, behind a foreign shrine,
The school house, or the jungle. Time
Is all oak's way, elm's way, unalarmed
It vegetates, knows every age came armed
Where legend's child walked with his national toy—
Stone, axe, or arrow—learning the huntsman's joy.
Death was once a barefoot boy.

Survival in Missouri

When Willie Crosby died I thought too much:
Sister and Mother and Uncle and Father O'Brien
All talked about me and how
It was all very touching: *Such sorrow.*
He really lived in that boy.
Here now, you gowonoff to the movies.
Give your grief to God.

But here I am in Missouri twenty years later
Watching the rain come down
That no one prayed for: a drowned crop
And the Mississippi rising
On a wet world still washing away the kid
Who thought too much about Willie Crosby
But went to the movies all the same.
It was a lovely wake and everyone admired me.

At night the Salt Hills go blue perfectly.
Having survived a theology and a war,
I am beginning to understand
The rain.

Hawk

It circled, hung, and circled. I watched it come
Halfway from nowhere, winding down
The whole look of the sky. From the horizon
To the next field it never moved a wing,
But spread itself as though its motion waited
Before it in the sky to be drawn in
On reels of wind it tripped simply by being
Rapt and immobile. Then it dove:

                          Its wings went back,
Part of the same motion that set its talons
And arced its head that was another talon,
All making one line of focus and intent
Condensed from miles of air like any storm.
It emptied all the air as it went down
Screaming there was [his] own life in every element
That managed to stay whole and arrogant
Above the dollar chickens pecking bugs.

I shot it halfway down. Its angles opened
Back into air, the focus fell apart,
And everything that was intent came down
Like laundry down a chute. What lay in the grass
Twitched one last look of hate when I ran up,
Then let its look go dark. So much has died
Pity must keep a waiting list. This wasn't pity
But admiration that what had filled a sky

Could lose itself in stubble and still make
A last look burn like that. A symbol died
To let the chickens live: it always will.
Then the cats ate it, who were perfect too,
Though tamer. They made another focus there,
Tooth, claw, and haunch.

                        Before I came away
I knew it had to end in philosophy
After such intersections of intent.
I cleaned the gun the way the army taught me,
And squinted down the barrel at a light
Like penmanship, all perfect flowing spirals,
Tooled for necessity or recreation,
And let it write its own efficient word—
To keep the symbol but to shoot the bird.

Letter from a
Metaphysical Countryside

Frankford, Missouri

A summer's pastoral looks on barn and bin
Through leafy shadows on unpainted sheds.
This is the private world: the sun and soil,
The hawk and hen, the buzzard and the dead.
Nothing I know is native to this place:
I roam it with a gun, lie under a tree,
And wonder what to do. In every field
I hear the tractors growling at my play
But I am smoking by a waterfall—
The lunar man stared at by martian frogs,
A food for bugs, a question for wary dogs.

This is as far as I shall ever go
Out of the world, uneasy to return.
This is the country where metaphysicians dreamed
Private virtue and the freedom of soul,
Until the statistician built his roads
Across the granaries of the absolute
And turned his traffic loose on every man
With a new law: *fate rides with a stranger*
At every turn: thou shalt not drive to endanger.

I am the political man out of his times
Trying to make sense of solitude,
Thinking of Rilke: shall I save my soul
Since nothing matters now for eight more weeks?
I think I'd rather try to raise the devil
Being hard put for any company.
And so I sit by the theosophic tree
To capture the commotion of damnation.
I have chewed the apple, but there is no temptation
Except to grow a beard or sleep too late.

What is the formula for tempting fate?
How are Blake's angels born? Byron's black soul?
What tortured Donne burning from fair to foul?
I putter and grow dull. I am out of place
Peeking through keyholes for a look at space.
This fling at metaphysics comes too late:
I have known too long our future is the state.
I am ready to venture a timid first prognosis:
Metaphysics must end in boredom or neurosis.

Letter to Virginia Johnson

Our Times, Virginia, of which you are a doctor,
Scholar and therapist of the wishing nerve
Whose balance is our sanity, whose rebuff
Hides in the intricate corridors of madness
Until a healing understanding reach
The memory of a loss and draw it back
From the neurosis of its retreating wish—
Our Times, announced in scientific journals,
Where to be lay is largely to be wrong,
Publish man in a scholastic tongue.

The gnomic notions of man's self-invention
Wither by dial and gauge, and we arrive—
Ascending or descending—to begin
A recognition of necessity.
I think what ages tortured at free will,
Or paused at the divinity of madness,
Looking forever from an inward eye
Across the deserts of man's ignorance
To search a theological concern
From the ambush of midnight, and from space
The starry outline of a father-face.

Virginia, our commonplaces keep
A native notion of the native's need,
But love, which is intelligence or nothing,
Knows nothing surer than the rule of change,
Where man, who is the product of his tools
—A plowmind from the plowman, speed from the flier,
And tribal gods sprung from the tribal fire—
Changes his vision with every change of dress
Yet keeps his native motives and address.

Man, whose childhood passion was his soul,
Shall be seen steadily and be seen whole:
A target for environment, the rhyme
Of all his memories from his earliest time.

We sit our maps a continent apart,
The evening paper open to dismay
All that we love from its prosperity.
While all our fears grow richer than Oklahoma
On the combustible sediment of our past
Tapped from the rock to run a hot machine.
Deeper than oil we drill for recognition,
To reach the total measure of our past.
I dream a billion years from cell to sight
On the distilling heat of evolution,
And think no fish has ever measured man,
And think how in one season of the womb
Eras from cell to blastopod, gill to lung,
Claw to prehensile hand reel once again
Down the whole traffic of our ancestry
To be the foetal child, redfaced and hungry.

Is it a forced analogy or a law
That all of us must move through all our past
Down all the species of unfamiliar terror
And so at last survive the mastodon
To be the measurement of what we were?
—Thinking again, no fish has measured man.
And too few men themselves, nor any until
They had evolved beyond the mental gill.

We who believe our half-emancipation
From legend to necessity, and believe
By diagram and dendrite that we shape
An accurate measure of the wishful mind;

And you above all who daily diagnose
The symptoms of the retreating mind's confusion,
Treating the curable and incurable
By the slow prescription of a learning process,
Tracing the mechanics of the mind,
Succeeding, failing, learning not to fail,
Learning to measure and at last be right—
Shall be the measure of man's improving sight.

Our Times, that are an end and a beginning,
Have closed the age of Faith, and need by need
Moved out of Heaven through the Ionosphere,
Believing man is prodigy enough
To be the measure of his own intent,
Believing the cavalcade to eternity
Starts gorgeously, but stumbles at the end
Into the courtroom of the laboratory,
Where, measured and confirmed, the question stands
As it has always stood: Man versus Time,
But now with Man the judge, by need and reason,
The Age of Evidence in a natural season.

The jungles of our childhood where the tiger
Was always silent as a superstition
Through thickets of wonderment and the dangerous caves
Whose mouths, like the cross-sections of a nerve,
Issued a menagerie of monsters
Into the swarming gardens of the brain
—Until you spoke a charm, spit over your shoulder,
Conjured an omen on the livid air
And ran at last, your terror unashamed
For mother's refuge from the thing unnamed . . .

That was our past with the invertebrates
Practicing our failures of recognition
To document a text-book summary:
"Ontogeny repeats phylogeny"

(That dark Bob Nichols dramatized for us
Through his Neanderthal hair, his arms awry
With something like an astronomer's excitement
When love and mathematics coincide
In one perfection of calculated silence
That brings the comet punctually down the lens.)

Man, in the province of his ignorance,
Where sun and rain were theological matters
Ruled by magicians, priests, and medicine men,
Defends his past with a patriot's nostalgia
For the assurance of a familiar law,
The comfort of his first inaccuracy
In solving the invading mystery
That tracked him where he went, lost and alone
On the vertical abyss of swallowing stone,
While lightning threatened in a personal tongue
Whose fearful mutterings drove him to be wrong.

By a semantic confusion of the thunder
The cumulous throne of energy flung down
A fiat to man's ignorance and God A
(A sort of filing cabinet for the unknown)
Became God B (an answer to all questions)
And by a nerve's dynamics rose
On nature above nature, till at last
The thunder-that-was-prayed-to (a face like father's)
Strode from the cumulous door down a mountain stair
To scatter the hooligan fates that pulled your hair.

Until the fates came faster than the rescue
(Rickets is a darker fate than Satan)
And a single moving century of the mind
Stuck telescopes into the eye of space,
Threw fossils at creation, reset the clock
From Israel to lead-uranium,
And found a paramecium in Paradise;

While priests and poets juggled and abstracted
An Emersonian last line of defense,
And God became a kind of thinning vapor:
A memory Wordsworth had, quiet Arnold wept,
And Hardy lost in a bitterness of Fate,
Until the high nostalgia for the infinite
Fell from the vision of natural tragedy
And brought him home to social necessity.

An exercise of centuries arrives
From all the parallel bars to its exhaustion,
And from the high trapeze of consequence
Man's aerial parabola from the ape
Merges with a jet's trajectory
Where rocket ships expand the universe

Into a calculus of the calculable.
The thunder closes like a symphony
And reason is the silence after strings.
The skies are silent through every telescope
Of everything but arithmetic and hope
That opens man to a final recognition:
A dendrite with a losing premonition
Caught in the natural storm of chance,
A cortex and a circumstance
With neither freedom nor integrity
Until he recognize necessity
And by a studious decision
Be the mechanic of revision.

Filippo Argenti

From The Inferno, *Canto VIII. Dante and Virgil are crossing the stinking lake that lies before the city of Dis, when Argenti rises from the slime before them. No one has explained Dante's savagery in dealing with Argenti.*

As our boat ran that dead gut, the slime
    Rose before me, and from it a voice cried:
"Who are you who come here before your time?"

And I replied: "If I come, I do not remain.
    But you. Who are you, so fallen and so foul?"
And he: "I am one who weeps." And I then:

"Weeping and waking may you stay for all of me,
    For I know you now, hell-dog, filthy as you are."
Then he stretched both hands to the boat, but warily

The Master shoved him back crying, "Down! Down!
    Back with the other dogs!" And the wretch embraced me
Saying: "Indignant spirit, I kiss you as you frown."

"Blessed be she who bore you. In world and time
    There was one haughtier yet. Not one unbending
Supples his memory. Here is his shadow in slime."

"How many living now, chancellors of wrath
    Shall come to lie here yet in this pigmire
Leaving a curse to be their aftermath."

And I: "Master, it would suit my whim
    To see the wretch dipped into this fine swill
Before we leave this stinking sink and him."

And he to me: "Before we leave, you will."

Letter to Dante

I'm doing you a wrong and well I know it.
It's incivility to simplify
A dead man's words out of his century.
Therefore, while incivility's still inchoate
Here's my apology to man and poet.
I'm told we've entered into valueless days,
But not so deep we're bankrupted of praise.

When masters and makers are no longer heard,
It is not silence but the noise of wrath
That warns the listening universe of death
To come and gather. Praise the singing word.
Ground-man scholar, praise you the man-bird.
And most, this eagle of the *duecenti*.
And now one question: What about Argenti?

I told you at the start I'd be uncivil,
And though there's no great grace in being candid
I'd like to ask the poet what the man did
That afternoon in hell when a calm devil
Whose sense of system nothing could dishevel
Sailed through the damned and entered in his log
"Halfway across we fended off a dog."

It isn't like you. You're a Florentine.
That's one of the few races whose men *relax*
Between political murders and the pox,
With none of this Teutonic *hoch* and *hein*
That drills the sadist to the party-line.
Confess—it was a battle to resist him.
And you'd have lost it too—without the System.

I meant to say, you lost it *to* the System.
That's how it stands with us eight centuries later:
We're such eternal slicks at gathering data

And such poor guts when it comes to digest 'em.
We get our facts half-straight, and then we twist 'em
To fit the system, God, or Harry Truman.
And that's an end to humans being human.

You see I'm talking past as well as to you.
There's that about the dead that doubles us.
We like to think you know what troubles us.
Then, too, you never contradict us, do you?
Well, as we say, "Qualunque cerc' il suo."*
I hope you found whatever the system leads to.
Maybe it's in that Heaven no one reads to.

You have to face it—of all that Gothic house
Only the cellar's saleable. A moral?
By now your forehead's dented with the laurel—
First prize in architecture—and your success
Becomes a natural law. Yet all confess
They *like* it, but except for the heating plant
The thing's a bit of a white elephant.

Well, that's enough of metaphor. I'm thinking
You system-makers have yourselves to answer
When pure idea runs wild, and like a cancer
Roars into living flesh. Argenti sinking
Into the swill has left whole empires stinking
Of perfumed chancellors and sweet aesthetes
Of Panzer-roses blooming in the streets.

Go back, go back and be a Florentine:
Drop him a tear. One mercy spring in all
The rock and *Reich* of Hell. It meant to fall
The first time through, but system made a sign
And there you were—hoist on the party-line.
Proving, I gather, that Hell's really Hell,
And if it isn't, that righteousness does as well.

That's all I had to say. This from a stranger
May seem offensive. No offense intended.
Oh, yes—there's one thing more before I end it:
If you've had Hell enough to calm your anger
I wish you'd tell your putty-nosed *doppelgänger*—
Converts, aesthetes, and all such *cognoscenti*—
That Hell's the place where Dante left Argenti.

Everyone seeks his own [Ciardi's note].

A Guide to Poetry

O che sciagura d'essere senza coglioni!

—the Eunuch's cry from *Candide*

For Cid Corman, who needs it least

One good poet gives an age its voice,
But twenty won't drown out the critics' noise.
For every poet somewhere on the scene
Two schools of critics start a magazine.
Pulpwood forests vanish in a day:
Our literature is not to read but weigh
On trucking scales. In time the gross pulp ton
Will build the New Jerusalem from Kenyon
To every headland of the fractured seas
Whose Jargonauts return with Ph.D.'s
From islands of the polyglot abyss
Where Mr. Eliot's hippopotamus
Plays Lorelei to the eclectic rocks
In the last language of the orthodox.
There, golden sheepskins hang upon the trees
And every death is possible—by degrees.

From farthest Index, see, the Voyagers come
Bearing the spoils of Text and Glossary home.
Beyond Sewanee in Partisan Review
Where New Directions tower upon the view,
Issue by issue, issues forth the chorus
Bent in italics from Lexicon and Thesaurus:
Presyllabic vowel, magnetic tension,
Caudate syntax, consonantal flexion,
Tangential sound, circumferential pause,
Strophic elision, presymbolic clause,
Fractional flux, conjunctive imagery,

And (borne on Mastheads soaring to be free)
Banners whose wind-torn typography
Scatters the holy word: Technology.

    If classic man with an unclinical air
Judged poetry by meaning and by ear,
That's old hat. Now it's done with cathode rays,
The poem's an augite of a diabase,
Its total voltage is its tensile strength
By metric volume, by metaphoric length
Charted on sine waves of syllabic fission.
Nothing is irrelevant but revision—
Whatever the subject, be sure the critics know it:
They've learned to recognize everything but a poet.

    Well, that's your cue, Cid: be at least omniscient.
And though life's short (as what in Boston isn't
Except the "A") and simple fools may be
Discouraged between Aardvark and Zymurgy
Thinking one lifetime is too short a go
For learning everything you have to know,
Don't worry: get your learning like a critic:
Go to school—but sit up in the attic,
And where the ventilator shafts converge
From every classroom hear all learning merge.
By studious application any dunce
Can learn a little—you learn all at once.

    Now write a poem. But first you must be taught
It won't be read if it's not polyglot.
Mention *Gestalt*, TO EV, the *id, esprit.*
Say *ergo* often. Refer symbolically
To Frau von Weltschmertz at the Kursaal table
Who turned (trailing a monotone of sable
Da uno braccio) and snapped your youth like matches
Because she spent the winter in Nome (or Natchez).

Ergo: the ice is bitter on the sea
And seaweed corpses float your memory.
Be fluent with Freud. Explain where Marx was wrong.
Quote the Upanishads (play that up strong)
And when you reach the crucial last parenthesis
(After four lines of asterisks for emphasis)
Clinch it with a hieroglyph or two.
The rule is—if it's meaningless it's true.

That makes you *modern,* but you're still not read:
You've quoted, paraphrased, and pirated
Till even Ezra Pound makes better sense:
Still you're ignored; no one comes off the fence
To nominate you for eternity
Or half a page in an anthology.
What's wrong? Only St. Clique will pull you through
(Understand John and John will understand you):
It's time you did a flattering review.

Begin with frame of reference and tradition.
Mention the poet's times are in transition.
State his dilemma. Say what he rejects.
(N.B. Avoid the question of his sex.)
Say something about *passionate incoherence*
("The wounded knife"), the spirit's reappearance
Despite the fracturing idioms of steel
("In every death I will repeat: *Love's real*"),
Analyze consonants on accentual staves
("We are the eyelids of defeated caves").
If you put nothing in, leave nothing out.
Never be clear, and never be in doubt.
Art is theology. In case of schism
There is no bridge like a neologism:
If there's no meter, say "syllabic slide."
If there's no image, speak of "structural pride

Freed from subservience to the graphic mood."
If there's no poem, you're that much to the good:
You're twice as sure you won't be understood.

Now you've done an essay explaining John:
He must do one for you—you're coming on.
Don't ever fear he'll falter in his praise:
He may think all your stuff is bouillabaisse
And tell his roommate so in sour asides,
But he knows bread is butterable on both sides.
So you're for John, and John is all for you,
And you've been heralded in THE REVIEW.

Next go to work on Tom and Bill and Chet.
And if they wait too long to square the debt—
A little pressure is the soul of trade:
Reputation is not born, but made
By gentle prodding. (There's no need to brawl:
Double entendre is single after all.)
Write them a breezy letter about Joe
Who thought their last few things were only so-so,
Until (poor soul, one has to pity him)
You clarified the personal idiom
"So full of implication, but here and there,
As for example, in *Embezzled Air,*
Could the ellipsis dominate the tone
Sounding an echo not entirely your own?"
—Digress at that point. Speak of "structural flaws
In so much modern verse—of *course,* not *yours*—
But still, well, could it be the poems relax
Their central vigilance, fall to parallax,
And thereby slip into a slack suspension
Of metric flux that dissipates their tension?"
You only mention it because you're taking
Notes for a little essay-in-the-making

About *Some Common Failures of Technique*
You hope to finish in another week.
It's a piece that Kenneth wanted for THE REVIEW,
But something you had planned for years to do,
A kind of "definition of the craft."
In fact when you showed Arthur the first draft
He wrote it was "definitive" and dared say
"Might set the critical tempo of our day
Were it conceived with a little less charity
To friends and fellow poets." But naturally
You'd be reluctant to dispraise the few
Dear friends whose loyalty to THE REVIEW
Has meant so much to poetry—and to you.
"Of course Kenneth's suggestion is quite wise,
But we shall see—there's still much to revise . . ."

It's foolproof, Cid, and if it's proof of fools,
Scribblers and mackerel still must feed in schools.
High art is somewhat lower than you'd think,
And the first rule of rising is to sink.
Then by an equal and opposite reaction
You'll be an *op. cit.* in the land of faction,
An *ibid.*, an *idem*, a *passim*, a *q.v.*,
And all you'll lack is sense and poetry.

From Time
to Time

—•—

(1951)

The Figure 𝄞 Drawn in Wire

To May and John and Dick and Dick

> *art has duties to—*
> *As well as to the "I"—the "You."*
> —Roy Fuller

The Curlicue Ego bends its own way—
A tangle, a small snare, or a fishhook.
There's at least that much choice of ways to say
I. And whatever pains I took
For whatever I took them for, there's some I suppose
Of all three in the I of this book.
Still I'd rather write prose
Worse than a clergyman's than wholly believe
I am the only I in the I I live.

    I as a tangle. The wire mess
    Of a sprung spring, and all of us in part,
    The Rabbit- and the Lion-heart,
    The inside-in who can't confess
    The reasons for or presence of distress.

    I as a small snare ankling a Crow,
    Or hanging the Rabbit by one foot in air,
    Or thorned in the Lion limping to his lair.
    Tricks of the deep wood. And one other I know:
    The Trapper dead in his own trap buried in snow.

    Then I as a fishhook spat upon for luck.
    This is the I of all oceans and possibilities,
    In every inlet a census of the seas.
    I dangling baited a foot above the muck.
    I at last hauling itself from sea ruck.

I, then, as all shapes: sea slug, man o'war,
Two-inch whale, or spirochetic eel,
All wonders and monstrosities there are,

Or only fish enough for a meal.
So catch by catch to empty the impossible sea.
Or only to talk of the big one that gets away
From every gaff, the white and hugest ray—
The all-in-all, the me in you, the you in me.

Manocalzata (Gloved Hand)

Outside my mother's town in Avellino
There stands a rock with a gloved hand chiseled on it.
And so it names a place: *Manocalzata*.

That's all I know of it. I've never been
Nearer to it than three thousand miles.
No one knows whose hand or why the glove.

How many times have I thought of it, needing a name
For what will not be named except by chance,
Or for some reason no one can remember?

As a tree mosses itself into twilight folding
The place of the tree into its presence in time—
Someone could be born there and believe it.

As a diver hangs forever in the eye
Between sea and rock, the arrest of the action glazed
Forever on the air of the place of the dive.

Or simply because it is more important
To remember being than to have been, I am
That hand in the glove and that glove on the hand

Of an unknown stone whose presence I shall someday enter
(As one arrives familiarly to twilight)
Being convinced at last of my presence there.

The Lamb

A month before Easter
Came the time of the lamb
Staked on my lawn
To frisk and feed and be
My loveliest playmate,
Sweeter for being
Sudden and perilous.

Fed from my hand,
Brushed by my love,
A most acrid and gentle wool
Grew clumsy and beautiful.
The lamb is a beast of knees.
A dear and slender bleat
Quavers in it.

The eyes of the lamb
Are two damp surrenders
To the tears of the world:
The child must love
The lamb's total disarmament:
It is the first life to which man
Grew wholly superior.

Year by year the lamb
Danced the black Lenten season.
On the Thursday of sorrow
It disappeared.
On the Friday of blood I knew
What business was in the cellar
And wept a little.

But ah come Easter,
My lamb, my sufferer, rose,
From the charnel cellar,

Glowed golden brown
On religious plenty.
How gravely it was broken
Sprigged for a bridal.

I praise the soil
In the knuckle and habit
Of my feeding parents
Who knew anciently
How the holy and edible
Are one, are life, must be loved
And surrendered.

My tears for the lamb
Were the bath it sprang from
Washed and risen
To its own demand
For a defenseless death.
After the lamb had been wept for
Its flesh was Easter.

Note: The text follows the revised version published in Selected Poems.

The Evil Eye

The belief in the Evil Eye is a still-surviving superstition among Italian peasants. One method of detecting its presence is to pour olive oil on a saucer of holy water. The shapes assumed by the oil can then be read by the gifted.

Nona poured oil on the water and saw the eye
    Form on my birth. Zia beat me with bay,
    Fennel, and barley to scourge the devil away.
I doubt I needed so much excuse to cry.

From Sister Maria Immaculata there came
    A crucifix, a vow of nine days' prayer,
    And a scapular stitched with virgin's hair.
The eye glowed on the water all the same.

By Felice, the midwife, I was hung with a tin
    Fish stuffed with garlic and bread crumbs.
    Three holy waters washed the breast for my gums.
Still the eye glared, wide as original sin,

On the deepest pools of women midnight-spoken
    To ward my clamoring soul from the clutch of hell,
    Lest growing I be no comfort and dying swell
More than a grave with horror. Still unbroken

The eye glared through the roosts of all their clucking.
    "Jesu," cried Mother, "why is he deviled so?"
    "Baptism without delay," said Father Cosmo.
"This one is not for sprinkling but for ducking."

So in came meat and wine and the feast was on.
    I wore a palm frond in my lace, and sewn
    To my swaddling band a hoop and three beads of bone
For the Trinity. And they ducked me and called me John.

And ate the meat and drank the wine, and the eye
    Closed on the water. All this fell between
    My first scream and first name in 1916,
The year of the war and the influenza, when I

Was not yet ready for evil or my own name,
Though I had one already and the other came.

Note: The text follows the revised version published in As If,
not the uncorrected version in Selected Poems.

Fragment of a Bas Relief

The knife, the priest, the heifer
Wander stonily into shadows of erosion,
Profiles of gem-eyed Egypt.

How shall I ever believe the world is real?

Credo

Today
Dr. William Carlos Williams
Of Paterson and Rutherford, N.J.
Delivered a child to its anonymity
And wrote the name of sunlight on a plum.

Mystic River

Medford, Massachusetts

I

The dirty river by religious explorers
Named Mysticke and recorded forever into its future
Civilization of silt and sewerage, recovers
The first sweet moon of time tonight. A tremor
More thought than breeze, more exhalation than motion
Stirs the gold water totem, Snake of the Moon.

"A most pleasynge gentle and salubrious river
Wherein lieth no hindraunce of rock nor shoal
To the distresse of nauvigation, but ever
Aboundaunce of landynge and of fisherie, and withal
Distillynge so sweet an air thorough its course
Sith it runneth salt from the sea, fresh from the source

"And altereth daily through its greater length
Thus, chaungynge and refreshynge the valleys breath,
That," wrote the Gods, "God grauntynge strength
We took up laundes, and here untill oure death
Shall be oure hearthes oure labour and oure joye."
But what the Gods will have they first destroy.

Still Mystic lights the wake of Gods—the moon
Dances on pollution, the fish are fled
Into a finer instinct of revulsion
Than Gods had. And the Gods are dead,
Their sloops and river rotted, and their bones
That scrubbed old conscience down like holystones

Powdered imperceptibly. Their land
Is an old land where nothing's planted
Beside the rollerdrome and hot dog stand—
Still Mystic lights the wake of Gods, still haunted
By the reversing moon. "Let me be clean,"
It cries and cries, but there are years between.

II

And I have stoned and swum and sculled them all:
Naked behind the birches at the cove
Where Winthrop built a landing and a yawl
And tabloids found a famous corpse of love
Hacked small and parceled into butcher's paper,
Joe La Conti stumbled on an old pauper.

Dying of epilepsy or DT's,
And I came running naked to watch the fit.
We had to dress to run for the police.
But did we run for help or the joy of it?
And who was dying at the sight of blood?
Weeks long we conjured its traces in the mud

And there was no trace. Later above the cat-tails
A house frame grew, and another, and then another.
Our naked bank bled broken tiles and nails.
We made a raft and watched the alewife smother.
But there our play drank fever, and Willie Crosby
Went home from that dirty water and stayed to die.

III

So I know death is a dirty river
At the edge of history, through the middle of towns,
At the backs of stores, and under the cantilever
Stations of bridges where the moon drowns
Pollution in its own illusion of light.
Oh rotten time, rot from my mind tonight!

Let me be lit to the bone in this one stir,
And where the Gods grew rich and positive
From their ruinous landing, I'll attend disaster
Like night birds over a wake, dark and alive
Above the shuttered house, and, bound and free,
Wheel on the wing, find food in flight, and be

Captured by light, drawn down and down and down
By moonshine, streetlamps, windows, moving rays.
By all that shines in all the caved-in town
Where Mystic in the crazy moon outstays
The death of Gods, and makes a life of light
That breaks, but calls a million birds to flight.

Note: The text follows revised version published in As If.

A Box Comes Home

I remember the United States of America
As a flag-draped box with Arthur in it
And six marines to bear it on their shoulders.

I wonder how someone once came to remember
The Empire of the East and the Empire of the West.
As an urn maybe delivered by chariot.

You could bring Germany back on a shield once
And France in a plume. England, I suppose,
Kept coming back a long time as a letter.

Once I saw Arthur dressed as the United States
Of America. Now I see the United States
Of America as Arthur in a flag-sealed domino.

And I would pray more good of Arthur
Than I can wholly believe. I would pray
An agreement with the United States of America

To equal Arthur's living as it equals his dying
At the red-taped grave in Woodmere
By the rain and oakleaves on the domino.

Note: The text follows revised version in As If.

Image of Man As a Gardener
after Two World Wars

On a theme by Tommaso Giglio

In the dead hour of the afternoon,
When the sun has overshot the sky
And the parched air stiffens
Like the stroke of a cracked bell, I stand
Hosing, householding my lawn.

The cat stalks ants on the flagstones,
Playful and murderous, but her paws
Are too gross for her victims
Who drudge on undeflected
Between and under
Claws and footpads.
I see there is a size too small to kill.

The paper thuds on the porch
From the helicopter newsrooms
That roar above the house
Bringing me worlds
Faster than I can use them.

I bathe green things
For their summer walk to light,
And think I am miscast as Fertility—
A tree of myth from a different time-turn.
The helicopters are dusting
Their acid gases on the braille of my bark.
It grows more difficult
To read myself by feel.

Still the principle green world survives,
And when vexation sours to despair
In the dry mash of memory,

The first star of evening gnaws through the sunset
Into the polaroid box of another dimension.
Its light lengthens all the universe.

Awaiting that lengthening light I play
Osiris to a grass patch.
I stand. I keep.
Those thousand years' householding in my blood
Take their green seriously. I am come
Of an old family of appetites
And I have too many fathers to deny their ways.
I stand. I keep.

Twice now the helicopters' dew
Turned maps to flypaper and gummed
The springs of all householding. Twice
The waterbottle mountains in the world's office
Shattered in blood on the Oriental carpet,
The tailor worked in wood, the woodsman
Shaved heads, the electrician
Wired the nursery chairs,
The plasterer served lunch,
The housebreaker became the new owner.

Already, what must never happen
Has happened
Twice.
I stand. I keep
A lawn for the world to wish on
Between two gas mountains
And the wind blowing.

When for the third time the helicopters
Roar on the wind like presses
To mash our calamitous ends onto yesterday's paper,
May one of us made small
Move to the green world again
Through every cat's-paw on the procurable stones.

Monday Morning: London

I

Sunlight crumbling from rooftops beheads
    Once more the equestrian conqueror of Monday
    Columned on the skyline he divides.

Sir, grant me, as you must, that to be human
    Man contradicts one minute with another,
    At violence with his own calms and occasions.

So these grenades of light shatter us all,
    A violence gathering at the heart of calm
    As a hearth-pot croons in gathering to a boil.

So in a sea of English roofs I stir
    Half waterlogged with ease in a hot tub
    Watching my naked body sail the sky—

A green-white corpse on a yellow rip of sun
    Floating on chimney pots by a plane's projection.
    A flowering bough on the waters I near shore

And rise from foam, a Goyan Aphrodite
    From my voyage of elements to a Turkish towel,
    A dressing gown, and coffee at the sill.

Below now bowlers roll in a swell of time
    Like buoys over their clerks, a squid-gray cat
    Licks itself on the red reefs of a bomb pit.

This might be calm and yet it is not wholly
    Calm nor violence. Slyly in air
    A ghost raises my hand in a glassy mist

And drains my cigarette. No time at all
    Or as good as any to be asking questions
    Out of the windows of another land,

A bathed rich idle man in his own reflection
    Under the tourist sun, a year, two years,
    Three years, perhaps, before his death in a war.

II

The water knocks in the pipes: di-di-di-DAH.
    V for Eroica. That's a pretty bathos
    Out of the guts of plumbing. My man in the window

Stirs in advance of his death like Chapter One
    Of a book I am re-reading. I buried him once
    On a last page. So he has no surprises:

I am re-reading him for style. On this page
    The equestrian conqueror rears on the reflection
    Of my man's head at a still center of time.

He gallops, but in no hurry. Everywhere
    After all is the center of a universe,
    The top of my man's head, the top of my own.

Unhurried my death waits at the center of all:
    At this moment exactly a man in a field
    Is planting the day I shoot him through the eye,

A recruit from one country is polishing in another
    A rifle butt I must prepare to gnaw
    On a chance curve. I am, of course, just supposing:

Graphically represented this would resemble
    A Dow-Jones average of 48 staple stars
    Computed on a base of 13 stripes.

And the wind blowing, and a brass band at the train.
    Di-di-di-DAH. Save us a way to grace,
    An index point. Give meaning to our graphs.

III

This question of my own private dying
    For public causes—I disapprove on principle.
    The morals of bullets are notoriously loose.

Physically, they are carriers of all infection,
    Camp followers. What war have I ever trusted
    Enough to die for?—Not that I will not go:

My man will say, "We might as well see the show."
    So we will see the show. But at once I imagine
    What heretofore only happened—I am in a plane

Miles over Japan. We have been hit. The flames
    Have washed the plexiglass out of the blisters. The air
    Is minus 50. Burning, I am frost bitten;

Frozen, I burn. There are perhaps ten seconds
    Before the explosion. Perhaps none at all.
    There is time for one thought only. What shall I think?

—My man smiles at the plot. Aesopian:
    The ice-colored goose in the jaws of the red fox.
    Everyone loves a story and a riddle.

What would you think? What would you think, Edward?
    You, Jane? Quick, there's a time limit.
    Yes, there's an answer, but it will spoil it. . . . Well,

The way it happened the goose had given up
    Wheedling the fox. It spoke to itself only,
    And all it said, which it repeated twice, was

"Well, you damn fool," and beat its wings and died.
    Which may or may not be moral enough for the action,
    And certainly is bad narrative technique:

Riddles are not to answer, and the well-made story
    Must not conclude but always be expected.
    Good hard truths. But wasted on the goose.

IV

But imagine, if you will, that we have met,
  The glass shattered between us and our voices
  No longer muffled by waking. Imagine

That you have watched a face change as in sleep
  And leaned over its breathing infinite
  As sleep itself, gently as a wish

Filters itself into a dream. Imagine
  That you have stood just so, and the face spoke
  And you heard your own question.—What has been answered?

Nothing perhaps, but so you will understand
  How a sky of rooks rips from the eaves of time
  Darkening all light with the heart of light.

I mean to say there is a dream as full
  Of wings as the wind from here to Hatteras.
  There, every honest meeting is two ghosts

Walking the mid-Atlantic of that wind
  Toward one another as through time itself
  Where no horizon's higher than an ankle.

V

The water knocks again. Di-di-di-DAH. Enter
  Mrs. Hamilton, poor old stick legs
  Carrying too much body nowhere exactly

Through the cost of living. A maker of beds for others
  And morning's witness to all nights. *Well then,*
  Did I Sleep Well? Thank you, I did, quite well.

A sheet flows on the air, subsides like water
  From two fat thighs. Aphrodite Bedmaker
  Bent to the waters of sleep. Out of that sea

It's a Fine Day, a sun to Warm a Soul,
    A Pity to Waste it. I retire to shave
    A face with a lather beard in a cracked glass.

The hour of examination: stretching of skin
    Over its bones. There's a pimple in the crow's feet,
    Hair growing out of the nose. How did these find me?

On whom are these visitations? (There were two kings
    As like to one another as two falcons
    And where one raised a dove the other dove.)

Knock on the door: *Is there Anything Else you Wish?*
    —Thank you, Mrs. Hamilton, all's well.
    —Then here's Clean Towels and I'll be Moving On.

(An epitaph.) Stick legs across the floor
    And a door turning into another bed.
    A day, that is, from toothbrush to shaving lotion,

At the window the ghost of a pigeon descending in light,
    Sun bursting the chimney pots. Thank you, all's well.
    All's well. All's well. All's well. All's well. All's well.

Elegy I

I fell from the bouncing tailgate to roll in traffic.
        Deaths whizzed about me broken on stone,
And burned by my falling and burned by my bleeding and burned
    By the scrape and peel of my skidding there I lay
        Snarled in horns and burning wet
  In my father's leak and bleed and retch of death.

Who rode the high seat and the open smiling
       Of his ride to beery outings in the trees.
My Big Tony of Jokes, so golden bellied
    Buddhas might sit to his smile. But waved and danced
        A rag-loose fling above his crash
  And let a curbstone drink his skull of blood. I

Fell from his airborne smiling luckier and lither.
       Hippolyte missed me with all his horses.
Christophers burst like grenades from dashboards
    —and missed me. Clang-clanging trolleys
        Threw sparks from under—and stopped short.
  So did all traffic stop and let me pick

My burning and my bleeding from my blood
       That none had drunk but I, not stone,
Nor speeding saint, nor clanging imp, nor my flying father.
    There began mercy and healing, a cold
        Septic discussion of knives and stitches.
  Then cigarettes on a balcony of the sun.

And the indifference of the healing to all but their wounds.
       For I had no father who was no flyer
And the traffic was only shadows on walls of fog.
    So was I laced together over incisions
        By fine puckers through the lips of flesh
  Till all my tears had whispered "Make me whole."

Elegy II

I dream awake in the uptown morning
    Thirty blocks and certain plausibilities
    North of St. Michael's and my father's flower party.

Now where's *l'anarchico* and *il presidente*
    dei Figli d'Italia, the huge pastries
    Of his smile unfolding layer by layer

Through the waxpaper terrors of his joke?
    What a thin country for a big man, that stony
    Suburb of anemic angels weeping.

I stir alive at the Statler gripping
    A dream's end. Letting go: dial coffee,
    Dial Western Union, dial a last look

South to the intersection of wheels and meat
    Where my Big Tony gave himself away
    For stones and flowers and the insurance checks

We ate him in. It took four hundred weeks
    For his letter to stop coming—an end of Tuesday.
    After a while there's no death left to eat.

But breakfast on a tray in a strange bed
In a dream-assaulted morning of the dead.

Elegy III, Cavalcante

"It was Cavalcante," my Mother said, "killed you Father.
  My son grow tall and avenge him." (And I was three
  and ready.) "He told him and told him
  not to go fast." But Cavalcante
was a bad man, and, speeding, he killed my Father.

And I who was the only son of that murder
  hunted a name in my dreams and posed for the death
  he begged me to spare him. "Spare you?
  Better," my pose said, "save your breath
for prayer, for I am the only son of that murder,

and my Mother's tears are in me frozen to knives.
  No man is dead who leaves a son in his name.
  Why Didn't You Go Slower!"
  And he begged me to spare him all the same,
but my Mother's tears were in me frozen to knives.

And I was six and seven and twelve and tall.
  I was twenty and grown. I was thirty and remembered
  nothing. And then his name
  came back, and I went to his wake dismembered
into three and six and seven and not at all,

and I stood by the death of the wreck that had been the blood
  and error and evil of all my Mother's tears.
  I stood and I was three
  and there was the dream again. Down all the years
I stood in the wreck of the death that had been my blood.

The Cow

A greensweet breathing
Wakes me from my noon nap
In the high grass by the fence.
Her head swings in above eye level
Weaving through the parade of grasses
Like a Chinese New Year's dragon.

You see a new cow this way:
A sod's-eye view of a munching dinosaur
Peeling the grass from time,
All sweetslobber and greenfleck
In the going going going
Of her machine jaws.

She sees me now,
And roundabout as a steamshovel's boom
Her neck swings its bucket
To the upper air of a question.

But she finds no answer,
Or is used to me and doesn't care,
Or does but forgets,
For back swings the boom
Into the sagebottoms of grass,
And here we are eye to eye
With a single daisy snarled between us
In the stem-tangle
Of sweetdrooling no-time
Going going going
In her machine.

Into the glazed eye
Of the munching cow
Leans the daisy
In a foreground of the hills.

The Cartographer of Meadows

I

The cartographer of meadows does not rose
His meridians. There is no north in a bramble.
Nor south nor anywhere is a scroll of thorns
In blue grass. They are simply consecutive with.
As the bee is born knowing the trumpet flower
Is at once everywhere he comes upon it.

This legend scales the hive to the meadow. The wind
That blows the forager from the wild rose
Can only blow him to another. Thus
All direction is one gathering:
There is only the place of the flower to be emptied
And the place of the bringing inward of sustenance.

This is a reality. Historied in amber
It gems the mountain's pores. Alive it drives
Spring through the valley, the scyther from the fields.
Drives or is driven: who will dare say
One thing is cause and one is consequence?
Do the bees chase the scyther or does he draw the bees?

It is enough to say there is no direction.
Flight is consecutive with flight. And life with life.
Should the man be pursued by the Adam of the bee that pursues him,
Would the Adam of the man run a different way?
The bee is all Adam as the flower is,
A continuous receptacle for the legend.

II

To the military and expedient mind
There is no such cartographer. At best
He could only exist as an impediment

To the line of march. At worst he must be the enemy.
Between extremes, it would still be inconceivable
To imagine him as fit for active service.

So it is aims that trample meadows. An Army
Enters a direction and the meadow
Is churned in that going. But the cartographer
Outlives his destruction. He makes of time
The map of his own presence. He is where he touches.
When he turns, that is another presence. A being.

The soldiers move north to battle and their bodies
Move south to burial in the ruined meadows.
The cartographer charts the projection of a grave,
A conformal of the wrong Adam. And at once
It is sprung with flowers where the universe of a hive
Expands once more upon the mounds of time.

When I am whole I will be that cartographer
And my right Adam. As the bee is his meadow
From gathering to bringing. As he wakes
Honeycombed with his own presences
Of mullen congruent with the piney mountain.
As he moves to amber from his resinous drowning.

Annals

I. Tricodon of Bruges, a Flemish
    Poet of no reputation and
    Of no talent but tears,
    Wept into his inkwell
    All one night, then hanged himself—
    His only gift to the dawn.

II. Aldo, the tragedian of Padua,
    Was another weeper. Passion in him
    Invited all accident. Sandbags
    Rained on his love scenes, flies
    Wavered on his battles, the doors of his castles
    Fell on him when he bolted them.

III. Malorca of Galicia was another.
     A defender. Shot at his wife's lover
     And killed the General's palomino.
     He left his tears on a wall in Estremadura:
     God grant me sustenance within myself
     To bear the dirty chuckle of the wind.

IV. Sophia of Montenegro died naked in a pie
    On her way to the Duke's table. Her own
    Golden surprise for him. But he
    Was dining in his chambers with La Guernerra
    When his firebird sank through its gilding
    Under the lorgnette of the Countess Merla.

V. Otto, the declaimer at the court of Saxony,
    Swore to the Elector on his head
    There were no Poles at Frieden
    That two dogs and one huntsman could not take.
    Smerzni, who felled him, sent the head to court:
    I hear, my cousin, your general owes you this.

VI. To remember what has never been is not
   To lie but to read the future:
   A place in nature where Polonius the pincushion
   Stitched into a tapestry of Clichy
   Speaks into Van Gogh's ear, and all perceive
   The action of incorrigible farce.

High Tension Lines across a Landscape

There are diagrams on stilts all wired together
Over the hill and the wind and out of sight.
There is a scar in the trees where they walk away
Beyond me. There are signs of something
Nearly God (or at least most curious)
About them. I think those diagrams are not
At rest.
        I think they are a way of ciphering God:
He is the hugest socket and all his miracles
Are wired behind him scarring the hill and the wind
As the waterfall flies roaring to his city
On the open palms of the diagram.
                There is
Shining, I suppose, in that city at night
And measure for miracles, and wheels whirling
So quick-silver they seem to be going backwards.
And there's a miracle already. But I
Went naked through his wood of diagrams
On a day of the rain beside me to his city.

When I kissed that socket with my wet lip
My teeth fell out, my fingers sprouted chives,
And what a bald head chewed on my sick heart!

Shore Piece

I.   It is someone's deserted private beach.
     (An astonishment: who dares to buy an ocean?)
     We have trespassed naked into the surf
     And naked in the sun and wet from sea
     Come spumed like myth onto a birth of sex.

II.   This is the statue of my woman beside me
     In a separation of myself. "Darling,"
     A mind at play in my mind records on the wind
     For monuments, "you are fiercer than a rape."
     But we have gone away into ourselves
     And nothing is said. We must wait to need one another.

III. So in the sun's bath of calm I float under
     A cloud whimsy: the sky's a lens under which
     I am the amoeba of my own passing
     Reflected in the blue eye of nowhere—
     A sequence of my own shapelessness.
     To cross any distance I must distort myself
     Endlessly into my own being.

IV.   I have never been
     Deeper into exhaustion and the sun.
     If you open my skull you will find a glass snowball.
     And a glassed-in wind over a glassed-in surf.
     There is a name sky-written there by a stunt pilot
     (Who was too much a boy) but it fades already.
     And so goodbye, my darling, where the clouds go:
     I am my own wind to erase myself.

The Clock in the Mirror

If A and B, two persons of identical age, depart from and return
to a given point on the earth's surface, and if they have traveled at
speeds greater than light, it can be shown that according to the angle
between the courses they take:

> *1. A will return younger than B.*
> *2. B will return younger than A.*
> *3. They will return younger than one another.*

—From a lecture on Relativity

This is the blur of dimension, the past arriving.
The clock in the mirror tells a different time
From the clock on the mantel, from the clock wavering
Through the trap door in the eye's reflection.

Kiss me Tuesday: it bends through the Khan's Empire,
Pre-viewed tomorrow on Pollux, re-run from Sirius.
On the main stem of Orion I took in a cutie
Billed as Eve de la Terre, a one-star attraction.

How far can a minute see its going? On Arcturus
I was again my waiting for will be.
Once I have learned to outrun my passing
I shall peel only the orange in the mirror

And the hair of that glass head and the nails
Of that glass hand, while mechanics of kisses
Repair us in time locks—visible memory
In a cubic mirror. Which of ourselves shall we be?

Two Songs for a Gunner

I. Firing Tracers

When I was dangerous tracers leaped from me.
What a wild fountain I sprayed at the zodiac
Falling how-many-colored to sea-dark
Of the world's body under, where powerfully
I rode it and rode it done. "Look, Mother, how gay
And luminous a sperm I spend in play!"

II. Being Fired At

When I was danger's the tracers' endless
Jeweled cobra struck at my running tomb
In a cloud. How chaste and sweet a womb
I covered in to praise its luminous
Waver and fall from power. And as it fell,
How deep an egg I curled in very well.

March Morning

Black snow, the winter's excrement
On the foul street, thaws
Oil-slick puddles traffic splashed
Back on black snow. Spring
Begins its rumor everywhere,
A new critique and weather.
The ripple is running under
The river's rotting ice,
The winter-lock jaws open.
There is no sun. Only a gray day
Warmer than most.

                    Warmer than most,
Colder than some, I mail

Three letters at the corner, turn
On black slush skirting puddles,
Shy from traffic splash, wade
The unclean graves of winter,
Drift-dregs of dead accumulation.
The first corpse is beer bottle green,
A honeycomb of filth on glass.
What's dirty passes. And returns.
What's clean . . .

              What's clean? My dirty death,
My death to walk on, rehearses
Days in a rotting season. Love—
The pulse in a skin glove. Time—
A civic trash on Spring's groundswell. The Scene—
Hellgate at the glacial recession,
Flower faces of children in red hats
Already wanton in water, splashing
Oil-slick puddles on the black snow,
Their mothers scolding from windows.

                 From windows,
You smile, and I,
Having mailed three promises
To the fiction of a world,
Return through these real Limbos
Balancing a bubble of myself
That shines, and is surprised it does not break.

My Father's Watch

One night I dreamed I was locked in my Father's watch
With Ptolemy and twenty-one ruby stars
Mounted on spheres and the Primum Mobile
Coiled and gleaming to the end of space
And the notched spheres eating each other's rinds
To the last tooth of time, and the case closed.

What dawns and sunsets clattered from the conveyer
Over my head and his while the ruby stars
Whirled rosettes about their golden poles.
"Man, what a show!" I cried. "Infinite order!"
Ptolemy sang. "The miracle of things
Wound endlessly to the first energy
From which all matter quickened and took place!"

"What makes it shine so bright?" I leaned across
Fast between two teeth and touched the mainspring.
At once all hell broke loose. Over our heads
Squadrons of band saws ripped at one another
And broken teeth spewed meteors of flak
From the red stars.

        You couldn't dream that din:
I broke and ran past something into somewhere
Beyond a glimpse of Ptolemy split open,
And woke on a numbered dial where two black swords
Spun under a crystal dome. There, looking up
In one flash as the two swords closed and came,
I saw my Father's face frown through the glass.

Note: The text follows revised version in As If.

Landscapes of My Name

*Calling a person by name is recognized as the best method
of awakening him when he is sleeping, or of awakening a
somnabulist.*

　　　　　　　　　　　　　　—Freud, *Delusion and Dream*

Like trumpets on a dry mountain, I blow
The high hot note of my name away
Brassy and far on the still Sierras.
John! John! The mountains cry and diminish.

Stone fall would do as well. The silence
Is time past and time to come.
The disturbance of the present sinks like squid
Into the upthrust sea bottoms
Where a different arrangement of a billion years
Suns the fossil by the eagle's nest.
　　　　　　　　　　　　　John! John!
I cry in the fossil present. My breath, my name,
Wheels once like nesting birds disturbed
From the endless lips of the crevice.
Then settles back into an after-image.

Was there a stir on the mountain? Does God
Believe in me? Did the mountain speak?
Something farther than I could hear blew back my breath.
The mountain and the mountain beyond the mountain.
I see them waver through the seas of time.
An army of my presence
Rang on the shore and the waters divided before me
And a voice woke crying
　　　　　　　　　　　　　John! John!
From the muddy throat of the gulf.

Anatomy Lab

I

Wavering his scums and incisions
Cadaver swims up like a vision
From the smile of his sleep in the brine,
From his casket and sour uterine
Ret in the slop jars of form.

So this is our shrivel to norm?
He lies at the root of the graph,
The totally distributed life
When the eyes have forgotten their face
But remembered the family place
And returned from traintables of time
For a souvenir look at the slime
And forgotten to wipe it away.

Now scholar and scholarship lay
Gloved hands on the fish of his heart,
On the litter of mice in his throat,
On the warren and sponge of his lung,
On the gray coral bed of his tongue.
> *We have opened his flesh for a hoax.*
> *We have rigged him for sophomore jokes.*
> *But the wire through his penis horseplays*
> *The sex of our own heavy days,*
> *Our bird in the cage of his ribs.*
Hic iacet Cadaver. His nibs,
The Marquis of Formaldehyde,
Is receiving. We hurry inside
Like inquisitors: "Sir, we ask
Whence and Whither. Now rip off your mask."
He gives us his answer in bone:
Undressed to skeleton

He drops from the slack of his jaw
The drunken last face of the Law.
Misgovernment lewder than hate
Grins from his obscene state:
"*L'état c'est moi!* For a price
Let any man have a slice."

II

Three Songs for Cadaver

i

Cadaver's a box of cold meat
And the scholar has opened him wide.
(Enter poets on little cold feet.)
Cadaver's a box of cold meat
And formaldehyde pickles him sweet
A feast of debris for the tide.
Cadaver's a box of cold meat
And the scholar has opened him wide.

ii

"Oh where is the soul in the meat?
And what of the stuff of our wish?
Is he only a bad thing to eat?
Oh where is the soul in the meat?
Did it rise from his death like a sheet
And soar out of sight with a swish?
Oh where *is* the soul?" "In the meat.
And what *of* the stuff of our wish?"

iii

At that supper the Paraclete:
"The feast and the feeder are one."
Let the hungry be had in to eat
At that supper The Paraclete
Gives Cadaver charge of the meat.
Of the brine, of the loaves of stone.
At that supper the Paraclete,
The feast, and the feeder are one.

Joe with a Wooden Leg

Joe with a wooden leg comes home
So deep into my heart, pity is lamer
Than wounds, whose flesh, like lumber,
Stumps all the hopeful experts and turns numb
The forward foot of time, whose dream is
Clumsy, kissless, and therefore backward to
Joe on the S-curve of a dive through
Summer-salt air where Joe is
Once more Joe and Mary
Throws him wish
Without
Pity.

Heatwave

By ten we know the day is out of order:
Heat jams a melted slug in the clock's turnstile,
Piles up in the house like mobs, breathes down our necks,
Trains of it stall in soot across the room.

Our lives that fled from climate
To an enclosed air, return to climate,
Strip naked to a swelter of endurance.
A day of the mind's South.

                              Winters of energy
Grow dim as adolescence, a furious nuisance.
We think, as of incredible ignorance,
Where Northern legends of industry and merit
Annoy themselves in air-conditioned dooms,
Trade latitudes of the equatorial door.

Better this resignation in stone shade,
The Latin defeat and calm—our sleeping dogs,
Too lax for savagery or acquisition,
Sprawled on the sun, their patient look
All given to being, a gentler way to die.

Elegy for Sam

Here's one more dead man, boxed, nosegayed.
The botanical garden of his last look
Where splinted roses limp on wire
And orchid bows gift-wrap him to himself,
Blooms us away again. Goodbye, Sam.

The family ruins itself on the debt
Of his last state. Marble says:
Dress him in new clothes, rouge him, shave him.
(Is he in the doll of himself? Is there
A doll in us?) Satin says:
He is, there is. Tallow says: Goodbye, Sam.

In China with fireworks to guard him,
In Bali cutting a string at the grave,
In Egypt coveting great tombs. Here, there,
Burial details with a bulldozer at the edge
Of the airstrip. Matter for mirrors:
Who sees whom as the bierside?

The more complex the chemical organization
The more unstable the compound. He rusts
Faster than iron. The violence of his breaking
Hurries him from his taint in us.
Flower him. Then down deep fast
Before lame roses stumble, spill. Goodbye, Sam.

Hello. Mrs. Buff-Orpington. Cluck-cluck.

Childe Horvald
to the Dark Tower Came

Well, they loaded him with armor and left him
All night by the altar rail, and he was young,
And darks have voices when you pray to hear them,
And in the morning his lord unbuckled
And blessed his shoulder, and most were drunk yet
From the night wassail, and all the girls . . . .

At, say, sixteen can you doubt the dark and the girls?
The grail, they told him, *the grail*. And he: *I swear it*.

And so the tower rose beyond his dead horse
In the valley of drifted bones. He blew his horn then
(Noise of the true man), and unbuckled, and came twirling
The folderol sword hilted with girls' garlands
And of course *Blut und Ehre* sloganed on it,
And worse nonsense brave in his head.

                              And what would you
Do if you were the magician hearing
His boy-murderous blast shaking your phials and silences,
Watching him come shouting *St. Poobah and the dragon!*
Into your library and uncertainty?

                              It takes
More than civility to civilize
The very young. I say send out a peri
If you've her address or her incantation,
Or drug him if you can, or conjure him on
To the bog of his own idiocy. But for Godsake
Don't let him into the house with his nice profile
All tensed for swordplay and lifting of heads
At arm's length over the fallen books.

Or if you've real
Magic, change him! change him!

Memorial Day

"Well," they were saying, "The war's over."
All the parades were coming back
And when they stopped
The uniforms went off and hung themselves in closets.
"Here's Johnny again," they were saying. "Hello, Nathaniel.
Heard you was hit at Shiloh. Welcome back."

Then they began saying,
"Lincoln's been shot."
They kept saying it all night over the wires
And by the time it came out the other end
It was already saying "Lincoln is dead."
And everyman's skull was a sky
And had a buzzard in it that wheeled and cried,
"I eat magnificence."

Now it's all pictures and parades and schoolbooks.
Johnny's fading out of the family album.
Nathaniel's wound is gone from Shiloh.
And any one can believe Lincoln is dead.

You don't even have to remember Nathaniel in '24
When the G.A.R. was already riding in touring cars
To keep up with the Spanish War Vets
Who were already too slow for the Legionaires.
Maybe I was the only one young enough to see
Nathaniel's change to a buzzard in the back seat
And stretch and fly. I had a big sky then
But he filled it all
Full of dreams I had
A long time running because

There are pictures and parades for all the rest,
But you have to dream the buzzard.

Another Comedy

Nel mezzo del cammin di nostra vita
mi ritrovai per una selva oscura,
che la diritta via era smarrita.

In storms of half-light, in a separate, dim,
    and swallowing air, I came to my own turning
    from the world's way. The night-light of a hymn

Quavered beyond that road, half sound, half burning.
    "Statistics, God, and will-it-come-to-rain?"
    world sang to world again, half prayer, half yawning

Between the dream-deep and the counterpane.
    —And so I found myself in a dark wood
    Where everything that flourished seemed inane

And nothing I could cherish came to good,
    and there's the hell of it. But in you must
    and in I meant to go. And as I stood

Wondering which way, there came a wind of dust
    out of a cavemouth, and a metal roar
    that left the whole wood smelling of exhaust.

"Hell," I thought, "must be diesel." But before
    I reached the cave a tank poked into sight,
    its hatches closed, its sides stenciled for war,

its gun-shield mottoed: "I am in the right."
    But at one gun port I read: "Hollywood."
    And at another: "Mother, hold me tight."

I waved. It answered with a burst that chewed
    the ferns I dove to—greeting and reply.
    Like water down a sluice I flowed through mud

counting each puddle one more place to die,
　　when a voice reached me from behind a rock:
　　"This way. This way." And still behind me I

heard voices shouting and the wet ground shook
　　with tank-tread. I cried out: "Which way? Which way?"
　　"This way"—It seemed almost the rock spoke.

And then, spotlighted in the sun's last ray,
　　I saw a face above a bush that sat
　　at some dark entrance into that dead clay.

A figure rose. The tatters of his suit
　　were denim. His scratched skin was fair.
　　He seemed a gentle and untidy brute

with a wild beard and four winds in his hair.
　　He beckoned and I followed. But the shaft mouth
　　gave off so foul a taint on the sick air—

as if the dead were given back their breath
　　after utter corruption—I drew away
　　thinking I would rather face than breathe death.

But his lantern disappeared into the clay
　　and with a shudder I ran after it
　　stumbling down the wet shaft. How shall I say

I knew it all already?—his lamp, the spirit
　　of that dead passage, a ghost more shadow than light.
　　Myself doomed there to follow and to fear it

in a dark dance through drainpipes of the night
　　as if a sodden firefly led a roach
　　into a nightmare's plumbing. And out of sight

a sound of sluggish water seemed to crouch
　　tainting the air. Then suddenly we came
　　to a stone cavern lofty as a church

and lighted at one wall by one flame
    and no door anywhere. Two shapes rose there
    in business clothes and cassocks: "Name? Your name?"

My guide walked on as if he did not hear
    and left me struggling for a name. But none
    would come. I thought. "I know this nightmare:

I dreamed it seven years running and woke alone
    on spikes of puberty. Is this its den?"
    But now my guide had turned to call, "Come on,

what's holding you?" And I: "These gentlemen—"
    And he: "Are never really there until you are.
    Do you remember me at all?" And I then:

"What must I do?" And he to me: "Endure
    a change of imagination: I did no wrong."
    The ghosts blew out. I led him back from there.

Goddamn the wood that made his death so long.

As If

———•———

(1955)

From *Poems to Judith*

Men Marry What They Need.
I Marry You

Men marry what they need. I marry you,
morning by morning, day by day, night by night,
and every marriage makes this marriage new.

In the broken name of heaven, in the light
that shatters granite, by the spitting shore,
in air that leaps and wobbles like a kite,

I marry you from time and a great door
is shut and stays shut against wind, sea, stone,
sunburst, and heavenfall. And home once more

inside our walls of skin and struts of bone,
man-woman, woman-man, and each the other,
I marry you by all dark and all dawn

and learn to let time spend. Why should I bother
the flies about me? Let them buzz and do.
Men marry their queen, their daughter, or their mother

by names they prove, but that thin buzz whines through:
when reason falls to reasons, cause is true.
Men marry what they need. I marry you.

Note: The text follows the corrected 1958 version from I Marry You.

Sometimes the Foundering Fury

Sometimes the foundering fury that directs
the prayer through storm, the sucking mouth;
sometimes a gentleness like a parent sex,
sometimes an aimless tasting mild as broth

or the drugged eye of the invalid, sometimes
the naked arm laid loose along the grass
to the brown-eyed breast and the great terms
of the turning flank printed by root and moss.

Sometimes a country in a white bird's eye
coasting the shells of cities in their past,
the roads that stretch to nothing but away,
a horseman wandering in his own dust—

say you were beautiful those years ago,
flush as the honey-blonde who rode the shell
in Sandro Botticelli's studio,
and what we are now, we were then,

and lost, and found again—what shall we wish
to visit from ourselves against that death
but their imagination on our flesh?
There is no other body in all myth.

The Deaths about You
When You Stir in Sleep

The deaths about you when you stir in sleep
hasten me toward you. Out of the bitter mouth
that sours the dark, I sigh for what we are
who heave our vines of blood against the air.

Old men have touched their dreaming to their hearts:
that is their age. I touch the moment's dream
and shrink like them into the thing we are
who drag our sleeps behind us like a fear.

Murderers have prayed their victims to escape,
then killed because they stayed. In murdering time
I think of rescues from the thing we are
who cannot slip one midnight from the year.

Scholars have sunk their eyes in penitence
for sins themselves invented. Sick as Faust
I trade with devils, damning what we are
who walk our dreams out on a leaning tower.

Saints on their swollen knees have banged at death:
it opened; they fell still. I bang at life
to knock the walls away from what we are
who raise our deaths about us when we stir.

Lovers unfevering sonnets from their blood
have burned with patience, laboring to make fast
one blood-beat of the bursting thing we are.
I have no time. I love you by despair.

Till on the midnight of the thing we are
the deaths that nod about us when we stir,
wake and become. Once past that fitful hour
our best will be to dream of what we were.

The Health of Captains

All wars are boyish and are fought by boys.

—Melville

The health of captains is the sex of war:
the pump of sperm built in their polished thighs
powers all their blood; the dead, like paid-off whores,
sleep through the mornings where the captains rise.

The gloss of captains is the flags of war:
the polished shoes of death, the brass of poise,
the profile fitted like a tool in leather
between the paddlewheels of marching boys.

The deaths of captains are the tic of war:
the bone-hinged jaw punched open by surprise
under the marshsmoke- and cycloning-air
whose devils suck the last light from their eyes.

Fife and drum dollops drop to bins of grass
the health and gloss and deaths of captains are.
The boys behind the dead boys change their brass.
The womb of woman is the kit of war.

Elegy

My father was born with a spade in his hand and traded it
for a needle's eye to sit his days cross-legged on tables
till he could sit no more, then sold insurance, reading
the ten-cent-a-week lives like logarithms from
the Tables of Metropolitan to their prepaid tombstones.

Years of the little dimes twinkling on kitchen tables
at Mrs. Fauci's at Mrs. Locatelli's at Mrs. Cataldo's

(Arrividerla, signora. A la settimana prossima. Mi saluta,
la prego, il marito. Ciao, Anna. Bye-bye.)
—known as a Debit. And with his ten-year button

he opened a long dream like a piggy bank, spilling the dimes
like mountain water into the moss of himself, and bought
ten piney lots in Wilmington. Sunday by Sunday
he took the train to his woods and walked under the trees
to leave his print on his own land, a patron of seasons.

I have done nothing as perfect as my father's Sundays
on his useless lots. Gardens he dreamed from briar tangle
and the swampy back slope of his ridge rose over him
more flowering than Brazil. Maples transformed to figs,
and briar to blood-blue grapes in his look around

when he sat on a stone with his wine-jug and cheese beside him,
his collar and coat on a branch, his shirt open,
his derby back on his head like a standing turtle. A big
man he was. When he sang *Celeste Aida* the woods
filled as if a breeze were swelling through them.

When he stopped, I thought I could hear the sound still moving.
—Well, I have lied. Not so much lied as dreamed it.
I was three when he died. It was someone else—my sister—
went with him under the trees. But if it was her
memory then, it became mine so long since

I will owe nothing on it, having dreamed it from all
the nights I was growing, the wet-pants man of the family.
I have done nothing as perfect as I have dreamed him
from old-wives tales and the running of my blood.
God knows what queer long darks I had no eyes for

followed his stairwell weeks to his Sunday breezeways.
But I will swear the world is not well made that rips
such gardens from the week. Or I should have walked
a saint's way to the cross and nail by nail
hymned out my blood to glory, for one good reason.

Days

Something in the wild cherry—
the cat or another caution—
triggers the starlings and the tree
explodes. Who would have thought
so many pieces of life in one tree?
The air shakes with their whirligig.
The first have already lit across the field
before the last one's out.

They fling their bridge of lives
and of some sort of reason
across the field, a black
rainbow over my surprise.
What is it I prize in these commotions?
The burst of the live thing
takes me wholly to praise.
And if there are no gods

shaking the tree, as once
the father of man would have knelt
to omens, there is still
principle in his blood:
what goes is all going,
and all going graces
the true quick fact
a taken man is. I am

man again in their going.
Deep in the field of my coming
and of my father's coming
I stand taken
in this one rush
of lives upon us all.
What I had forgotten
was the suddenness of the real.

Now I remember
my mother wept for me
watching her man in this field
go slower and slower
while over him faster and faster
the wind shook out
the inexhaustible lives
that all life leaves.

The empty cherry quivers
in balance, spinning the light
inside itself. I had forgotten
how gradually the real is.
These two thoughts answer me:
between the exploded instant
and the long weather,
what walks the field is man.

Thursday

I

After the living, the attic. Then the rain,
and children prowling indoors turned into the attic
to treasure-hunt the remains.

So Thursday when the wind turned.
Whistles blew: No school. No school.
Northeast from the Atlantic.

Rummage day under the eaves. The dressmaker's dummy
that was Aunt Clara welcomed us. The rain
scratched like a kitten. *Let's play store.*

Not much imagination but let them be.
Sea-blown kittens over aunty's ghost
change no habits. They *like* to play store.

Then Jenny brings me the album she bought for two papers.
"Look! Look at the man in the funny hat!"
—Hello, Father.

Is heaven the cave above us, under the rafters
aged the color of leather? The dead are dusty
everywhere we touch them. Jenny brings me

Paul at three in his grandmother's lap:
the gray-leather smile at the suede child I think
means nothing. Age is no skill but a nuisance.

Store it away.
The rain is its own arrival. It needs nothing.
If accident follow the act, is that an action?

Yes, Jenny, it must go back.
The faces need their time, as time needs faces.
Someday even Jenny will need to be sad

as great grandmother's talons on the child,
as Aunt Clara's dummy, as Father's easy thirties
in a funny hat.

But oh, Mother, what eyes my father had!

II

Order? The son of the man beside his children
has no other. Why should I teach them the rain
who know already they can play in it?
Now they are dressing the dummy in old curtains.
Well, what if Aunt Clara's heaped in one more dust rag?
Father's a laugh in a derby?—let them be:

time's for a time. I'm here to beg not preach.

III

Fingers drum on the roof. *Ratapan, ratapan, ratapan.*
Snakes writhe on the sea.

                 And the big wind.
Ratapan. For the dilatory man.
For the literary, tutelary

             capillary man.

I know no artery to the dead nor vein dark
as the Cretan's river:

             a smallest mesh
webs Uncle Cesar to his handlebars
(very gay nineties)

          and the great stance
seeming to say: "Throw me a live bull; I'm hungry."
No more. It's after dinner

         And Father again,
with Mother a beauty beside him; this man's woman
in the flower time of starting:

             veils, smiles,

initiation rituals—the solid seeming
places of the tribe.
                    And Father's father,
photographer- and Sunday-scrubbed and scarved,
Sorrento painted behind him
                    Con affetto
al mio figlio lontano. And over his ear
a rip in the photographer's Sorrento.
                              Canvas too
turns to a leathery dust. A dusty sea
sneezes in the wind.
                    Clara, Cesar, Lorenzo.
Licked by the flaming children. Felice, Cristina.
Ratapan, ratapan, ratapan,
                    for the fritillary man.

IV

And the Sunday paper. Last Sunday's.
Already an archive under the pitched roof.
THE ROYAL LIFE ON THE PORTUGUESE RIVIERA.
FOG ENDANGERS JERSEY TURNPIKE.
DIOCLETIAN PONDERS DIVIDED EMPIRE.
P. VERGILIUS MARO PREDICTS CHRIST.
DANGER OF GLACIER SEEN AVERTED.

Tom Ferril. That's his trick for a World Edition
of a One Star Final.
He wants to publish a paper for Mount Massive.
Well, haven't I stolen more than that. Or begged it?—
Have an emotion for me: let me live:
shall I need less than a child the child's perfection
at rummage under the rafters? Let any man store me.

—And so the temptation to prayer. The exultant refusal
to let the dead go dusty under the rain.
Men have missed death but worms have eaten them

in love with life.—And there's another steal.
As the children must be stolen
out of my father's archives. Traveler's gear
forgotten in the dust of a lighted fog.

V

And what road?
"The Turnpike's record to date stands
at 5.8 fatalities per
100,000,000 vehicle miles,
As compared to a national average
of 7.6." As compared—
to what?
       At an average rate
of 11 miles per hour the Tiber flows
96,426,000 miles per millennium,
with a record to date of
one civilization.
          Over the Tiber,
looking down from the Ponte del Risorgimento,
I saw a hawk float by.
Not a reflection in the sky.
The bird itself in its own death,
wings outspread on the water,
clouded by flies in its going,
a nebula.
       The stars are no further
over Sioux Falls than over the Coliseum.
In Jersey City
I saw the day-moon over the wood
of the video aerials. When I entered the Turnpike
the fog came. By Entrance Eleven
the wreck waited. The corpse grinned out of metal.

VI

And the rain. The rain.
Pattering the car top.
Coming too fast for the wiper.
My daughter slept at my back
in a portable bed.
The ambulance came
for tidiness only.
There was nothing left to save.

The dead man lay
openly in the rain.
Morbid, I waited,
pleased by my own revulsion.
The man is dead
when the rain falls openly.
There are roofs on the living.
His rain is another sound.

For him the box is ripped.
The kittens have scratched it.
The flies await their constellations vainly.
The river is stone to the crematorium;
the embalmed vein, a solid.
There is nothing the stars
may gnaw in their swarms
but dark.

VII

Muddle, muddle, muddle, says the rain
on the roof. The sea's hissing.
The fog's stuck to the world.
Somewhere a bank gulps gone.

So Thursday among the children who do not see
days but games, places but games.
A singleness of the blood at its round flowing.
Why play at less than life?

Muddle, muddle, muddle, says the rain.
Roundness is all. The round game like a music:
the first sound calling the second into being.
Lightly, lightly, *graziosamente.* Follow the music

into itself. A road like any other.
Past children in the rain, past the stone news,
beyond the rip in the old man's Sorrento.
Ratapan. For the cinerary man.

But oh, children, what eyes our father had!

Three Views of a Mother

I

Good soul, my mother holds my daughter,
the onion-skin bleached hand under the peach-head.
Ti-ti, she says from the vegetable world, *la-la.*
A language of roots from a forgotten garden.

She forms like a cresting wave over the child;
it is impossible not to see her break
and bury and the child swim up a girl
and the girl reach shore a woman on my last beach.

Ti-ti, la-la. I will not fight our drowning,
nor the fall of gardens. I am curious, however,
to know what world this is. The honey-dew head
of the child, the cauliflower head of the grandmother

bob in the sea under the garden. *Ti-ti, la-la.*
The grandmother rustles her hands like two dry leaves
and the child writhes round as a slug for pleasure,
leaving the trail of its going wet on the world.

II

I see her in the garden, loam-knuckled in Spring,
urging the onions and roses up. Her hands
talk to the shoots in whispers, or in anger
they rip a weed away between thumb and fist.

When the jonquils open she makes a life of them.
Before the radishes come she is off to the fields,
scarved and bent like a gleaner, for dandelions.
When the beans are ready she heaps them in a bowl.

The Fall is lit by peaches. As if they were bubbles
she balances them from the branch and holds them out
one by one in her palm. Her eyes believe
the world self-evident in its creation.

Last of all the chrysanthemums take tongue
from the spikes of November. She lingers by glass boxes
coaxing the thickened earth a little longer
to hoard the sun for sprigs of mint and parsley.

But Winter comes and she is out of employment
and patience. She is not easy to be with
here by the buried garden. Winter mornings
she wakes like shrouded wax, already weary

of the iron day. *Ti-ti,* she says to the child,
la-la. A piece of her life. But her mind divides:
she knows there is seed enough for every forest,
but can she be sure there is time for one more garden?

III

Three rainy days and the fourth one sunny:
she was gone before breakfast. At three she hobbles back
under a flour sack bulging full of mushrooms.
Well, scolding will do no good. I see her eyes
hunting for praise as she fishes up a handful
and holds them to the light, then rips one open
for me to smell the earth in the white stem.

I think perhaps this woman is my child.
But right now what do we do with thirty pounds
of uncleaned mushrooms? If I let her be
she'll stay up cleaning them till one o'clock
and be all aches tomorrow. I get a knife;
and here we sit with the kitchen table between us,
one pile for root ends, one for the cleaned sprouts.

Her hands go back with her. I see her mind
open through fields from the earth of her stained fingers.
"Once when I was a girl I found a fungus
that weighted twenty-eight kilos. It was delicious.
I was going to Benevento for the fair.
I cut across the mountain to save time,
and there it was—like an angel in a tree.

"You don't see things like that. Not over here.
My father ran from the barn when I came home.
'Didn't you go to fair?' he said. But I laughed:
'I brought it home with me.' He wouldn't believe
I'd carried it all the way across the mountain,
and the path so steep. I made a sack of my skirt.
He thought some fellow—I don't know what he thought!"

Ti-ti. La-la. The memory works her fingers.
"Oh, we were happy then. You could go in the winter
and dig the roses and cabbages from the snow.
The land had a blessing. In the fall in the vineyards

we sang from dawn to sunset, and at night
we washed our feet and danced like goats in the grape vats.
The wine came up like blood between our toes."

We finish at last, the squid-gray fruit before us.
"Leave the root clippings," she says. "They're for the garden.
See how black the dirt is. Black's for growing."
She sets her hoard to soak. "I'm tired now.
Sometimes I talk too much. That's happiness.
Well, so we'll eat again before we die.
But oh, if you could have seen it in that tree!"

Two Egrets

"Look!" you said. "Look!"

On Easter morning two egrets
flew up the Shrewsbury River
between Highlands and Sea Bright

like two white hands
washing one another
in the prime of light.

Oh lemons and bells of light,
rails, rays, waterfalls, ices—
as high as the eye dizzies

into the whirled confetti
and rhinestones of the breaking blue
grain of lit heaven,

the white stroke of the egrets
turned the air—a prayer
and the idea of prayer.

Poem for My Thirty-ninth Birthday

Itchy with time in the dogday summer stew,
    flesh melting at its creases and salted raw,
I drove the day for breezes. The children blew
    kisses to traffic. In the stubbly jaw
of the bay my wife went wading. In the wood
    a mouse lay torn on stone beside a pool,
an anthill raging in him like a mood
    of the dogday, a weather of the soul.

Waiting by pools for the fish that spins all water
    and the mouse that will come. Steaming on lawns
in a tinkle of gin. Spraying my birdy daughter,
    my guppy-bubbling son, and nodding like bones
on the leash of love, I heard the wind go over
    like jet-scream, the fact gone before the sound
ripped at the world. And naked as a lover
    I watched a pointed moon sprout from the ground.

It was too thin to die to. Fat as meat,
    I stood alive into my thirty-ninth year
from the deaddog day of summer, the shag heat
    still matted like wet wool on the midnight air,
and took my death for reason. Here it was
    the red worm pushed a nerve-end onto rock.
The world began with women in the house,
    and men with wine jugs waiting on the walk.

Over and through the reefs the thin moon skids,
    the great squid of the storm squirts down the air.
A clam of light glints out of swollen lids.
    Flying fish leap at the barrier.
There goes the moon, shipwrecked on churning stone.
    What holds the weather up? A raging Morse
flickers along the reef. Let down! Let down!
    But the moon rides up and holds, dead to its course.

A specimen ego pokes into the hour—
        news from the sea my mother's screaming broke.
I ate her in her pain. Manchild and sour
        from the sea's gland, I sweetened as I woke
out of her milk. But if the land was love,
        it was half-terror and too big to dare.
In a great plain, the ticking grass above
        my head and reach, I waited with my ear

to the thudding ground. What passed me out of sight?
        My father was one. When I had died enough
I made a perfect pink boy of my fright
        and used him to forgive time and myself.
Thirty-nine dying birthday years behind,
        he listens at the children's sleep and goes
sighing with love and pity to the blind
        and breathing love's-bed at the long thought's close.

Here is the thought, outside my house in time,
        the year comes where it is. I watch it down
under a moon rubbed like a garlic spline
        to a last skin. The river, thick as stone
sweats beads out of the air. A waiting man,
        itchy with time and damp as I was born,
I count my birthdays grave by grave, and stand
        watching the weather tremble to the storm

that cooked all day while I strolled death by death
        by pools, by lawns, by sea, and all my loves.
Time as it is. A laboring to breath
        in the clogged air. A nudging at what shoves.
A tapping at what blows. A waiting still
        at the sweet fear and bittering appetite.
A ghost that will not and a ghost that will
        burn faster as it burns out of the night

where all men are their fathers and their sons
     in a haunted house of mirrors to the end.
I have walked my deaths out of a day of bones
     and put my loves to bed, and free, and found
in the laboring summer flesh of man, I wait
     easy enough for the lit nerve and hover
of thunderheads to bolt the moon and break
     the stuck air open, like a death blown over.

A Thought about Sheik Bedreddin

I read in a tattered book about Sheik Bedreddin
who on his best day sank ten thousand axes
into the Royal Heir's ranks, and broke eight thousand.
Men, that is. Snapped brittle at the handle
for what's crazy in everyone. Called a glory.
With, of course, a gallows. Some want *that* badly
to be taken in righteousness. Of Sheik Bedreddin,
it is written he was hanged between two rivers
preaching firm faith to his two thousand "survivors,"
their heads under their arms in strict attention.

Now there's a day's work: ten thousand wraith
decisions sopped up into history
like garlic gravy, leaving a bad breath
somewhere among the back smells of Turkey,
and everywhere. The slops did very well
the day Bedreddin preached the way to hell
to his last two thousand rags of crazy cloth.
I almost wish I knew what they thought they were doing
aside from that day's immediate hacking and hewing.
There must be something to say of that much death.

Elegy for G. B. Shaw

"If I survive this, I shall be immortal."

Administrators of minutes into hours,
Hours into ash, and ash to its own wedding
At the edge of fire and air—here's time at last
To make an ash of Shaw, who in his time
Survived his times, retired, and for a hobby
Bred fire to fire as one breeds guinea pigs.

In time, one can imagine, schoolchildren
Will confuse him as a contemporary of Socrates.
For a time, the fact is, he confused us:
We half believed he really had lived forever.
Sometimes, perhaps, a man can. That is to say,
Civilization is one man at a time,

And that forever, and he was that man.
For this we will not forgive him. Neither
The ape in me nor the ape in you, tenants
Of the flag-flying tree and drinkers of blood in season.
We meant to resemble the agonies of statues:
He left us only a treadmill in a cage.

Consider his crimes: He would not commit our diet.
He opened our tombs. He sold his medals for cash.
His laughter blew out our anthems. He wiped his nose
On the flags we die for—a crazy Irishman
Who looked like a goat and would not be serious.
But when we are finished, he will be our times.

And all times will be nothing in his eye.
All marshals, kings, and presidents we obey.
His presence in men's minds is contempt of court,
Of congress, and of flags. So must we pray
That he be born again, anarch and rare,
The race we are not in the race we are.

The Invasion of Sleep Walkers

(What I shall say to my Father)

They were weeding out the dead at the funeral home
to reduce the overstock. Rack after rack
the wire-hung bones chattered their loneliness
and even the drunkenest angel wept and sang.
But the coroner's men were stuffed too full for hearing,
the trucks were backed to the wind, and the sleep walkers
already were pacing the streets, their eyes like spit,
their arms out stiff before them, their knees unbending,
their heels hitting too hard. They had no faces,
or, more exactly, they had the look of faces
that could not happen or that had not happened—
once on Fifth Avenue I watched five miles
of faceless cops march on St. Patrick's Day
and learned that face forever—
                              There's not much more:
when the dead had been thinned out they put that face
over the skulls and gave them back to us.
We marched all day and night with flags and torches
to celebrate our thanks. The Great Good Face
stared down from photographs ten stories high.
It had no eyes but it saw my guilt at once
among a million marchers. I never learned
what signal passed between it and the Law,
but something certainly—and here I am.

Can Hell be taken more seriously than the world?

Temptation

Volgiti indietro, e tien lo viso chiuso:
chè, se il Gorgon si mostra, e tu il vedessi,
nulla sarebbe del tornar mai suso.

St. Anthony, my father's holy man,
was tempted by a worm-shop, spills of guts,
soft coupling toads, blind fish, and seeing maggots.
The whores the devil sent leaked through their skin.

Now who would leave off heaven for such stuff?
What in the devil was the devil thinking
to try to turn a man with such a stinking
parcel of shoddy? Or were times so tough

he hadn't one small kingdom, or at least
one final Lilith to give sin some standing
a man could sell his soul for without branding
himself a damn fool before man and beast?

The devil's a better fisherman than angels
or he'd have starved long since. When slobs die poor
on rotten kingdoms and a nagging whore
still in her heat when every other chills,

the devil keeps that last bait for the ardent:
my father bit bare iron to go damned:
I see the leakage through the door he slammed:
I think the devil almost hooked his saint.

Flowering Quince

This devils me: uneasy ease at my window
    discussing the day with quince, flowers of the quince
    almost upon me in tree time, in slow
    dazzles of budding and bending asprawl since
        Spring began my consideration again

of the angels of the blind eye. *This must mean*
    the angels sing from the many-folded falls
    of the open light, from the twist and gnarl and sheen
    of the airy works of the tree, from the writhen scrawls
        and mobile arms of its tilt and balancing.

But at once the wind shakes free a fall of light
    from undiminished light, the light-machine
    sends and goes in an ample-handed sleight.
    This devils me: can worlds be made to mean
        whatever they are about when they shape a tree?

can the angel-blinded eye be made to enter
    a presence without intent whose devils sprawl
    calmer than angels in the windborne center
    of the quince-bursting Spring? is quince a moral?
        The form of a tree is a function of the air

and its only possibility, say the devils.
    But the eye sees by religions and recollections.
    What shall the green bough care for rites and revels
    or the angel imagination whose paeons
        moralize the strictness of God's chains

in a world that cannot worship but only answer
    one urgency with another? Spring
    is no more intricately bloomed than cancer,
    nor than the dreams of angels which they fling
        age after age at the invincible world.

Measurements

I've zeroed an altimeter on the floor
then raised it to a table and read *three feet.*
Nothing but music knows what air is
more precisely than this. I read on its face
Sensitive Altimeter and believe it.

Once on a clear day over Arkansas
I watched the ridges on the radar screen,
then looked down from the blister and hung like prayer:
the instrument was perfect: ridge by ridge
the electric land was true as the land it took from.

These, I am persuaded, are instances
round as the eye to see with,
perfections of one place in the visited world
and omens to the godly
teaching an increase of possibility.

I believe that when a civilization
equal to its instruments is born
we may prepare to build such cities as music
arrives to on the air, lands where we are
the instruments of April in the seed.

Thoughts on Looking into a Thicket

The name of a fact: at home in that leafy world
chewed on by moths that look like leaves, like bark,
like owls, like death's heads; there, by eating flowers
and stones with eyes, in that zoo of second looks,
there is a spider, *phrynarachne d.*,
to whom a million or a billion years
in the humorless long gut of all the wood
have taught the art of mimicking a bird turd.

"It is on a leaf," write Crompton, "that she weaves
an irregular round blotch, and, at the bottom,
a separate blob in faithful imitation
of the more liquid portion. She then squats
herself in the center, and (being unevenly marked
in black and white), supplies with her own body
the missing last perfection, *i.e.,* the darker
more solid central portion of the excreta."

Must I defend my prayers? I dream the world
at ease in its long miracle. I ponder the egg,
like a pin head in silk spit, invisibly stored
with the billion years of its learning. Have angels
more art than this? I read the rooty palm
of God for the great scarred Life Line. If you
will be more proper than real, that is your
death. I think life will do anything for a living.

And that hungers are all one. So Forbes reports
that seeing a butterfly once poised on a dropping
he took it to be feasting, but came closer
and saw it was being feasted on. Still fluttering,
it worked its woolen breast for *phrynarachne,*
pumping her full. So once I saw a mantis
eating a grub while being himself eaten
by a copper beetle. So I believe the world

in its own act and accomplishment. I think
what feeds is food. And dream it in mosaic
for a Church of the First Passion: an ochre sea
and a life-line of blue fishes, the tail of each
chained into the mouth behind it. Thus, an emblem
of our indivisible three natures in one:
the food, the feeder, and the condition of being
in the perpetual waver of the sea.

I believe the world to praise it. I believe
the act in its own occurrence. As the dead
are hats and pants in aspic, as the red
bomb of the living heart ticks against time,
as the eye of all water opens and closes, changing
all that it has looked at—I believe
if there is an inch or the underside of an inch
for a life to grow on, a life will grow there;

if there are kisses, flies will lay their eggs
in the spent sleep of lovers; if there is time,
it will be long enough. And through all time,
the hand that strokes my darling slips to bone
like peeling off a glove; my body eats me
under the nose of God and Father and Mother.
I speak from thickets and from nebulae:
till their damnation feed them, all men starve.

On Looking East to the Sea
with a Sunset behind Me

I

In a detachment cool as the glint of light
on wet roads through wet spruce, or iced mountains
hailed from the sea in moonfall, or the sea
when one horizon's black and the other burning;

the gulls are kissing time in its own flowing
over the shell-scraped rock—a coming and going
as of glass bees with a bubble of light in each
running errands in and out of the sunset.

Over the road and the spruce wood, over the ice,
and out the picture of my picture window,
the exorbitant separation of nature from nature
wheels, whirls, and dances on itself.

Now damn me for a moral. Over and out,
over and in, the gulls drift up afire,
screaming like hinges in the broken air
of night and day like two smokes on the sea.

And I do nothing. A shadow three feet under
my window in the light, I look at light
in one of the years of my life. This or another.
Or all together. Or simply in this moment.

II

Lead flags of the sea. Steel furls of the surf.
Day smoke and night smoke. Fire at the smoke's top.
A passion from the world in a calm eye.
A calm of the world in the eye of passion.

The day that sank birdless from staring Calvary
was another. And only another. And no other
than the clucking calm of Eden fussed to rest
from the black bush afire in the first eye.

A calm-in-violence like Aegean time.
Day smoke and night smoke over the palled sea
tensed for a clash of tridents. Far ashore,
a staring army camped beside a temple,

the base of the temple black with powder stains,
the pediment flashing wild in light above.
—A day of the world in which a part of the world
looked at another, two parts of a mist.

At Cassino the dusty German wetting his lips,
his eyes crashed in his face like unhatched birds' eggs
splashed from their nest, looked East from the burning night.
There was no West. Light came from nowhere behind him,

slanted, flowed level, drained. He looked out, waiting.
Where had it come from, the light of his terrible patience?
A dead man waited to die on the shell-scraped
stones of another God, dust of the stones

caked to his body, rivers of blood within him
ran to their dusty sea beside the world.
Calm in his changes, risen from his changes,
he looked his life out at the smoking world.

III

I have no more to do than what I wait for
under the changing light and the gulls afire
in rays of rose-quartz. Holy ghosts of the sea,

they rise in light from behind me. The light lifts
long from the edge of the world and juts away
over the top of the dark. My life sits

visible to itself, and I sit still
in a company of survivors and the dead.
Jew, Greek, German, man at the edge of himself

in the long light over the worlds he ran to
to save unsaved. I practice the man in all,
clutching the world from the world to praise it.

Lines While Walking Home
from a Party on Charles Street

Suffer, do you? I think if wounds were art
you'd fill a gallery with scars on plaques,
extractions on red velvet, rare amputations

stuffed and varnished and set out on mirrors
under magenta lights—then throw a party
for Jesus and Mother and Father and all Charles Street.

As for being a beast—you'll have to move outdoors.
Not conscience but the unconscious
stiffens the stallion to the dancing mare.

And one temptation by Hieronymus Bosch
over the radiator won't qualify,
even with Baudelaire propped on the table

between two coupling boys in terra cotta.
Piddle's no rape, rape's no vocabulary,
and Hell's no hobby. One family of Sicilians

has more beasts in to breakfast than you to your nightmares.

Elegy for Jog

Stiff-dog death, all froth on a bloody chin,
sniffs at the curb. Skinny-man death, his master,
opens the traffic's hedge to let him in.
Jog was his name, silliness his disaster:
he wasn't satisfied to scare the truck,
he had to bite the tire. Fools have no luck.

Cézanne

When I returned from you in the blue of midnight
I sat by my lamp holding a pear in my hand
and hearing you say: "Tell me again you love me.
Say the words to me. Let me hear the words."

And I could no more understand
the words I said to please you,
than you could have seen that pear, which was also
a word love could ask of me. The pear

was the yellow of a glaze but sanded dull
then lit again by my lamp. These first two lights
were then burned red from below. And up through that,
the black and umber of ripeness freckled it.

And somewhere never placeable in that yellow
a memory of green misted its presence.
I held the pear in my hand and could not tell
where its outline entered the light that made it.

"I will need six colors and all desperation,"
I said to myself, "to bring this pear to truth.
Yet she believes a man may say 'I love you'
on arriving, leaving, and all the night between."

Fragments from Italy

I

Nona Domenica Garnaro sits in the sun
    on the step of her house in Calabria.
    There are seven men and four women in the village
    who call her *Mama,* and the orange trees
    fountain their blooms down all the hill and valley.
    No one can see more memory from this step

than Nona Domenica. When she folds her hands
    in her lap they fall together
    like two Christs fallen from a driftwood shrine.
    All their weathers are twisted into them.
    There is that art in them that will not be carved
    but can only be waited for. These hands are not

sad nor happy nor tired nor strong. They are simply
    complete. They lie still in her lap
    and she sits waiting quietly in the sun
    for what will happen, as for example, a petal
    may blow down on the wind and lie across
    both of her thumbs, and she look down at it.

II

One day I went to look at the Mediterranean
and I found myself on an infected hill.
The waves under the sky and the sky over the waves
perfected themselves in endless repetition,
but the hill stumbled and twitched. A desert ate
into its sea front and a gully cankered
its piney back, or what had been
its piney back before that eczema
of stumps and stones and landslides. At its top
like a trollop's hat knocked cockeyed in a brawl
there leaned a tattered strawwork of gray grasses

that fizzed and popped with a plague of grasshoppers.
The grass was salt-burned and seemed wiry enough
to cut the hand that pulled it. And at its roots,
under the leaping gas of the live grasshoppers,
I saw a paste of the dead. There were so many
I thought at first it was the clay-sand soil
from which the wiregrass grew. I could not see
any of the living fall from their leaping
but the dead lay under them, a plague they made
invisibly of themselves who had come to feed
where the grass ate them on an infected hill.

And I saw there was no practice in the sea.

III

A man-face gathered on the eyes of a child
    measures me from an alleyway. The child
    stirs, but the face has lost its motion:
    the face stares at the traffic and the child
    picks with one finger at a scab on his knee.
    Not looking at it. Not knowing it is there.

He stares at me. I am part of what he knows.
    I am the traffic forever in his eyes
    and damnation, the way all worlds go
    leaving him neither admission nor understanding,
    as, somewhere in a thicket like the mind,
    a gargoyle might stare down at running water.

IV

You would never believe to watch this man
    open his pocket knife to cut his cheese
    (his bread he tears with his hands)
    and lay it down precisely on a leaf
    and tip his bottle off against his mouth

(which he wipes with the back of his hand)
and lift the knife again to peel an apple
so carefully from stem to bud it is all
one red spiral, and toss it on a bush
to see it against green and color of loam
and slap the crumbs from his lap for the birds to have
before he sleeps with his hat over his eyes
(for a pillow he joins his hands behind his head)

that all the guns and lances looked to him
    all the maps and marches centered here
    and all the charges climbed this same small hill

that it was always this man in this field
    through all of Europe and the island-South
    the kingdoms and their kings were told about.

V

What the Roman sun says to the Romans
    (a boy fishing the Tiber with a seine
    while two old men and a tourist watch from the bridge
    that leads to Castel Sant' Angelo, where once
    a cypress forest mourned across the roof
    for a faded emperor gone like his forest
    into the stoneworks)
                  what the Roman sun
    (a species of tumulus or burial mound
    as for example pyramids cairns barrows
    and similar monuments common to many cultures)
    says to the Romans (the present structure
    visible on the Tiber being simply the base)
    I have said to you in all the tongues of sleep.

VI

The mountains quiver like a low flame
    on the horizon. They flicker and reappear,

flicker and reappear. Sometimes
there are no mountains and sometimes
they are always there.
                    Mountains
have no need of being seen. They can outwait
all but these repetitions of the air.

VIII

Naples

Hanno vinto le mosche

I saw at a table of the bombed café
a fat man in shirtsleeves,
the stuff of his jersey sweated
to his woman's breasts and belly
so close that the texture of the fat
(like the texture of cottage cheese
or of brains or of boiled cauliflower)
showed through the cloth.

All he had chewed and swallowed
lay ruined in the fat
which pressed at his skin for escape,
a skin strung on a net
of round holes, while through the holes
the fat pressed for escape
held only by the strands of the net
through which, perhaps, his blood ran.

The air was soaked heavy
with the oil-sweet smell of corpses,
that taint which breathes from all
the summer cities of ruin,
their rubble and broken sewerage.
He sat at a table of the bombed café
brushing away the flies that came for him.
Especially for him. There were no others.

He wore his cloud of flies
as a saint wears patience
after his knees have been abused
too long to feel the pain itself.
The flies were his vocation
and he theirs. There can be no
accident in so much meeting:
he was a St. Anthony of flies.

And all of ruined Europe fell about him.
Tiles lay wedged in the gross ruff
at the back of his neck. The dust
of an exploded temple caked
muddy on his bald head and flowed
like half-thickened blood
down and over his eyes,
which were sealed in his fat like navels.

He sat at a table of the bombed café
by the ruined temple, a pediment at his feet,
its writing cracked and crazed. His chair
was a split capital. When he waved his arm
to brush away the flies
a column fell. When he waved it back
another. From every crash the dust
changed into flies and drew a cloud about him.

I Marry You

—·—

(1958)

Snowy Heron

What lifts the heron leaning on the air
I praise without a name. A crouch, a flare,
a long stroke through the cumulus of trees,
a shaped thought at the sky—then gone. *O rare!*
Saint Francis, being happiest on his knees,
would have cried *Father!* Cry anything you please.

But praise. By any name or none. But praise
the white original burst that lights
the heron on his two soft kissing kites.
When saints praise heaven lit by doves and rays,
I sit by pond scums till the air recites
Its heron back. And doubt all else. But praise.

Morning: I Know Perfectly How in a Minute You Will Stretch and Smile

As pilots pay attention to the air
    lounging on triggers wired into their ease;
    seeing what they do not see, because their eyes
    are separate cells; hearing what they do not hear,
    because a life is listening in their place;
    and so with their five senses and a sixth
    cocked to their element, free and transfixed,
    slouch as they hurtle, ticking as they laze—

so in the mastered master element
    love is or nothing, silences unheard,
    flickerings unseen, and every balancing
    and tremor of our senses still unsensed,
    joins and enjoins, and, nothing left to chance,
    spins our precisions in us as we nod.

The Stills and Rapids
of Your Nakedness

The stills and rapids of your nakedness
in the bird-started morning mist of sun
spill from my sleep like April's waking rush
into the groundswell and green push of May.

All days tell this. Season and season, this.
This apple to my mind's eye. This new bread.
This well of living water where the bell
of heaven is. This home's door and first kiss.

Darling, to see your eyes when you, too, stir,
turn all their inner weathers to a smile
I write you this: a jargon in the sky
twitters about your sleep; and like a churning

the dawn beats into gold; and, like a field
the wind turns over, all your body lives
its circling blood; and like the first of leaves,
I start from wood to praise you and grow green.

In the Rich Farmer's Field

A black stallion and a white mare
are posed in the field nearest the road
as one enters the model farm.
Magnificent and sudden they are, and yet
too obviously of the rich farmer's pride;
too obviously matched and put just there
that no one might miss seeing them. And thus
not wholly nature, and not less than nature,
but an exploitation: true, but overmanaged.

I should not have invented them. Not surely
since Freud and the freudlings, real or posed,
parsed out the sample- and too-obvious-dream
the farmer, being obvious and illiterate,
sets up to be his nameplate in this field.
I should not have invented them, and yet,
there they are centering the morning air,
and I walk past again to look at them,
too perfect to be likely or to avoid.

I watch *him:* a wound quiver of inner balances
built rippling to brute bulk: Greek head and neck,
bulwarked Arabian chest, haunches light-coiled
and rounded huge from all the wars of kings—
an ease awaiting its next chemistry.
As *she* waits in the swan arch of herself,
all dove white and all coiled and all at ease,
till he flame in the terror of his making
and she shake all the forests under him.

Three days ago I passed them in their storm,
clear as the kind of truth schools are about;
but every lesson lied, and the truth was
a bloodshock drummed, the air stampeded,
a black and a white energy crazed and rearing
with an agony like a lion on its backs,
from which real blood flowed black, unholdable, driven,
he to her battered ecstasy in pain, she
struck and still plunging to his battery.

And I saw watching from across the field
the rich farmer—too rich even to care
that nature is striped with injury—watching,
too obviously repaid by what he was not
to care for one scarred mare. Her coat would heal.
Would heal enough. And he had brutes enough

to waste these two perfections from the rest
of his manhandled teasers and iced sperm.
He wanted what he wanted in itself.

And if I saw his staging overstaged,
any man living could sneer back my lie
should I deny the sweats that broke in me,
the thud of self on self that beat afire
out of the night-thought of a whole illusion
where once, black stroke on white stroke, seized,
monstrous and inGodding, we reared from time.
Then burst apart, coiled down as they are now,
at ease till our next chemistry upon us.

What rich men can afford, others may still
stare at inside themselves. I have walked back
morning by morning to an energy
I need to touch again, rank with ourselves.
The white mare and black stallion strike their poses
into a memory that makes again
the world's well at the roots from which we sprang.
I hang upon the rail as on a limb
of the whole tree up through time, and watch again

original energy in its place below,
too obvious to invent or not to know.

For My Son John

Jonnel, this is for you—my river-saint-named
and first-born son, the lamb
for whom the prophets flamed their beards to God
and rolled their eyeballs inside out to praise.

Nothing so grand, so rank with twitching sweats
of holy rapture does
for the tousling hand across your mop-top. Oaf-cub!—
a long noise off from glory, but my own pup.

And glorious for all that. Spit on my lie
if ever I allow
the dry-hack of a wordless generation
to rack up in my throat and choke my praise

of that blazed glory-bed where, blood to blood,
man-beat and woman-beat,
like swollen pods lashed by a golden wind,
we burst you from our love into our love.

All men brag this. So let it praise all men.
The bed that bore you
was no garden but a nature, and there
the great man and great woman touched their tree.

Then when that great woman slowed and swelled,
a langorous long smile
grew in her eyes and mine, and the first thump
beat our two bellies at once where we lay locked.

Whatever glory spoke in those flame-bearded
God-knocked and goatherd deserts
whose gales blew through the prophet's mouth-at-law;
or roars here in the speed-run of flag-extras—

this is for you, the son of praising man
up from the glory bed
in the weathers of the touched tree chosen.
The first life and the first and still the first.

Ten Years Ago When I
Played at Being Brave

Sleep was what deviled it. The days were easy.
The going itself was nothing—once in air
there was the next thing and the next to do.
We would come back or burn. Would or would not.
Whatever would happen was already going.

It was that sleep before—which was no sleep
but a long whisper: "By this time tomorrow
you may have burned."—"Well, and suppose I do:
what do I want tonight? If I could have it,
what's the last thing I really want forever?"

—I need to say this to you as it was.
As nearly as I can. What *could* a man want?
A woman, yes, but this was for perfections:
a last night on the Universe, and paid for.
I wanted Eve, her nightname of the blood.

—Then—in one moonquake—it was worlds ago.
Three thousand nights, and more, and numberless,
I've hailed your body's tropics from the moon
and sung your surfs out of my sleep, and come
to every Eve and nightname in my need.

This is to dream what thousand dead men bless you:
you were their one most reason not to die.
Were I where they have gone and could some dream
patch that torn sleep, I think I could make whole
the flesh of all wish in one dream of you.

I wake then—as I woke once to be born
out of their dark—locked to your rustling islands,
whole as a flood tide flowing to your shore,
a thousandth and a thousandth time again
come from the shapeless waters under time.

Two Poems for Benn

I. Romping

Silly. All giggles and ringlets and never
about to stop anything without fussing:
get down I say! Do you think I took your mother
to beget me a chimp for my shoulder?
I'm forty, boy, and no weight lifter.
Go find some energy your own size.
Get down!—Well, just once more.
There. Now get down, you baby-fat incubus.
Go ride your imagination. No, I don't care
how many kisses you'll write me a check for.
A million? Some banker you are. Still—
a million of anything is a lot of something.
All right. Once more, then. But just once. You hear?

II. Stopped Suddenly That He Is Beautiful

It happens at once and unthought of: what bumbled zooms,
what clattered turns to speech, what sprawled
leaps and becomes a balance on the air.

It is an elegance beyond all choosing.
As an elk is sighted. As a partridge
explodes from under the hunter's foot.

As a porpoise breaks the surface like light.
As a pear tree one morning blooms, its scroll on scroll
tiered in the sun at perfect random—

Yesterday you were all yolk and today
there are gulls in your laughter, and land and sea
in the light from you, and a name

in the measure of your eyes. Little boy, little boy,
I feel an absence beginning. You are touched already
by the shape of what you will be:

the stranger I go to my grave for and give my house to,
as once it came from a stranger stopped in love
to cry: "My son! My son! I am well traded!"

Most Like an Arch This Marriage

Most like an arch—an entrance which upholds
and shores the stone-crush up the air like lace.
Mass made idea, and idea held in place.
A lock in time. Inside half-heaven unfolds.

Most like an arch—two weaknesses that lean
into a strength. Two fallings become firm.
Two joined abeyances become a term
naming the fact that teaches fact to mean.

Not quite that? Not much less. World as it is,
what's strong and separate falters. All I do
at piling stone on stone apart from you
is roofless around nothing. Till we kiss

I am no more than upright and unset.
It is by falling in and in we make
the all-bearing point, for one another's sake,
in faultless failing, raised by our own weight.

Letter from an Empty House

The hour pings like a bird hatched from a bell
as I come in. And the last stroke is silence.
The house is a hoaxter's garden—all in glass:
not one leaf withered, banks and borders trim,
every stem gleaming like a flower—but flowerless.
Neat nothing. A lit emptiness on file.

"Well, come now," I begin, "a week, ten days,
two weeks at most . . . two weeks out of a year . . ."
I could count year by year how far I am
since midnight racked me sobbing on its moon,
and having you was more than I could stand,
and leaving you was more than I could stand.

And what if I *should* count? What could *that* change?
I shall not die of flames I lived in once.
But if I need fire less, I need warmth more.
I cannot stand this glassblown winter garden
without your summering colors, or the spring
and breakage of the children's insolence.

It is three days now and I am already
emptied. I have touched nothing. I come and go
like a bellhop through a suite. Even the ash trays
are polished bright as a doll's funeral.
Nobody lives here and nothing happens. I wait,
not wanting to go to bed, and then I go.

Say I am cranky with habit and middle age.
A not-much and no matter. It is as if
I had left my pulse in the next room, like glasses:
I cannot wholly breathe nor wholly see.
And though I put the light out, and my breath,
nothing turns off, and nothing falls in place.

I cannot sleep. My sleep is in your hand.
Until you touch me with it, I stare blind
into the waking dark. I cannot wake;
my waking is a stir that is not here—
a babble, and a tumble, and a yell
that ends in kisses, tears, or a new babble;

but is the tick and bell note of the house
whose one last bird pings in its egg downstairs,
and then again, and then again. I hear
the hours I cannot use fall and fall still.
I lie on absence, a white frozen moon,
and cannot sleep, and then at last I do.

The Stone without Edges Has Not Been Mined

The stone without edges has not been mined,
and the kiss that does not lie has not been joined.
Nothing falls from Heaven but of its weight.
    I love you of my loss.

What day begets the child of no nuisance?
In a tantrum after tenderness, for nothing,
I have slapped the child of our impudence.
    I love you of my shame.

Be old leather. Dry, as a hide in sun
cracks and turns dust and puffs at a touch,
once airborne pastes of life have smeared it.
    I love you of our death.

The bride without escapes has not been kissed,
nor the groom without terrors. Having dared
our own tears and a child's, we have our healing.
    I love you of that health.

Letter from a Death Bed

This afternoon, darling, when you were here,
I meant to say some true and final thing
and could not. I am not all myself
but a chemical changeling, a tide of salt and juices,
a shore from which I sink, wash back, and sink.

Then in a rhythm and for an interval
I am again. I know then—now—exactly
what was my best. That instant—this—I seize,
which is no memory but the being again. At last,
for this instant, I can say "I love you."

I have it here: that first night and the first
again, and always, incredibly—thank you—the first
from the instant of your turning, your dropped silks
a froth at your feet, and like a grained flame
the leap and repose of your nakedness in its giving.

Let the tide wash that from me if it can.
A dark like your body's fuzzes and crinkles takes me.
Then blanks. But is always the last of me.
The last of me going from me is you. And returns.
Goes and returns. Goes and returns. Holding you.

No, I am all going. All arrows set from the wind.
All out and away. Skewed only by cheer and nurses.
Damn them, I will die in my own climate.
What breath have I ever drawn from the wax-weathers
under their hothouse skulls and fogged windows?

I tend a refusal better than their prayers,
these flour-faced angels with their piano legs
who don't think I notice. Today that doctor,
his smile put on with adhesive tape, came poking:
He'll have me out of here in nothing flat.

I know damn well he will. Nothing and flat.
He wants to know my religion. "Refusal," I tell him.
"The Church of the First Covenant of Damned-if-I-Will."
Fool. Does he think what a man lives by
gets changed by his dying? Well, I'm cantankerous—

must I *like* dying to gossip?—Oh, I hear them:
"Twelve, he's a queer one. Won't be told what's wrong.
Just doesn't want to know." I know all right.
If they think what I'm dying of's any one thing,
they haven't healing enough to mend a rip.

. . . What was it I said? "Some true and final thing."
I meant a better end to that beginning.
Well, maybe cantankerousness is true and final.
—No. No it isn't. Your eyes are true and final.
Your smile even in pity and enforced. Your hand . . .

Thank you for smiling, darling. Don't come back.
Come bury the bones. Come take away the clothes rack
they'll hang my tatters on. But the end's here.
This is my last stroke as myself. My going.
My meat has this last energy and no more—

to praise you as you are from all I leave.

39 Poems

—•—

(1959)

Abundance

I

Once I had 1000 roses.
Literally 1000 roses.
I was working for a florist
back in the shambling 'Thirties
when iced skids of 250 roses
sold for $2 at Faneuil Hall.
So for $8 I bought
1000 roses, 500
white and 500 red,
for Connie's wedding to steadiness.

I strewed the church aisle whole
and the bride came walking
on roses, roses all the way.
The white roses and the red roses.
White for the bed we had shared.
Red for the bed she went to
from the abundance in her
to the fear in what she wanted.
The gift was not in the roses
but in the abundance of the roses.

　　　　　　　　　　　To her
whose abundance had never wholly
been mine, and could never be his.
He had no gift of abundance in him
but only the penuries of sobriety.
A good steady clerk, most mortgageable,
returning in creaking shoes over
the white and the red roses. Returning
over the most flowering he would ever
touch, with the most flowering I
had ever touched. A feast of endings.

II

This morning I passed a pushcart
heaped with white carnations
as high as if there had fallen all night
one of those thick-flaked, slow, windless,
wondering snows that leave
shakos on fence posts, polar bears
in the hedges, caves in the light,
and a childhood on every sill.
Once, twice a year, partially,
and once, twice a lifetime, perfectly,

that snow falls. In which I ran
like a young wolf in its blood
leaping to snap the flower-flakes
clean from the air; their instant on the tongue
flat and almost dusty and not enough
to be cold. But as I ran, face-up,
mouth open, my cheeks burned
with tears and flower-melt,
and my lashes were fringed with gauze,
and my ears wore white piping.

There is no feast but energy. All men
know—have known and will remember
again and again—what food that is
for the running young wolf of the rare days
when shapes fall from the air
and may be had for the leaping.
Clean in the mouth of joy. Flat and dusty.
And how they are instantly nothing—
a commotion in the air and in the blood.
—And how they are endlessly all.

III

My father's grave, the deepest cave I know,
was banked with snow and lilies.
We stuck the dead flowers
into the snow banks dirty with sand
and trampled by digger's boots.
The flowers, stiff and unbeckoning,
ripped from their wires in the wind
and blew their seasons out as snow.
Purer than the snow itself. A last
abundance correcting our poverties.

I remember the feasts of my life,
their every flowing. I remember
the wolf all men remember in his blood.
I remember the air become
a feast of flowers. And remember
his last flowers whitening winter
in an imitation of possibility,
while we hunched black
in the dirtied place inside possibility
where the prayers soiled him.

If ever there was a man of abundances
he lies there flowerless
at that dirty center
whose wired flowers try and try
to make the winter clean again in air.
And fail. And leave me raging
as the young wolf grown
from his day's play in abundance
to the ravening of recollection.
Creaking to penury over the flower-strew.

IV

This morning I passed a pushcart
heaped beyond possibility,
as when the sun begins again
after that long snow and the earth
is moonscaped and wonderlanded
and humped and haloed in the
light it makes: an angel
on every garbage can, a god
in every tree, that childhood
on every sill.—At a corner of the ordinary.

Where is she now? Instantly nothing.
A penury after flower-strew. Nothing.
A feast of glimpses. Not fact itself,
but an idea of the possible in the fact.
—And so the rare day comes: I was again
the young wolf trembling in his blood
at the profusions heaped and haloed
in their instant next to the ordinary.
And did not know myself what feast I kept
—till I said your name. At once all plenty was.

It is the words starve us, the act that feeds.
The air trembling with the white wicks
of its falling encloses us. To be
perfect, I suppose, we must be brief.
The long thing is to remember
imperfectly, dirtying with gratitude
the grave of abundance. O flower-banked,
air-dazzling, and abundant woman,
though the young wolf is dead, all men
know—have known and must remember—
                    You.

A Dream

I had a dream once of dancing with a tiger. As it took
  my arm off, I heard a dancing-master
who came by on a bus with his dancing class on an outing
  say to the class:
"Note and avoid this dancer's waste of motion—more
  violence than observance."
And as I died and woke, I heard him add: "Dancing, my dears,
  is a selection of measures."

Once at St. Joseph's, asked by Father Ryan something I have
  forgotten, I answered, burning,
something I meant for love. He grabbed my hair and hauled
  me to the Virgin.
"Pray for your soul!" But I stomped my heel on his instep
  and ran damned
my first long race from God, to hide by the river till
  I dared go home and be strapped.

I was what had been done to me. There in the grass
  I lay outside my action.
Whose was the act? Whose will, not mine, was in it?
  How was it chosen
that the thing done had been given me to do? I envied the birds
  the eyes they could eat from my head
for a little waiting. I lay already dead in God's eye
  upon me.

You think perhaps it's a child's tale, that nose of
  Pinocchio's?
All boys are born of the guilt that sprouts from them
  in a wrong world
whose Virgins and Good Fairies accept prayers, tears,
  and apologies
from the block-head who becomes a man at last by the act
  of cutting his nose off.

There in the river reeds, outside of God and the happening
    act, I learned
my tiger to dream to. When I laid my face in the river
    to cool my tears
a rat swam under my eyes, no further away than this paper.
    And came swimming
into a thousand dreams I screamed from. Rat? Tiger? I
    forget now which was which.

But that dancing-master—why had my face been put
    between his wig and ruffles?
Which of my acts was done to me so in secret that I
    wake here
at forty in a white shirt and a striped coat of manners,
    and bow and bow,
teaching the children songs and kisses and curtsies,
    to one side of all tigers in my arms?

After Sunday Dinner
We Uncles Snooze

Banana-stuffed, the ape behind the brain
scratches his crotch in nature and lies back,
one arm across his eyes, one on his belly.
Thanksgiving afternoon in Africa,
the jungle couches heaped with hairy uncles
between a belch and a snore. All's well that yawns.

Seas in the belly lap a high tide home.
A kind of breathing flip-flop, all arrival,
souses the world full in the sog of time,
lifting slopped apes and uncles from their couches
for the long drift of self to self. Goodbye:
I'm off to idiot heaven in a drowse.

This is a man. This blubbermouth at air
sucking its flaps of breath, grimacing, blowing,
rasping, whistling. Walked through by a zoo
of his own reveries, he changes to it.
His palm's huge dabble over his broken face
rubs out the carnivores. His pixie pout

diddles a butterfly across his lip.
His yeasty smile drools Edens at a spring
where girls from Bali, kneeling to their bath,
cup palms of golden water to their breasts.
His lower lip thrusts back the angry chiefs:
he snarls and clicks his teeth: "Stand back, by God!"

And so, by God, they do, while he descends
to rape those knobs of glory with a sigh,
then clouds, surceased, and drifts away or melts
into another weather of himself
where only a drowned mumble far away
sounds in his throat the frog-pond under time.

O apes and hairy uncles of us all,
I hear the gibberish of a mother tongue
inside this throat. (A prattle from the sea.
A hum in the locked egg. A blather of bloods.)
O angels and attendants past the world,
what shall the sleeps of heaven dream but time?

Ballad of the Icondic

It was the year the ICONDIC
    was sighted (hush, my pet,
for it has slewn the GAWNOSE WATT
    and it is slewing yet).

It was THEOLGARD shook its head.
    THENOOGARD likewise its.
And having knit a BITTAPPEASE
    they raveled it to snits.

"Now what shall save us?" ICONDIC
    cried out, as if in thought.
"O gird about your gat, set out
    and slew the GAWNOSE WATT!"

The GAWNOSE WATT is slew and slew.
    Was never seen such slewage.
And GAWNOSE WATT went up the spout.
    And GAWNOSE WATT went down the sewerage.

I only know the ICONDIC
    slewed on and still is slewing.
(Now sleep, and may you dream just what
    the GAWNOSE WATT was doing.)

It Is the Same Place
Always Once Again

The most truth of what is most usual
can be spoken backwards only and only after
some part of all is finished. Zinnias,
in their commonplace rank blazes bordering
a day, are a color of something/nothing,
glad and ordinary to the eye that accepts thanks.
. . . But that you will never again be the hand that plants,
nor the step between them on the walk—*that*
is the one measure of the going of all color.

The hedge grows wild or is trimmed by another.
Come twilight and star-twitch, the young lions prowl again
up the same walk to the same step, and there,
like a moonrise in the doorway, a girl
who could almost be you, waits, glowing and sudden.
They do not know what they will have to remember—
not she in her power, nor they in their dance around it—
and therefore they believe only
the extraordinary of themselves, and cannot hear

when they stroll melded in poolside shadows
how I whisper of you behind them,
wishing them the great tremor and tenderness
of your body again as they at last must find it
if ever they may learn to endure in themselves
their returning and returning past the same hedge
in its other hands, the border of zinnias
doused in darkness, the door of their night kiss turning,
from which they turn once, and never again.

The One Dull Thing You Did
Was to Die, Fletcher

For Fletcher Pratt

To you, Fletcher, from my dark house asleep
in the sound of its lives breathing, at three
of a tired morning, and, as it happens,
in Rome—which could be Oslo or Shanghai
to any sense of mine: a place like any,
a distance equally anywhere from you
engraved in your dull death—and a damn poor likeness. . . .

I read a fool's book late, then puttered
along a marble hall a block long nowhere
at a hundred-thousand lire a month, and poured
my last shot of real Armagnac.
                                        And now,
here I stand, a sheep-face in the mirror,
the drink raised in this crazy Italian dim
of every bulb too small for what it does
and everyone saving a lira the wrong way.

Here I stand in this light that sticks to shadow
without half changing it, and there you are
as long as rent, and time wherever *it* is
in a lira's worth of something saved from dying.
God, what a silly way to keep a budget!
Well, here goes: from your budget's end and mine,
the last of what there is—to you, Fletcher,
maudlin, but in the best that money can buy.

To Dudley Fitts

(Some mortal lines while lying in bed with a jangling
sacro-iliac)

Patience, Dudley, we are two dried paltries.
Two sticks of season bloating at the bark.
Think what it is to think and still to be
at the stick-end of economy in the same wood
where once there were not thighs enough to squander!
But smile, old hobbled horse, days are worth something:
that smile at least, a head cocked to old jazz.

Or should we go down solemn and unbudged,
toga'd in our own fat like statuary?
as heavy set as those last senators
who sat in their stone places to the end
as if at Law, while through the balanced arches
the redbeards lurched to topple-in the day?
It *is* an Empire we outsit at last.

Or should we rail back moon-mad, damning all?
—I lie in bed, the ape-tail at my spine's end
jangling a buzzer of pain at my least stir:
part of a bedpan reading Robert Browning.
Bah! I wish I had the Henry Miller
I smuggled in from Paris but lent and lost.
It takes a madman to see all the moon.

But patience, patience. I smile at the madman's children
caroming in and out; bless his bright wife,
her flower trays of surprises and hot broth;
pat her behind, a melon from the moon;
lie naked to be washed, feeling her hands
soft as a birth's first night-knock at the womb.
—I drift toward my own embryo in sleep.

If death has such small hands, why, let it in:
some idiot snuggle at the pit of day

wriggles from self into the opium rot
that clings to all wet rooting where the dead
let out their gas of life to be first food.
Idiot sweet, I drowse there till the buzzer
grates once more at the ape-end of the spine.

Jangled awake and bursting at the bladder,
I reach for the goose-neck: gone to tidiness.
Damned if I'll yell for help: twinge and be damned.
But minutes later my wife comes sweetly clucking
to find me stiff and sweating on all fours,
stranded in my own hall like some obese
and stinking hound at its arthritic end.

Thank you. Thank you. Thank you. Thank you. Sorry.
I knew I shouldn't have, but I had to try.
Thank you, darling. Easy. All right. Now.
She gets me turned about and inch by inch
eases me back into a hotpad's rat's-nest,
a scolding mercy gentling me to bed.
It is the same bed in the same day's glare.

It is the same smile softening at the end:
patience in love, a coddle for a fool.
So am I changed to drizzle in the same field
where once I was all thunder. *Mop me, love.*
But if you dare forget the nights this bed
bucked in the moon . . . but if you dare forget. . . .
Ah, Senator, senators remember Rome!

. . . Paltries, Dudley, we are two shrunk paltries.
But bless us both, and for a sort of blessing
I trace this invalid drifting of the light.
That dead dog in the hallway sniffs through time
to its rooty end in the stiff sweat of damn.
Easy does it. Take this prattle for praise,
Old Paltry Bones, these two sticks clacked together.

Bridal Photo, 1906

A ceremonial rose in the lapel
a horseshoe wreath of pearls in the tie-knot,
a stone-starched collar bolted at the throat,
a tooth on a gold chain across the vest—
this is the man, costumed for solemn taking.

Pompadoured and laced and veiled for giving,
the woman sits her flower-time at his side
badged with his gifts—gold watch on a fleur-de-lis
pin at the heart, gold locket at the throat—
her hand at total rest under his hand.

What moment is this frozen from their lives
as if a movie stuck in its lit tracks?
Between the priest's gilt cave and their new bed,
ducking and giggling through the rowdy friends
who scattered rice and waited to get drunk,

they ran out of their day to the rigged cave
of the unknown hooded man who took their look
and made it into paper. Here they are:
stopped with all eyes upon them in his eye,
so solemn and so starched, they must have laughed

a thousand times, when they could laugh again,
to see themselves carved from themselves like stone.
And yet what moment is this of their lives
who hold their lives so open to all looking?
Was this the bridal and all else the dance?

Half-man, half-woman, not yet one another,
but in a first time and a last between
that separate morning and all joined good nights,
they stood to think their lives into one look
and hold the unfinished bridal to its hour.

Oh man and woman tranced in your new flowers,
your eyes are deep as churches, but as far
as you look out unseeing, the years look in!
Sweet strangers, I am left across your lives
to see the flower day taken from its flowers.

I follow this long look into its dark
where, leathered as an Indian chief, the woman
sags through this lace to keen for the bashed corpse
that drops from the man's steadiness in his hour.
I hold this study by the hooded man

and pray to that held hour from its last love:
Bless the unfinished bridal to its bed.
This day becomes this day. What others follow
have touched their flower. By all flowers and all fall
I am the son of this man and this woman.

Palaver's No Prayer

Palaver's no prayer.
There's a nice-ninny priest
at tea in everyone,
all cosy and chatty as auntie,
but a saint comes
and throws rocks through the window.

S.P.Q.R. A Letter from Rome

Sono Porci Questi Romani

I

It does for the time of man to walk here
    by the spoken stones forgotten, a criss-crossed empire
    sticking its stumps out of cypress. Not a name,
    though stone-carved, but what a name
    is plastered over it. Not a god in town
    but watched his temple changed into a quarry.

And could smile: "Let them change Heaven and Earth
    if they can: nothing changes the Romans.
    Men as they were, beasts as they were, they are.
    Their God across the Tiber has stone arms
    stretched from his dome like crab's claws. Can claws hold them?
    A thousand kings have held Rome; none, the Romans.

Who knows the goats better than the goatherd?
    We piped their lambing from burnt rock
    and made a people of them. Rank and graceless
    they are a people yet. And ours. All arches
    are one to them. Whatever name is on them,
    they read their own. Exactly as we gave it."

—You hear that gods' pique everywhere. A jobless
    immortality fallen to sneers and gossip.
    They'll rob you blind, kick your shins bloody,
    elbow you over the edge, then smile and say *"Scusi."*
    History? Rome's no history, but a madhouse.
    So, I suppose, the original of history.

It does for all time to walk there
    over the unchanged changes—like a guard mount,
    the same before and after. What's there to change?

You go to the Vatican or the Pantheon
in the same mob.
                              And keep your pockets buttoned:
leave one flap open—you'll learn history.

II

On stone, her stoned knees throbbing like a pulse
    in the concussion of holiness, Sister Pia,
        vowed to meditation, unwashed, unflinching,
        prayed in her stones that days and men be laundered.

"If I am worthy, teach me what I must suffer."
    Ten years upon her knees in the odor of grace.
    Spoon-fed a broth a day by those who cleaned her;
    the prayer bubbling on through every spoonful.

Ten years on her knees while the stone cell
    became a Colosseum and the blood
    steamed, hymned, to Heaven from the beasts'
    muzzles and the glory was said and said.

"If I am worthy, bless them." And was tolled
    by bells and the praying shadows of stone,
    the Convent black with triumph.—While, at the gates,
    a hundred thousand Fiats snarled and screeched.

III

Till one claxon of all rang statues quick:
    Mussolini ha sempre ragione. And he came
    out of the stones like yesterday-made-easy.
    A new statue sprung from every footfall.

Empire! And the mob remembered! It rained stone chips
    in Rome all one generation as the masons swung
    again. A thousand, ten thousand, a million
    stone-thrust-chins for piazzas, dressers, export:

in the mud at Addis Ababa, an Arch of Triumph;
      in Libya, on the sand grill, a Colossus;
      across the Mare Nostrum in the moon,
      a bust of glory on the binnacle.

Till all hung upside-down on a northern wall,
      suffered as Sister Pia to its stones, and the mob
      sang: *"Fatto! Viva l'America!"* Turned, praying:
      "If I am worthy—Joe, a cigarette."

IV

It does for the time of all to walk here
      by the saved arches and the forgotten surrenders.
      An empire of ego figging its thumbs at heaven.
      A museum of famines lurking to snatch bread.
      A propriety of dressed scorns promenading.
      A cradle of prayer bubbling.

As time is. Half a nonsense. Like a guard mount:
      the same stone godwatch before and after,
      a grandiose serenity with its lips cracked,
      smirking: "Let them change Heaven and Earth
      if they can. Nothing changes a Roman."

And still a marble marriage pomps the light.

Massive Retaliation

Saipan 1944–1945.
Aerial Offensive Against Japan.

I gaped, admitted, at some of what we did
those days at skip-ocean, watching the shore towns blow
like spouts below us, staring into volcanoes
at the half-closed red eye under everything.

One moon-mist night six miles above Nagoya
we let our fish go, banked wide over mountains.
A searchlight from the world washed us in green,
lost us to black, returned, lost us again.

Those wars were all waiting. I waited, looking down
into the dark of one more thing set fire to.
Then we were over ocean and alive.
The blaze went out. We dove into the dawn.

It was as far from home as we could go.
I remember the teeth of the mountains of the moon
and the meteors falling in. By afternoon
it was official. Something had been done.

We acted boredom but lived better. Once,
above the sea, circling a rendezvous rock,
we filled the east and west with silver sharks
pinwheeling like a marriage race of gods.

It was a thousand of ourselves we saw.
A thousand theorems spiraled from the sun
to some proof statelier than the thing done.
A sky-wide silver coming of the Law.

Even toward murder such possibility
meets and becomes. Like empires on their shields
we circled over time, and the great wheel
blazed like a reason on the lighted sea.

I gaped for all good men at what we were,
dressed in such bridals, spilling from the sun,
stuffed with such thunderbolts, and come
so far from home, almost beyond return.

In Place of a Curse

At the next vacancy for God, if I am elected,
I shall forgive last the delicately wounded
who, having been slugged no harder than anyone else,
never got up again, neither to fight back,
nor to finger their jaws in painful admiration.

They who are wholly broken, and they in whom
mercy is understanding, I shall embrace at once
and lead to pillows in heaven. But they who are
the meek by trade, baiting the best of their betters
with the extortions of a mock-helplessness

I shall take last to love, and never wholly.
Let them all into Heaven—I abolish Hell—
but let it be read over them as they enter:
"Beware the calculations of the meek, who gambled nothing,
gave nothing, and could never receive enough."

To Lucasta, About That War

A long winter from home the gulls blew
    on their brinks, the tankers slid
    over the hump where the wolf packs hid
    like voodoo talking, the surf threw
    bundles with eyes ashore. I did
    what booze brought me, and it wasn't you.

I was mostly bored. I watched and told time
    as enforced, a swag-man
    under the clock. The bloat-bags ran
    wet from nowhere, selling three-for-a-dime
    and nobody buying. Armies can
    type faster than men die, I'm

told, and can prove. Didn't I find
    time there, and more, to count
    all, triplicate, and still walk guard-mount
    on the gull- and drum-wind
    over the hump? I did, and won't
    deny several (or more) pig-blind

alleys with doors, faces, dickers,
    which during, the ships slid
    over the hump where the packs hid.
    And talking voodoo and snickers
    over the edge of their welts, I did
    what I could with (they called them) knickers;

and it was no goddamn good,
    and not bad either. It
    was war (they called it) and it lit
    a sort of skyline somehow in the blood,
    and I typed the dead out a bit
    faster than they came, or anyone should,

and the gulls blew high on their brinks,
    and the ships slid, and the surf threw,
    and the Army initialed, and you
    were variously, vicariously, and straight and with kinks,
    raped, fondled, and apologized to—
    which is called (as noted) war. And it stinks.

The Verbal Generation

As the hostess said,
it was really nothing,
and not even the flowers
bothered to nod
but posed,
cut and expensive,
between the martinis
and the elbows

after two hours of which
the author
and the painter
and the composer
and the poet
and the moderator

were taxied to the Hall
and went on stage
and talked
and answered questions
about being a generation.

The Baboon and the State

A dog snout puzzles out the look of a man.
The wrong smell of a stranger tweaks the air.
"Fangs! Fangs! Why should we run? We are
Born of the chosen, first, and tallest tree!
Sons of the Sacred Banyan follow me!
Baboons are born to kill because they can."

Clemenceau said to the American
With the blue jaw and the fox-terrier hair,
"Above France, civilization." He made war
As if he strangled a mistress—tenderly,
But with a certain competence. A man
Must sacrifice for his own family.

Guido came trembling from the Vatican,
Roped up for God, God's moonspot in his hair.
"How shall I overthrow the Lateran?"
The Fat Pope said. "Speak up. God lives in me.
In His name teach me my cupidity."
And Guido spilled the malice in his ear.

Odysseus, that seven-minded man,
Piled up his kills to honor prophecy—
And indispensable, most Ithacan
Justification for a blood at war.
He spoke tongues and heard God-talk on the air,
But all his men were told was, "Follow me!"

Is man wrong for the State, or it for man?
High reasons and low causes make a war.
It is the Baboon kills, because he can
But Presidents hear voices from the air.
So packs and parishes cry equally:
"God's first and last Law sounded from a tree."

The voices come to rest where they began.
Clemenceau nods to the American.
Guido comes praying from the Vatican.
And indispensable most Ithacan
Baboon snout puzzles out the look of a man.
The killers kill. They kill because they can.

The Gift

In 1945, when the keepers cried *kaput*,
Josef Stein, poet, came out of Dachau
like half a resurrection, his other
eighty pounds still in their invisible grave.

Slowly then the mouth opened and first
a broth, and then a medication, and then
a diet, and all in time and the knitting mercies,
the showing bones were buried back in flesh,

and the miracle was finished. Josef Stein,
man and poet, rose, walked, and could even
beget, and did, and died later of other causes
only partly traceable to his first death.

He noted—with some surprise at first—
that strangers could not tell he had died once.
He returned to his post in the library, drank his beer,
published three poems in a French magazine,

and was very kind to the son who at last was his.
In the spent of one night he wrote three propositions:
That Hell is the denial of the ordinary. That nothing lasts.
That clean white paper waiting under a pen

is the gift beyond history and hurt and heaven.

Captain Nicholas Strong

The moon with Venus in her sickle blade
made a masonic bangle in Orion,
then dimmed from gold to platinum in the haze,
not yet a dawn, that dusted up the sky
pale shade by shade, then dimmed again to pearl,
then sank into the ice-age before light,
shimmered from a blue depth, and, as a bird
skimmed on the surface, sank into the day.
Then the first fire ray shot above the earth.

    All turned to day. Ambushed in history,
three guards on their last tower looked to the West
and saw it move, at first only a little.
A little was enough. The three descended,
opened the gate and waited, a white scarf
tied to a broomless broomstick. So it ended.
The trucks pulled in. A corporal took the guards
under his gun. The Captain called them up:
"Show us who's here." The three led through the yard;
but the thing had snapped already—like a dust
swirled forward by the wind, the corpses boiled
out of their graves and boxes, sullying
the light they moved in. With a shriek like joy,
but crazy, they blew past both armies, blind,
and crashed against a locked shed. As if noise
were force enough for all, the gray wall climbed,
the roof cracked, tilted, and the shed went over.
And there they clawed, each corpse mad with its find.
And when at last the Captain, forcing bone
apart from bone, got in to take a look,
he found it was flour-barrels, and the corpses
stood cramming flour into their mouths, both hands full,
and gagging as they swallowed, but still cramming,
choking and cramming, dying at last for food.

There was nothing else to do: he signaled back
for water, which was jostled to the ground,
and the dead men ate the paste out of their hands,
lay in it till they retched, and came unwound,
and let themselves be hauled away to life,
quivering and limp. And so within an hour
that, too, had ended, and some seemed to be
the parts of men again, if parts are men,
and if what men are parts of can be healed.
The Captain was no healer. He had wept
nothing in twenty years. He took two drinks
and shot the guards himself. And when the medics
arrived at last, he had no more to give,
and left the gates of Hell, sure he was right.
Still bleached with flour, pale as the day moon's finger,
he opened two more Hells before that night.

It takes no training to be dead. The Captain
was trapped in his own name—Nicholas Strong—
and made a muscle of it. Before he tracked
that shaved moon out, and, at the second dawn,
saw Venus drown alone, he had set free
six circles of the damned. What had he done
in all his life before that let him see
what he did now? He hated what he did—
their stink, their burls of bone, their slimey beards:
they clung to life so hard they dirtied it.
He would have shot them sooner than the guards
had he been God. The Captain *had* to kill:
only a violence could wash him. Sparks
shot from his hand, and part of every death
was that his face must never move.

                              What part
of anything the Captain was in Hell
is all of us in time, I do not know.
In four moons more the Captain had undressed

from war forever. Home, and back again in
—of all things—Nick Strong's Haberdashery,
he dressed again, but never quite completely:
that day showed through no matter what he wore.
He knew it had meant something. Of his years
from dunes to bunkers, it was that first day
lurked in hat boxes and the racks of tweeds.
The Captain knew but never learned to say
he had been happiest when he stood most still,
letting one finger blast the world away,
carved like a rock and right, almost a will.
Grateful for what he killed, that being plain,
and loathing what he rescued, which, being sick,
troubled his health for mercies with no name.

A Thousandth Poem for Dylan Thomas

Waking outside his Babylonian binge
    in the wet and cramp of morningstone, the sot
begins his daily death. A first stiff wince
    numbers his bones, each like a tooth of God.

Where did night end? Girlies in a red flame
    squeal through his broken memory like pigs:
Hell's barnyard burning or the zoo of days,
    stampeded shapes exploded from their skins.

He tastes again the ooze of a first sigh
    dead in his throat; his mouth, a rotten fig:
his sex, a broken glue-pot in the thighs;
    his breath, a shudder from below the will.

Sooner or later he must break an eye
    to look at what he sees of what he is.
An angel beating at the trap of time?
    A bird-heart pulsing in an idiot's fist?

Both. Either. Floated open from its muds,
    that moment in the clear, the sot's eye sees
as much as saints could bear of the fireblood
    God's heart pumps in its seizure of the skies.

Then how the man could sing his ghost to tears,
    there in God's eye and blood, for that lost place
where he was innocent, before his need
    changed to a thirst inside the worm of waste.

He pours his celebrations of regret,
    tormented joyous from the throat of mud,
hawk-hearted as Augustine in his sweat,
    dove-eyed as Francis' bridal with the wood.

It is the age of sots. Our holiness
    wakens outside the minareted fronts
of a jazzy, airless, and expensive hell.
    He sings our wish. He drinks his death for us

who have no throats to die of or to sing.
    He is Saint Binge at death in his own meat,
the blaze meant in the char we make of things,
    our addict, and our angel of defeat.

Some Figures for Who Must Speak

I

Forget understanding. There will be none.
A condition natural as weather is between us.
Our lives are in separate airs. Our memories
are seas and mountains: sometimes and for a while
in sight of one another, but across an element.

You mountain Congregationalists—will you believe
however faithfully at every risk
I dredge it from myself, the existence of squid?
I carry an oar on my shoulder, and who
in all these uplands knows it moves a world?

You sea-going mackerel snatchers by the sputtery pumps—
would you answer, though I break my back for it,
to September hay sweated from ledges
in the sight of four weathers at once
there in the sluices and bowls below my footing?

Whatever is, is the natural day of who goes there.

II

It takes a habit of living. Poetry
is the family talk of the generations:
you have to have lived in the house of that name.

When an outsider happens in, it stops or changes.
The young, being someways truest, prattle
to confuse him. The old may try, for politeness,

to say a little something. But whatever
was going on there round the table,
or by the fire, or squealing through the hall,

dressing, undressing, and piggy-back to bed—
whatever was going on before the stranger
came popping smalltalk from somewherever else—

the faces sit re-arranged and the fun is over.

III

Is it possible to say it without memories?
As if in answer to a questionnaire? squared
like columns in a statistician's eye?

It is a plain thing. Plain enough for saying.
A white elk, for that matter, once you come on it,
is as visible as a jackass: there it is.

The trick is to happen next to it *and*
to be ready for what happens. I've known men
to see that elk and think it was a ground fog.

It is a plain thing, then, but one must have eyes.
I can see it as it is: I cannot name it
by any names you know. "Poetry," I say,

and you think of Longfellow, and I
of the race in its going: the family at its days:
the young at the edge of the thicket where the elk sleeps.

I mean the thing behind the name of the thing.

IV

Perhaps it could start with an exchange of pictures:
you may think of me as a knob-kneed wheezy paunch
too old to hunt, but left on guard at the cavemouth.

(There is more to it than that, but that will do.
I sit here watching the cubs spill in the sun,
and think: "Tonight I shall try again to carve an Elk head."

It is something to think about, a way
of leaving that much of myself to the cave forever—
if I can truly remember the lines of that head.)

You are also a man of intentions. I see you
(you must not let the change of time and scene
confuse you: this is all times and all scenes:

I speak for the family in all its ages)
—I see you also as the keeper of a propriety,
both in your nakedness, and naked but wearing a collar.

You are something and believe something (that
is not necessarily the same thing). And you distrust me
with your certainties. I waste the family's time.

It was so I met you once in Florida
in the image of a Baptist graduate student
who told me that the Absolute in Aesthetics

was the same as the Absolute in everything else.
When I asked what that might be, he tossed his mane,
and pointing his finger and his whole arm, said:

"The Triune God!"—Now suppose you're as saved as he is
(as all of you are somewhere inside yourselves)
how shall I not be read in your own image?

And how shall I carve that Elk's head
which is the Elk's head truly remembered? the presence
of life in the thicket named for my hunting tribe?

the picture of themselves my people are?

V

It can also be half-seen half-truly.
I could show you what an elk is.
Even what a white elk is. But can I

show you, or you see, the elk in his stance?
musky and rank in the great steam of his presence?

It is in the elk and equally in the life
of the elk people that the seeing happens.
After the first son who was killed in the hunt
was buried with the elk's horns on his cairn,
we tore the flesh of the beast hot from the fire.

VI

It can also be half-said half-truly.
But remember of what is half-said
that it must be twice heard: once
in the words of the saying, and again
in the burial and the feast between two bloods.

I am, for plainness, a tribesman speaking
to other councils. "See what a land of plenty
we war in," I say. "Let us possess our difference
and hunt our need in peace, to die as that first son
at whose grave we wintered; not in these games of stones."

And there you sit in your feathers and Absolutes,
pointing your finger and arm. Do I see three heads
thrown back? Well then, the pow-wow is ended.
Your people are not mine. And yet, whoever
wins this war must hunt that Elk or starve.

A Praise of Good Poets in a Bad Age

To the memory of Wallace Stevens

Any man—God, if he had the money—
could rip the sagebrush back for terraced gardens
and tilt a pearlstone Hollywood between
the swimming pools and the Pacific.

Lord, what we know of doing badly!
the nerve's reach for order gone huge,
eye-catching, and moneyed. How shall I say this right
who say "Lord" and mean something else?—

Something not Heaven nor Hell, but something.
The tongue is wrong in the mouth to say it, the words
soggy from the prayers of lace-curtain angels.
We lack a vocabulary for admiration.

And still a man could take a train to magnificence:
to Rutherford for Williams, to Hartford for Stevens,
to Cambridge for Frost—and not have it, and yet
have touched the most of it in one day's going.

How much higher in its own mind could the age stand
than these three have stood for it?
Now Stevens is dead from meaning-as-it-is,
and that day's ride to the age's best

longer by an absence as it goes shortened
by stone-imagined forests of stopped birds
and voices windborne from a midnight river,
an oarlock's birdcall from the gist of time.

Imagine any man at that train's windows,
watching the world from this death and these lives,
hearing the carried voice of their alert—
what shall defend Newark from his arrival?

Harlem from his revulsion? South Station from his defeat?
Once in Connecticut from such a window
I saw three egrets statued by marsh-reaches
as if posed for the eyes of Egyptian lovers.

What a suave possibility they made of the sky!
But before the next-to-prayer in my heart could open
we broke the soot of Somewhere-on-the-Line
and my eye crashed like a flung egg on its walls.

Is it a symptom only or a source,
that permission of ugliness in American houses?
Arson could be a creed, and a vote for Nero
a vote for a compassion corruption.

Call the dead poet from his imaginings:
"Soit!" he chimes back from that pixie passion
that made his belltowers tinkle as they bonged.
"Waa-waallee-waa!" the whistle learns to say.

Nonsense. But nearer than the age to being.
It is no chin-thrust figure angel-high
the ardent man lifts from his ordering:
leave those grim doughboys to the yokel squares.

By bong and tinkle he dwarfed back the fronts
of the age's skew and sooty imagination.
Now he is dead: one gone of the three truest,
and poverty, drowned in money, cannot care.

Soit! To be a poet in an age of prose
is to hear more than the age is ready for.
Caroo, Caballero! the States lack word of cockles.
A bronze pear hanging is not news enough

now Congress has the language by the throat.
Let it strut for nothing. "Fat! Fat! Fat! Fat!"
When the age has found a memory near enough
his news from bronze, most houses will come down.

To W. T. Scott

with thanks for a poem

I like that poem, Win. There's a green world in it.
Not just green acreage—any nature boy
can rhyme on that a dozen lines a minute:
put in a bluebird if you're out for joy,
put in a hayloft if you're out for plot,
put in a dead tree if you're out for thought.

I mean what's green in being what a man
touches to leave. Say, Mark Twain at the end;
the green of his last thought. Suppose it ran
to Huck or Jim drifting around a bend;
then stopped there with a sigh or with a smile,
or even wondering had it been worthwhile,

but still a life to think about that stood
green to itself. As God might lose a world
yet think back and be sad that it was good.
All green dies. But the sere manfingers curled
to their last pulse, touch in a memory.
Touch, and I think are justified. For me

that green is first. The green thought more than green
of Walden is Thoreau. The man unspared.
As queer as he was green. An in-between:
half-Cod, half-Buddha. But a system bared
to its own pulse. He had a mind with wings.
But best of all he had an eye for things.

God, how he could see green! He must have died
with time ablaze around him like spring fern
caught in a single ray of sun inside
a glacier-rumpled Stonehenge, while a churn
of swallows buttered him his last of light.
—All nothing till he held it in his sight.

That green. Say, Whitman like a stricken bear
thinking: "What is a sea?" Say, Henry James
thinking: "What country is it over there?"
on a long foggy walk beside the Thames.
Say, Melville thinking: "What have I left done
that will stay green to time for anyone?"

And *all* done. What a sea or country is.
What world can grow to, shaped round from the mind.
Such forests deeper than Yosemites
a man walks thinking in and leaves behind.
That last green, Win, after the first unrolled.
The eighth day of the world, by a man told.

An Inscription for Richard Eberhart

I do not intend the people I know to believe me
    outside themselves: belief is inside the self.
    "It is the not-me in my friend delights me,"
    Emerson wrote. It is my friend in me
    that lets me see my friend.—These are convictions
    one sleep this side of poetry. But in time,
    with sleep dissolving from me like a mist,
    I find the shape of a scimitar still in my hand
    and know what holy wars I should have gone to
    in the right season. When I say to my friends:
    "We are that invisible war," they smile
    with a smile I know from myself. It is so we learn,
    one from another, our difference is no war
    but the delicate jointure of the parts of a skull.

But is the articulation of bones a meeting?
    I have slept on ruined Rome and wakened green
    with the squeal of birds and the power-hum of the bees
    sealed in the air like amber. In the atrium,
    a laborer was eating bread and cheese
    in the noonday of his wine. I watched his ease.
    It was longer than the ruin. *"Buon appetito!"*
    I cried like God in the Sunday of my pleasure.
    He raised his wine flask and called back *"Salute!"*
    Then did he turn to stone? Or the stones to him?
    Something stayed fixed in time out of that meeting:
    a signal from my friend in me, a placement
    of holy banquets in their atrium,
    a vision of the bones that speak themselves.

In the Stoneworks

—•—

(1961)

The Sea Shines

The sea shines. Wind-raked, the waters run light
strand by strand. Wind-plowed, they fold
light into the furrows. Wind-winnowed, they toss
spume ends; and rainbows and the ghosts
of rainbows leap, drift fading across an
enormous look, like breath at the poles.
All burning in motion. All sanctioned and told.
All sent of the creature's warmth in the world's cold.

The sea shines. Tremulous over its crushing hunch
to the world's end, it shakes the entire
tree of light to the sky-top, and the gulls
blow off like leaves that seem never to land
but to catch fire in air and be wholly consumed—
all back to fire and air before
they can take weight and fall. A day,
another day, burns upward in the great eye, and away.

It takes a god to say "the sea shines" each first time
into the day, as his eye goes, thought by thought
before him, calling forth from lead-deeps and blazings,
from far-silver and shore-mica, imagination
by imagination, the dazzle
of what will be sung and sung, age by age,
man by man, of the god in him, as each
stands churned in his lit veins on his lit beach.

The man stands in god's place on that shore,
opening the eye there is—
man's, god's, or beast's—for seeing the world lit
in the wind from origin. "The sea shines,"
he says, and god could say no more,
having once begun entirely to imagine
by what world he stands, in the pour
of what abundance, on what hammered shore.

The Dolls

Night after night forever the dolls lay stiff
by the children's dreams. On the goose-feathers of the rich,
on the straw of the poor, on the gypsy ground—
wherever the children slept, dolls have been found
in the subsoil of the small loves stirred again
by the Finders After Everything. Down lay
the children by their hanks and twists. Night after night
grew over imagination. The fuzzies shed, the bright
buttons fell out of the heads, arms ripped, and down
through goose-feathers, straw, and the gypsy ground
the dolls sank, and some—the fuzziest and most loved—
changed back to string and dust, and the dust moved
dream-puffs round the Finders' boots as they dug,
sieved, brushed, and came on a little clay dog,
and a little stone man, and a little bone girl, that had kept
their eyes wide open forever, while all the children slept.

Back Home in Pompeii

Back home in Pompeii
birds crunched underfoot,
stones flew away,
statues began to bow.

Government wrote
our clauses and conditions,
then as now.
But, egged in stone,
a saved worm curled alone
to hatch through the inscriptions.

Some thought to run and were
the first down.
The weather laid a ton
on every breath.
I brought you water there
and watched it hiss away.
"It's an elaborate death,"
I heard you say.
And then the rafters broke.

Storms later, we awoke
and strolled among ourselves
in the excavated bed—
stone castings on stone shelves.

How had we fled,
leaving so neat a foot
cast in the mountain's soot?
these hands in a glass case?
and, like an artifact,
the fragment of a face?

One of us lay intact
for anyone to see
the stone-stored human form
curled like the stone-saved worm
in a last agony.

Well, that's that.
Settled down
and starting to get fat
in another town
oceans away,
we only come to see
a curiosity
on holiday.

A Memory of the Sad Chair

All in a dream of the time it was
(Kissing the corpse on its bombproof nose)
I winked at a peach that gave me a buzz,
But when I rubbed her she had no fuzz.
A sad chair stared, heaped with our clothes.

All in the light of the moon that came
(The bottles empty, the switches thrown)
I lost my wallet, I changed my name,
I saw the colonel go down aflame.
There stood the chair, our only one.

All in a heap on the chair that stood
(Polaris neither rising nor setting)
I told no evil, I saw no good
Except those sad few sticks of wood,
Like a ghost I had been forgetting.

All in a row in the law that wrought
(Some still listed and some still lost)
I sighted squinty, my tracers caught,
The sad chair blew up like a thought.
She snored her whiskey. I turned and tossed.

All in a dream of the thought that blows
The moon in the window, the ghost on the chair,
The one sad chair heaped with our clothes,
I kissed her corpse on its bombproof nose,
And left her dead and went out for air.

All in a dream of the time it is
(The colonels coming, the colonels going)
Since Tokyo sizzled her star-spangled sizz,
I got a medal for writing this,
And an oak-leaf cluster because it was snowing.

All in the hush of the snow that fell
(Tojo dancing for everyone's crime)
We swung the hammer, we rang the bell,
But the only reason it wasn't Hell
We went to was—we won, that time.

All in a haggle of what we won
(The corncob rampant above the noose)
The sad chair stood, our only one.
I wish, now all is said and done,
We had shared that sadness, but what's the use?

Epitaph

Here, time concurring (and it does),
Lies Ciardi. If no kingdom come,
A kingdom was. Such as it was,
This one, beside it, is a slum.

Song for an Allegorical Play

Ah could we wake in mercy's name—
the church mouse in each other's eyes
forgiven, the warthog washed in flame
confessed—when paunch from paunch we rise,
false and unmartyred, to pretend
we dress for Heaven in the end.

To look and not to look away
from what we see, but, kindly known,
admit our scraping small decay
and the gross jowls of flesh on bone—
think what a sweetness tears might be
in mercy, each by each set free.

Only Success is beast enough
to stop our hearts. Oh twist his tail
and let him howl. When best we love
we have no reason but to fail,
in reason learning as we live
we cannot fail what we forgive.

The mouse is in your eyes and mine.
That warthog wallows in our blood.
But, ah, let mercy be our sign,
and all our queer beasts, understood,
shall rise, grown admirable, and be,
in mercy, each by each set free.

The Tree

There was a tree whose leaves were flowers.
Rainbow deck by deck it tiered
Into original light—a weird
And central system blazed with towers.

The black trunk gnarled and sent away
Whole horizontal nebulae,
While the main shaft, split into three,
Struck through the dome of night and day.

It was my tree. Its leaves my flowers.
I woke under it all one lawn.
Like small monks who had died and gone
To Heaven, bees intoned great hours.

Like small humped monks with lighted souls
They prayed their spirals to its blooms.
And radiant as the promised tombs
Of martyrs, rose in aureoles.

It was my tree of dappled swings.
I floated under it all one weather.
The bees and I turned gold together.
Time stroked us with first wings.

'Till wind by wind, in storms of shreds,
The flowers spun off, the buds stood bare.
One winter I was passing there
And saw its fruit—like shrunken heads.

The Little One

And if you do not weep,
at what are you used to weeping?

—Ugolino

The little one
chilled paler and paler
till the smile in her
wisped off
like breath in a frost.

Then, last, her eyes went out.
By that nightfall
the snow on the sill
had let out glass claws,
and what man was not scratched
could have no tears in this world
nor hope of dear smiling.

All our silences walked those rooms,
walked us,
tore and took
what we did not say.

"This is what Nothing is,"
said our silences.
"And this," said the winter mounds
that had to be blasted open
even for so little a one
to slide into
        to Nothing.

Dialogue

"Good-morning," says the Fine Brisk Man in the mirror,
"And what shall you do today?"
"I shall part my hair, I suspect, as I always do.
Or maybe another way."

"That wouldn't work long," says the Excellent Man in the mirror.
"A man's hair leans like all the things of his life
into habituation. It would only tousle
once it has dried. That would displease your wife."

"The hair of her pleasure," I grin at the man in the mirror,
"does not grow on my head, though I part it with care."
"*Today*, I said," says the man. "Save that for night."
"The time to shoot is when the quail's in air."

"Not very clever," says the Good Sound Man in the mirror.
"Have you no serious thought, no thought
appropriate to my better sense of composure?"
"No, sir, I have not."

"Well, what of China and Lebanon and Algeria?
What of the bickering flags on the winds today?
How can you see life steadily and see it whole
in that irresponsible way?"

"Sir," I say to the Clean-Shaven Man in the mirror,
"I recall you when your face was stuck with sleep,
and your chin draggled with whiskers.
You were not, I think, quite so deep

poised and sententious then. Can soap and water,
lather, a razor, and a dash of smell
have wrought all this in something like five minutes?
Try it on someone who doesn't know you so well,

or I swear I'll tousle you till you never slicken,
gum up your eyes, and dangle hemp from your chin.
You shined accessory to an attaché case,
you're not taking me in.

Aren't you the brat who used to steal from Woolworth's?
And your own mother's purse to get to the show?
Haven't I seen you puking drunk?" Says the Proper
Prosperous Middle-aged Man in the mirror, "Really now!"

"And who cried like a ninny when that girl chucked him—
what was her name? And though he took the jam
and wore the medals, almost froze on the triggers
when the Zeroes tried to ram?

And who do you think was saving the world's sobriety
the night you bit the garter-belt from Nell?"
"—Well," says the Very Suave Man in the mirror, "so it goes.
But we mustn't—now must we?—tell."

Bedlam Revisited

Nobody told me anything much. I was born
free to my own confusions, though in hock
to Mother and Father Sweatshop's original stock
in Boston, Mass., four families to a john.
The spire of the Old North Church, like a tin horn
upside down on the roofs, was our kitchen clock,
and dropped the hours like rock onto a rock
over the Hull Street graveyard. "Gone. All gone,"

it thunked above the dead. The smells were sad.
And there were rats, of course, but nailed tin
could keep them down (or at least in)
to a noise between the hours. The graveyard had
left us a son in real estate and the lad
had grown to father our landlord, though Frank Glynn
was the wart-on-the-nose that came with a sneaky grin
to collect the rent. Till he died to Hell. Too bad.

Nobody told me anything much, and that
so wrong it cost me nothing—not even love—
to lose it. All but the Boss, the Cop and the Ghost of
the Irish Trinity. Those I sweated at
so hard I came up hating. But still grew fat
in a happy reek of garlic, bay, and clove.
I was crazy, of course, but always at one remove.
I tried on faces as if I were buying a hat.

Home was our Asylum. My father died
but my mother kept talking to him. My sisters screamed.
My aunt muttered. My uncle got drunk and dreamed
three numbers a night for a quarter with cock-eyed
Charlie Pipe-Dreams who moseyed along half-fried

every morning at seven. The old boy schemed
for twenty years that I knew of before he was reamed
by Family Morticians. But I'll say this—he tried.

Nobody told me anything much. Nobody had
anything much to tell me. I rolled my own
and scrounged for matches. How could I have known
everything about us was full-moon mad?
Or that I'd find few saner? It wasn't bad.
Someone always answered the telephone
when it had rung too long. You got only a tone
when they finally called you—far away and sad.
But it didn't matter. There would have been nothing to say.
Later they changed the number and we moved away.

Aunt Mary

Aunt Mary died of eating twelve red peppers
        after a hard day's work. The doctor said
        it was her high blood pressure finished her.
        As if disease were anything to Aunt Mary
        who had all of her habits to die of! But imagine
        a last supper of twelve red peppers, twelve
        of those crab-apple size dry scorchers
        you buy on a string at Italian groceries,
        twelve of them fried in oil and gobbled off
        (Aunt Mary was a messy eater)—and then,
        to feel the room go dizzy, and through your blood
        the awful coming on of nothing more
        than twelve red peppers you know you shouldn't have eaten
        but couldn't help yourself, they were so good.

Now what shall I pray for gluttonous Aunt Mary
     who loved us till we screamed? Even poor Mother
     had more of Aunt Mary's love than she could live with,
     but had to live with it. I am talking now
     of a house with people in it, every room
     a life of a sort, a clutter of its own.
     I am talking of a scene in the palm of God
     in which one actor dies of twelve red peppers,
     one has too many children, one a boy friend,
     two are out of work, and one is yowling
     for one (offstage) to open the bathroom door.
     This is not the scene from the palm of God
     in which the actors hold God in their palms,
     nor the scene in which the actors know their prayers—

it is the scene in which Aunt Mary died
     and nobody knew anything, least of all
     Aunt Mary. In her red-hot transformation
     from gluttony into embalmer's calm
     and candlelight, I cried a hypocrite tear.
     But it was there, when I had seen Aunt Mary
     bloodlet for God, that I began to see
     what scene we are. At once I wept Aunt Mary
     with a real tear, forgiving all her love,
     and its stupidities, in the palm of God.
     Or on a ledge of time. Or in the eye
     of the blasting sun. Or tightroped on a theorem.
     —Let every man select his own persuasion:
     I pray the tear she taught me of us all.

A Dialogue in the Shade

Said the Damaged Angel to the Improved Ape:
"Time is a hard road. I've come from others,
and longer, but never
so choking a dust, nor stones
so honed to the instep. This way's a crippler."

Answered the Ape, fingering the strings
of a first thought: "Measure's
whatever you're used to. I've
traveled no easier, ever, and, yes,
it's a crippler at last, but it does for what's doing."

"A thought!" said the Angel astonished. "And worthy
of me, though I say so. I'm learning there's more
to you, surely,
than met my eye first
when I stopped in the shade to lament like a creature."

"Your arrogance," answered the Ape, still improving,
and scratching a memory dark in the Tree he was leaving,
"reminds me of something
near as a mother tongue saying
we've more here in common than shade and the need of it."

"Enough," said the Damaged Angel, his legal training
still evident. "Our natures teach our natures
no trespass on common ground.
We've nowhere, it's certain, to go
but each other, and shall we begin, since we must?"

"There arises at once," said the Ape, now improving
faster and faster with practice, "the questions of sex.
The 'begats,' you recall
take particular doing. Myself,
I am partial to being the male of whatever we sign to."

"No, no," said the Angel, "though damaged, I'm still
the more heavenly part of what follows, and clearly
the aspirant, therefore
the male, of whatever
told species may flow from the womb of commandment."

"If mind is your weapon," the Ape, now concerned
not to improve too fast, replied, "I must tell you
you haven't convinced me.
Which leaves it, I'll argue, my turn
to suggest. Let's fight for it: power's a sure master."

So they fought and begat and the book of their doing
is long in the telling, with most left uncertain,
and endless the names
of their children, and not one
among them soul-sure of his father and mother.

It Took Four Flowerboats to Convoy My Father's Black

It took four flowerboats to convoy my father's black
Cadillac cruiser out to St. Mike's and down
deeper than all salt. It was a very successful
funeral my mother remembers remembering. *Imagine*
what flowers! Even the undertaker was surprised,
he told me! He came with only two flowercars.
He had to send his son all over town like crazy
to find two more, there were so many. Imagine!

And when the funeral went to circle the block three
times—those days they did that: it was like the man
coming home again three times for his soul to remember—
we started, and when the first cars came around, the last
ones were still blocking the street! Even
the undertaker was surprised! He had to go around two
blocks instead of one to make the circles for the soul!
You were too small to remember, but imagine!

. . . It was my first cruise: the streets ahead a groundswell
of flowers, the wind ripping petals like spume from a wave,
the hearse bobbing nattily in the troughs, powerful
and in ballast, dead into the flower-stripping wind, and steady.
Man! what a big day at sea it was in that wind past all
the shores that stood-to and moved with us through
the ports of the black cabin my mother made of her flesh
in the black Cadillac cruiser I midshipped in. I mean, God,

it was a regatta, I tell you, she told me,
half of which I remember, and half of which
I remember being told after I had forgotten it once.
There were thirty-three powerboats from the Figli d'Italia
alone; seventeen (sometimes nineteen, and once, twenty-seven)
from Metropolitan; and half the North End in the rest. That's

ninety, or over a hundred, and, some days, more, not
counting the flowerboats and the hearse.
                                              I had to go
(well, so I did, but I mean years later) to Venice and lean over
a cortege of gondolas stroked under the Ponte di Rialto
and out the big circle to the Campo Santo, like a trooping
of black swans on a fire-glaze, before I remembered clean
what an armada my father died into, sailing his flower-storm out
on the wind of the longest going my mother ever
sailed to sea or success on; and still breathes the forty-year-
old salt of new, between black and triumph.

A Plea

I said to her tears: "I am fallible and hungry,
and refusal is no correction and anger no meal.
Feed me mercies from the first-bread of your heart.

I have invented no part of the error it is
to be human. The least law could jail me
and be upheld; the least theology, damn me

and be proved. But when, ever, have I come to you
to be judged? Set me straight to your last breath,
and mine, and feed me most what I need not deserve

—or starve yourself, and starve me, and be right."

Launcelot in Hell

That noon we banged like tubs in a blast from Hell's mouth.
Axes donged on casques, and the dead steamed through their armor,
their wounds frying. Horses screamed like cats, and men
ran through their own dust like darks howling. My country
went up in flames to the last rick and roof, and the smoke
was my own breath in me scorching the world bare.

We fought. May the clerk eat his own hand in fire forever
who wrote I would not face Arthur. Iron sparks iron.
We fought as we had been made, iron to iron. Who takes
a field from me tastes his own blood on it.
Three times I knocked him from the saddle. What's a king?—
he'd had the best mare ever danced on turf

and couldn't sit *that* saddle. Well, I rode her:
king's mount from bell to cockcrow while bed, castle, and country
shook under us, and he snored holiness to a sleeping sword
from the fairies. Excalibur's ex-horseman. Yes, I fought him:
I took my damnation as it came and would have hacked
a thousand Arthurs small to mount her again.

He did better by a warhorse. That saddle, at least, he knew
how to climb into. Iron to iron he charged, and could have knocked
a castle over. But still a fool, too pure for a feint
or sidestep. Three times I dumped him with his ribs stove
and could have finished him backhand, but reined and waited
with my own head split and a puddle of blood in my pants.

The fourth, he hove dead already into the saddle and came on.
But even a king won't work with no blood in him:
his point dropped till it grounded, and poled him
over his horse's rump. And I did not rein but took him
clean in air, though I broke my arm to do it. And there he lay:
my two horns on his head, my third through his back.

What can a clerk know of the day of dead kings and dead countries?
I blew and no one answered. The men were dead

and scarcely boys enough left to carry a king's bones
to the smoke of the burned chapel. What other burial
was done that day was done by crows and gypsies. And in my heart:
where would I find another worth damnation?

I never turned back and I never looked back. My country
burned behind me and a king lay skewered on a charred altar,
his sword in blood at my feet. I took it up and flung it
into a swamp. He had bled into it: why hold back his sword?
No fairy arm reached out of the muck to catch it. That
was another life and spent, and what was there left to save?

Except the mare! Even bled down to dust and my bones shivered,
my veins pumped at the thought of her. Why else
had I cracked king, castle, and my own head? I rode,
and mended as I rode—mended enough—enough to be still alive—
or half alive—when I found her. And when I had waited
a cool two hours at her door, what came to meet me?

A nun! Eight thousand men dead and the best iron in England
black in the burned stones of a burned shire, and my own bones
stitched in by nothing but scars, and there she stood,
black as the day we had made of the world, and gave me
—a litany of tears! A whore of heaven wailing
from a black cassock as if she stood naked in a hollow tree!

With her eyes turned in unseeing: as if to Heaven:
as if there were no world and we had not dared it
beyond damnation! That was the death of all:
she dared not even look at what we were! And for *this*
I had fed the best meat in England to carrion crows
and left a crown in mud for a gypsy's picking.

I did not turn back and I did not look back.
I had left a king and country dead without turning.
Should I turn now for a mare? Let Heaven ride her spavined:
I had the heat of her once, and I'd sooner
have turned Saracen and ripped the crosses from Europe
than deny my blood spilled into his in the field that made us.

Once of a world she danced like flame, and the man who would not
die to be scorched there was dead already. Dead as the clerk
who rhymed us to a moral. There is no moral. I was. He was. She was.
Blood is a war. I broke my bones on his, iron to iron.
And would again. Without her. Stroke for stroke. For his own sake.
Because no other iron dared me whole.

Divorced, Husband Demolishes House

—News Item

It is time to break a house.
What shall I say to you
but torn tin and the shriek
of nails pulled orange
from the ridge pole? Rip it
and throw it away. Beam
by beam. Sill, step, and lintel.
Crack it and knock it down.
Brick by brick. (I breathe
the dust of openings. My tongue
is thick with plaster. What can I
say to you? The sky has come
through our rafters. Our windows
are flung wide and the wind's
here. There are no doors
in or out.) Tug it
and let it crash. Haul it.
Bulldoze it over. What can I say
to you except that nothing
must be left of the nothing
I cannot say to you? It's
done with. Let it come down.

Damn Her

Of all her appalling virtues, none
leaves more crumbs in my bed, nor
more gravel in my tub
than the hunch of her patience
    at its mouseholes.

She would, I swear, outwait
the Sphinx in its homemade quandaries
once any scratching in the walls
has given her to suspect
    an emergence.

It's all in the mind, we say. With her
it's all in the crouch, the waiting
and the doing indistinguishable. Once
she hunches to execution, time is merely
    the handle of the switch:

she grasps it and stands by for whatever
will come, certainly, to her sizzling
justice. Then, inevitably always daintily
she closes her total gesture
    swiftly disdainfully as

a glutton tosses off a third dozen
oysters—making light of them—as if
his gluttony were a joke that all
may share. (The flaps and bellies
    of his grossness

are waiting, after all, for something
much more substantial than
appetizers.)—"Bring on the lamb!" her look
says over my empty shells. "Bring on
    the body and the blood!"

A Rhetoric for Danny Keough
to Recite at the Bar

Leaving—for the present—sunsets, bluebirds, pussywillows,
and all that is not in itself saccharined,
sentimentalized, or otherwise disgusting, but which
has been marzipan'd, or, to phrase from the French, enmerded,
by the fact that there are females in our culture,
and certain attitudes evolving those females
into a species of converging vacuities
(as befits, in time, the mothers of storm troopers,
sleepwalkers, enuretics, and total abstainers),
and considering nature not as décor but as energy—
a dynamics best observed in the corruption
of all organic compounds, each of which,
in process, tends to magnetize to itself
gnats, midges, maggots, rats, piranhas, buzzards,
molds, flies, beetles, hyenas, lobsters, gulls,
and all that locus of forces implicit
in the unwinding of the nebulae and the blast
of the gassy galaxies cooling into life,
of which the sunset is a modulation, and bluebirds
and pussywillows two variations
in the key of mothermilk and the clutching gut;
and any one of which stands ready to convert
my eyes, the adenoids of the dean of women,
or the soft tissue of Lydia Pinkham's
cerebellum, genitalia, viscera, et cetera,
into the soft tissue of everything else
(and the shell around it), wherever and whenever
anything waits with a food-sac to be filled—

I can think of no valid reason whatever
for not ignoring the most part of all ladies
(and gentlemen) at the weekly, bimonthly, or annual
meeting of practically everything with teacups,

or against the utter damnation of all Good Women,
and I will recommend accordingly
the debauchment of daughters, the extinction of maiden aunts,
sterilization of clergy, reallocation of zippers,
an embargo on tombstones, the impeachment of Congress,
the immediate promotion of all bartenders
to the status of customer, and, for a beginning—
with a pause for a black damnation on all opposed—
the bottle on the bar and a round on the house.

Watching a Kettle Boil

Watching a kettle boil, a puddle
burst into pollywogs, light
catch in an ice-edge and ray open,
one thinks—nothing to say. There are

rays in things and they open to silences.
All wet is a mother whose seeds
rage up to leave her. There is fire
under wet, and a fist sound there

of forces forming through seas.
As time hissed once, uncontainably,
from the shell cooling. "Go down, Weather,"
said the Principal Midnight then,

"and set light, seed, and fire adrift.
Let there be demonstrations of courage.
I am tired of propounding theory
to my angels. Let them see practiced

how life will dare itself from any wet."

On Meeting Miss B

I should have something to say of/to this
woman who has had so little to say to
me, but who has said something, certainly,
to someone; while trying, with all the intensity
of the emancipated female, to speak to
all. Something. I do not like her, but she is
a poet, if only as The Free Woman. Something.
Well, then, what?

Emancipated, the slave
kept his chains for sentiment and making, now,
the motions of the free man, set them to clanking
so hard at every sweeping gesture, that his
free words were drowned in the sentiments
he brought to his freedom.

That is one
thing I might say of/to her. And of freedom,
that the line between eternal vigilance and some
clinically noted anxiety states is a jittery
one.
Well, have it out. What else?

By a certain age, virginity is no longer
a preserved possibility but a lost chance.
Whatever had been an act of will in such
purity, changes into an enforced condition.
There comes to mind, also, a friend of mine
who saved a bottle of Calvados for a
sufficient occasion. He had brought it from France
in 1919, and had not found an occasion sufficiently
sufficient until 1945, when he opened it to celebrate
V-J Day; only to find that it had spoiled,
though the bottle remained as authentic
as one could wish.

I could say that to this
woman/poet. And of apple juice,
that it will not necessarily keep till another
war is over.

But I am only speaking distrusts.
She is, after all, a poet of some accomplishment.
And if one cannot trust poets toward humanity,
we shall all be at the mercy of preachers,
politicians, and related et ceteras.

What, then, shall
I say toward meaning, of this woman I do not like
who is an accomplished poet I do not admire,
because, as I see it, no amount of accomplishment
undoes silliness?

How do you do, Miss B?
Isn't it a lovely day for painting bearded irises
on the walls of the girls' locker room?

—And so I have either found nothing to say
in honor of my own profession, which is in praise
of the power of the enlarging word; or there is nothing
to say except what must be said of us all:
that there are no pure human states, and that any
pretension to one is an assertion of inhumanity.

An Island Galaxy

Once on Saipan at the end of the rains
I came on a flooded tire rut in a field
and found it boiling with a galaxy
of pollywogs, each millionth micro-dot
avid and home in an original swarm.

For twenty yards between the sodden tents
and a coral cliff, a universe ran on
in a forgotten dent of someone's passing.
Clusters and nebulae of whirligigs
whorled and maddened, a burst gas of life

from the night hop of unholdable energy.
Did one frog squatting heavy at the full
of its dark let out this light, these black rapids
inside the heart of light in the light-struck dent
of the accidental and awakened waters?

There on the island of our burning, in man's place
in the fire-swarm of war, and in a sunburst
lens, I stood asking—what? Nothing.
Universes happen. Happen and are come upon.
I stood in the happening of an imagination.

Ten days later, having crossed two seas,
I passed that rut again. The sun had burned
the waters back to order. The rut lay baked.
Twenty upthrust shoreline yards of time
slept in the noon of a finished imagination.

And the bed and the raised faces of the world
lay stippled with the dry seals of the dead,
black wafers with black ribbons, as if affixed
to a last writ, but with such waste of law,
I could not read its reasons for its proofs.

Dogmatism

Between my right big toe, sir, and my bent
first podlet, is a blister with my
very self's rubbed acutest small
part inside, swollen.—And why
tell you?—Because I
am too easily nothing to invent
sweats and itches for the ball
of any foot. As flesh is true,
every one of my toes is all about you.

I say "I" in the big name of
everyone's most likeness to
whatever is nearest the one who
rambles to sleep down crooked nerves,
but strait and straight dreams love.
I dream what whispers as it curves
kissing fingertips, skin by skin,
to the very I of what's locked in.

Every "I" I think to name
is a first person and singular
as any self that rose and came
out of its skin and fistula
since skin began to take its lumps;
from the missing link to the missing name
of the dream from which the monkey jumps.
And "Better to itch than not, God knows,"
whispers a truth between my toes.

And where is there any itch to feel
but singular, personal, and first?
"I" is the only I that's real
and "I" the only thirst:
everyone's "I" to the smallest cleft
hidden away in the tiniest peel

of the only skin we all have left.
"I" from dandruff to flaking toes
is everyman and how he goes.

Where is there any "They" within?
And where a skin too thick to itch?
Every dog is a son of a bitch,
sniffing the unders of all there is
and flea'd fast to his own dog skin.
"They" come dressed. But where is
any dog with any flea
but scratches naked as you and me?
Every dog is the dog there is.

Creeping near or running far,
every dog is the dog there is,
first person and singular.
And I am just the dog you are.

Goodnight

An oyster that went to bed x-million years ago,
tucked itself into a sand-bottom, yawned (so to speak),
and woke a mile high in the Grand Canyon of the Colorado.

If I am not here for breakfast, geologize at will.

At Cocktails

For Fletcher and Inga

Benny, the albino marmoset,
eighteen years old, balding, and arthritic,
crawls upside down in his cage by the geraniums,
his skin flaps heaving cords
and knots of labor.
                    Eighteen for a marmoset
is older than nature, longer than Law allows
acrobats to stiffen and heave
on perches hunted by such talons
as even the quick must answer to.
                         Benny
puzzles a man-face out against the mesh,
two million years away from the cocktail party
we left the tree to come to.
Two by two
                we pause and look at Benny.
His life outside the Law
makes eyes from nature to décolletage.
A mistress mercy tends him as we watch,
curling him in her palm.
                  He,
coils and languishes, and then, put back,
grinds out his acrobatics for a grape,
from this world into that, one mesh
further from or nearer
                    some reality
martinis imagine in us or forget,
some day as it is with objects side by side,
looked at unequally by those pink eyes,
and ours, and thus, in fact, unequal.

Faces

Once in Canandaigua, hitchhiking from Ann Arbor
to Boston in the middle of December, and just
as dark came full on a stone-cracking
drill of wind that shot a grit of snow,
I was picked up outside an all-night diner
by a voice in a Buick. "Jump in," it said. "It's cold."

Four, five miles out, in the dead winter of nowhere
and black as the insides of a pig, we stopped.
"I turn off here."

          I looked around at nothing.
"The drive's up there," he said.

             But when I was out,
he headed on, turned round, drove back, and stopped.

"You haven't thanked me for the ride," he said.

"Thanks," I said, shuffling to find a rock
I might kick loose and grab for just in case.
But he wasn't that kind of crazy. He just waved:
"You're welcome, brother. Keep the rest for change."
Then he pulled in his head and drove away—
back toward Canandaigua.

          I thought about him
a good deal, you might say, out there in the sandblast
till a truck lit like a liner picked me up
one blue-black inch from frostbite.
And off and on for something like twenty years
I've found him in my mind, whoever he was,
whoever he is—I never saw his face,
only its shadow—but for twenty years
I've been finding faces that might do for his.
The Army was especially full of possibles,

but not to the point of monopoly. Any party
can spring one through a doorway. "How do you do?"
you say and the face opens and there you are
back in the winter blast.

But why tell you?
It's anybody's world for the living in it:
You know as much about that face as I do.

Everywhere That Universe

Even wisteria, sufficiently looked at,
will do for a galaxy. Nebulae
coil and flare on the trellises
of invisible principle much as these
gnarls and bursts grow to a house
they obliterate. With care then,
with waiting for a leaf to turn,
you may see the lives take place
in the great gaps of the system.
As at the porch corner there,
that nest full of raging fluffs,
half bald yet, who work mouths
the size of their entire heads
up into space. A nest of birds
is a nest of flames leaping,
novas of the insatiable energy.
Only the mercies of size save us—
imagine fledglings the size of rhinos
and full of just such rages—
what would a man do then
for the courage to look thoughtfully
into the throat of principle there
behind any leaf his waiting turns?

Joshua on Eighth Avenue

A man can survive anything except not caring
and even that's not mortal enough
to stop his drinking, except of course
that even drinking can be a kind of
                            caring.

Sometimes it takes a kind of at least
heroism to look entirely at Eighth Avenue
without anesthetic. Where would a man
get the sort of courage that risks
                            pity?

Frontiersmen maybe. Those whiskery hermits
that had to prove themselves to every
bear and redskin. But those were haters.
Which of them had the courage to risk a
                            tear?

Not anyhow Joshua, the old rumpot. He's
not daring anything sober, least of all
the question. Assuming there's one left
in him. What question? You crazy? This is
                            Joshua

you're talking about. "Hey, Mac," he says,
"buy a ticket to my funeral. Ringside
for one drink. Or sell you my left leg
for a pint. Going out of business. Everything must be
                            sold.

Whattayasay? Everybody needs a funeral
to go to."—And so for the third time
this year I buy his left leg. And once more own
more pieces than I can put to one
                            man.

Dragons

Dragons are not the only beasts
God forgot to make, and which, therefore,
man had, himself, to invent. The Phoenix,
the Griffin, the Sphinx, the Unicorn,
and such nightworks as the Vampire
and the Werewolf, are all
in the nature of the Imagined Kingdom.
And what good, in the long run, is Dominion
unless it is given over all
necessary beasts, real and imagined?

Therefore the Dragon, which—if it is true
that man must imagine at least one shape
moving alive for every dream in him—
images that dark in the jungle of dendrites
one man must run from and another attack,
to which every daughter must be thrown once,
and out of which any man may think to marry
a princess.

       Dragons, moreover,
being fire-breathers, do not catch cold—
and certainly all men need to imagine
not-sniffling.

      All these are realities, but
if you actually see a Dragon, check carefully
which reality you have been living in.

          To do so
may be very much to your advantage.

The Bird in Whatever Name

A bird with a name it does not itself
recognize, and I cannot recall—
if ever I knew it, and no matter—
lives off the great gross Rhinoceros of Africa.

The slathering hide of the great gross Rhinoceros,
slabbed like a river in a stiff wind,
is rancid at the bent seams, and clogged
with lice and fly-grubs at the pores and pittings.

The Rhino-bird, whatever its unknown name,
attends its warty barge through the jungle,
the feast of its own need picking the tickle
of many small corruptions from behemoth,

who, impervious to all roarers, is yet defenseless, alone,
against the whine of the fly in his ear, and stricken
to helpless furies by the squirm of the uncoiling grub
tucked into the soft creases of the impenetrable.

My bird—and oh it is my bird and yours!—crawls
him as kissingly as saints their god, springs
circling over him to foretell all coming,
descends in the calm lapses to ride a-perch on his horn

or snout. Even into the mouth and nares of the beast
he goes—so some have reported—to pick infection
from power. And can the beast not love
the bird that comes to him with songs and mercies?

—Oh jungle, jungle, in whose ferns life dreamed itself
and woke, saw itself and was, looked back
and found in every bird and beast its feature,
told of itself, whatever name is given.

Peaks

One day when I was feeling absolutely healthy
I climbed a mountain, and there at the top was
(just as I had absolutely foreknown—and what else
are mountains for to the absolutely healthy?)
the woman all mountains were standing for my health
to climb to.

Very few residents of Bronxville and/or their colleagues
transiently voting from a suburban address in
Connecticut, Jersey, or Long Island will know at once
the necessity of mountains to absolute health, or why
there is always that absolute woman there to be
climbed to.

As an absolute guess, I should say, at least one out of
every three thousand Tibetans might have an inkling of which mountain
such days as I mean come to. But perhaps I respect Tibetans
more for their distance from everyone I know than for
whatever they absolutely are inside themselves on their
best days.

Of you, my near brothers to nowhere on our level days
untopped, and of the imperfections of my own health
again and again in the days between topmost, and of the not-mountains
(like rotten nuts) that one forces only to find empty,
and of the anthills one falls from dusty into the splints
of sobriety,

and of the abysses between the ice cubes at 4:00 P.M. of a
Madison Avenue, and of all the partial women in cars
who wait in line for the 5:37 from Universe, and of all of us
plunging from the smoke-sided day at its stations, I make up
absolute Tibetans in an upper air of their best days
to dream us whole.

In Fact

—•—

(1962)

Selectivity

Now mist takes the hemlocks and nothing
stirs. This is a gray-green and a
glassy thing and nothing stirs. A plane
to or from Newark burrs down idling on
its flaps or grinds full-rich up its
airy grade, and I hear it. Mrs. Levy calls
her kids and I hear her. A train eight
blocks away rolls and I hear it. And
tire sounds. And a car door closing
dully. And a whole helluva caterwaul
when Richard hits Benn again and Benn does
stir. He comes running. And I hear it.
And then the phone rings and, carefully,
I do not hear it. I am listening selectively.

Come Morning

A young cock in his plebe strut
mounts the rail-fence to some
reviewing stand he has in mind
and practices commanding all those
blazed regiments eastward.

> *Not bad, boy!*
Not quite full-toned, but willing.
You'll make it yet!

        But suddenly
the damned Daddy-Colonel of them
all unfurls above our shavetail
like a flaming umbrella in a high
wind, and that's all brother! Our

lad's mustered out and running like
any civilian with hot hell on his tail.

Go it, boy! Old Jab-and-Spur has
blood in mind!
                    Till here comes
the Colonel back again strutting
posh as the dream of horse guards,
sets himself in place like Victoria's
best bustle, and, sucking a sky in,
lets go with the right high hot sound
for it, and makes it official. It's
morning!

Note: The text follows revised version in Selected Poems.

On Being Sure and of What

Salmon are very sure
of something. They endure
the eating sea, the falling
river and its hauling
edges of nets and spears,
and otters, too, and bears.
Then when at last they win
to the still waters in
the rock-pools of the sky
they spend their eggs and die.
What saint flings harder at
his martyrdom? Our cat
finishing the can
that we began
completes the commentary.
Here ends this bestiary.

My Tribe

Everyone in my tribe hates
everyone in your tribe.

Every girl in my tribe wants to
be there when we bring in anyone
from your tribe. Our girls save faggots
in their hope chests for you.

Every boy in my tribe has a peg
from which to hang the scalp of
anyone in your tribe. Our boys
hone knives in their dreams of you.

Everyone in my tribe is proud of
our boys and their dreams, of our
girls and their trousseaus. Our lives
have dear goals across which we

shall all finally kick all of your
heads. We are united.

A Fable of Survival

One of my neighbors began digging himself
an air-raid shelter week-ends. He had religion:
eight hours Saturdays, eight Sundays, a cubic yard
a day, starting in March. By mid-August,
even though, by then, he needed rigging
to hoist the dirt, he made two yards a sweat.
On the long Labor Day Weekend he made seven
with a clever bucket and pulley and his wife.
I guessed she had read Noah, too. By October
they had their hole dug twelve by twelve by fourteen
and thought it wouldn't do, but stopped for winter.

We had them in for cocktails to celebrate.
No strings attached. I pledged him in good bourbon
I wouldn't crowd in if the skies let go.
But what, I asked, if it happened before the thaw?
Or if his hole wasn't deep down enough.
How deep *was* deep enough? Suppose next fall
he had it twenty-four by twelve by fourteen
and guessed it wouldn't do and had to wait
another winter, and it happened then,
with his hole still open? Wouldn't it be simpler
to take a boat to China and dig from there?

He took my drinks but wouldn't take my jokes.
A man can't dig that long unless he's preaching
inside himself at every shovel-full.
He had a sermon to the cubic yard.
And data, blueprints, catalogs, specifications.
He couldn't have sounded more in Godly earnest—
or grander, or more memorized, or more saved—
had he been selling cigarettes on TV.
He had the Truth. He had, by God, the Truth.

I told him we were rival denominations.
That he swore by the shovel and I by bourbon.
He did point out that bourbon had first to be saved.
But he wasn't joking. Only being polite.
He was so saved he could be tolerant.

It was his wife took me aside and scolded.
"Good heavens," I told her—we had been friends once,
before survival—"don't tell me you're bitten, too?
If you want sermons, I can preach you one:
that mind's the only shelter left—whatever
shelter there is in that—though even that's
harder to come by than a hole in the ground,
and won't be shoveled at as clean as dirt."

I had a lot to say—or bourbon did—
of how I'd rather take it on the roof.
I said I had a case stashed by the hatch
and the ice-bucket on alert. I hadn't,
but I liked the notion better as I said it.
Then I was off on statistics. I invented
enough to feed the press for seven months.
She shook her head. "*I'll* join you on the roof.
But *look* at him! He's twenty good pounds younger.
Tough as nails. And, brother, he's got *fervor!*"

That's when I understood about survival.

Orders

Gulls in Wyoming, Utah, follow the plows,
picking the small jet lives from the turned furrows.

It half unfastens nature, their being there
a mile up and a thousand in from the sea.

In Gloucester, yes. In Manilla, Capetown, Dover—
by all the salt-shot names of the edges,

and slid beyond the edges, following, wide
and easy on the wind, the turned wakes, there—

at home where all mind trespasses and prays
and the impossible is a habitat—

there a man can answer with a psalm
from true-salt the blue dream a gull is.

But these landlubbers, half-hen and half-buzzard,
picking black lice out of the desert's pores—

call these things gulls? I call them bleached crows!
—Or did. Until I saw the sea still leaving,

first in Red Desert country, then in Salt Lake.
It must be salt deceives them from themselves:

somehow they smell it but can't find the water.
How could they guess at years-ago by millions?

I think they're queerly lost by a right instinct.
Or else they're only waiting, their instinct sound,

to be on hand when the next ocean starts here.
I wish they'd go to sea where they belong

and let the hawks and buzzards have the desert
in their own terms, as if it meant to last.

And then again I'm glad they're queerly home:
their presence teaches possibility

another range. And every man a moral:
put wings to a stomach and all the world is reached.

4:00 A.M. on the Terrace

I should—but anyone can and
therefore why?—go to bed. I
should get more sleep. I should
be rested when I go tomorrow to
do what anyone can—and bring
it home. I should think more of
my health. I should keep regular
hours as anyone can.

                But where,
tomorrow, will this night be full
of frog-beep and bug-Morse among
these stars that no one might
time-travel if I should not and
regularly never bring home?

Miss Olivia Branton

I remember Miss Olivia Branton, which
wasn't her name, but let that go. She was
the dumbest high-school teacher I ever
felt superior to, which I did instantly.
I don't think she had even read the books
she asked us to read. And she certainly
had never read anything else. Not that I
objected to her making a living. Everyone
has to one way or another. But why
couldn't she have been an honest char-
woman? Certainly she could have learned
to wring out a mop with a little practice,
which would have been a damned sight
better than saying "aren't I" and "like I
say" and "it's very unique" and "I'm truly
enthused" to, mind you, an English class.

She was so dumb that once I discovered
she simply did not understand how insulting
my papers were, I began to feel protective
about her. She thought I was some damned
kind of genius, poor clod. She was especially
a push-over for Greek mythology, and my God,
even when I wrote that Leda was a goose-girl
that pulled a feather from a gander's tail and,
using it as a magic wand, changed herself into a
narcissus, she—Miss Olivia Branton, that is—
wrote: "Another splendid example of the appeal
your imagination has for wide reading, and
beautifully expressed, like always. You will go
far."—I mean, my God, there comes a time when
you have to love the helpless just because they
are helpless, than which no one more uniquely was.
I didn't even have sex-fantasies about Miss Olivia

Branton, and those days I could have had sex-
fantasies about a female totem-pole if it had a
skirt on it. Half the time when I was called to
recite, I had to bend over the desk nearly-double
to keep from being obvious. But any bulge I stood
up with in her class was pure and detached plain
overflowing joy-juices. Not that Miss Branton was
bad-looking. She was all right in a confused-dolly
sort of way, but she was so lost that her own
husband (had she had one) would have felt like a
rapist if he so much as kissed her goodbye in the
doorway after breakfast. She was so helpless and
dumb I kept feeling like everybody's father (which
is a hell of a sex) whenever she opened her mouth and
let another moth flutter out of her cocoon brain.

And that, I guess, is why I fell in love with her,
though it was more nearly the way you love your
baby-sister, if you have one. I didn't have any
baby-sisters. Not aside from Miss Olivia Branton.
I ran her errands, and washed her blackboards, and
explained *The Decline of the West* to her (I had a
Spengler jag then) which she didn't have a dream
of understanding how much I misunderstood. She
thought it was wonderful to know a damn genius even
if she couldn't tell the difference between a genius
and a McCormick spreader with a vocabulary attachment,
or, as a matter of fact, just because she couldn't
tell the difference, and neither could I. I loved her
about twice as purely as you could imagine and with no
sex-fantasies, and when she left town I was very adult
about saying goodbye, but when I got home I cried.

In Pity As We Kiss and Lie

Softly wrong, we lie and kiss,
heart to heart and thigh to thigh.
Like man and woman. As if this
were how and who and when and why.

Some two in the time of man
and woman found it sweet
to trade what such half-bodies can
that both be made complete.

Some two in a place that was
hardly right but softly true
found themselves and founded us—
he to her and I to you.

Softly wrong and hardly right,
heart to heart and thigh to thigh,
in each other's arms tonight
we lie and kiss and kiss and lie.

If he by her and I by you,
like man and woman, now and then
find each other softly true—
what of how, who, why, and when?

Till hardly wrong, as mercy is—
when and how and who and why—
softly right we lie and kiss
in pity as we kiss and lie.

Credibility

Who could believe an ant in theory?
a giraffe in blueprint?
Ten thousand doctors of what's possible
could reason half the jungle out of being.
I speak of love, and something more,
to say we are the thing that proves itself
not against reason, but impossibly true,
and therefore to teach reason reason.

Vodka

Vodka, I hope you will note, is
upwind from all other essences.
Drink it all night and all day
and your aunt's minister could
not track you to perdition, not
even with his nose for it. Vodka
has no breath. Call it the dead-
man's drink. But praise it. As
long as he can stand, a vodka-
drinker is sober, and when he
falls down he is merely sleepy.
Like poetry, vodka informs any-
thing with which it is diluted,
and like poetry, alas, it must be
diluted. Only a Russian can take
it straight, and only after long
conditioning, and just see what
seems to be coming of that!

Fast As You Can Count to Ten

Fast as you can count to ten
commandments, I would count to
twenty forgivenesses, could I
think which twenty, and till I
can, let me offer all and with-
out number and beg for myself,
if you please, your used mercies.

Returning Home

I want to tell you a
gentlest thing. Like light
to you. Like old faces
being fed a good memory
from inside themselves.
Like eyes that do not
watch but slowly meet
across a room in which
everyone is, and no one
need hurry to what he is
sure of. I want to say
before we run out of
rooms and everyone
that I am slowest,
surest, gentlest, too,
across whatever room
I look at you.

Saturday

The power-mown morning of this spang
green world we have moved to opens roaring
from all house-held lawns. Daddy's home
up and down all the street, his growlers
spinning the other side of the thickets
to right and left and over the hedges
I hear him up and down at his sentry—
go that this world may stay trim and
told in its duty loudly.

                    So summoned
I wake and dutifully do my own bright
blurrer to its loud life and up and down
over my grasses make the noise of this
place in straight rows from thicket to
thicket and between the hedges while
from the tree-fort my sly gunners sight,
their arms shouting commands I can
glimpse but not hear, mowing me down
or suddenly pointing upward to blast a
plane from anywhere in its last traffic-
pattern to Newark, and then lunch.

Dawn of the Space Age

First a monkey, then a man.
Just the way the world began.

Eggs

The egg a chick pokes its head out of
is a process of nature. The egg I
bit by bit got my head out of was a
process of propriety.

There are great
chemistries to be recorded of the
natural egg. Of these confections in
which we systematically embalm the
young, there is to be said only that
they are generally too sweet, that
in hot weather they get sticky, and
that they are all hell to fertilize.

Bird Watching

Every time we put crumbs out and sunflower
seeds something comes. Most often sparrows.
Frequently a jay. Now and then a junco or
a cardinal. And once—immediately and never
again, but as commonly as any miracle while it
is happening, and then instantly incredible for-
ever—the tiniest (was it?) yellow warbler
as nearly as I could thumb through the bird
book for it, or was it an escaped canary? or
simply the one impossible bright bird that is
always there during a miracle, and then never?

I, certainly, do not know all that comes to us
at times. A bird is a bird as long as it is
there. Then it is a miracle our crumbs and
sunflower seeds caught and let go. Is there
a book to look through for the identity

of a miracle? No bird that is there is
miracle enough. Every bird that has been is
entirely one. And if some miracles are rarer
than others, every incredible bird has crumbs
and seeds in common with every other. Let there
be bread and seed in time: all else will follow.

Every Time You Are Sleeping and I

Every time you are sleeping and I
am not I like to watch your far
breathing wakefully counting this
and far nights tenderly dark with
thoughts closely and farther yet
nights when you will not be closely
thus thought of in any way nor I

Poetry

Whether or not you like it is not my
business/whether or not you can take
it is, finally, yours/whether or not
it makes any difference to you it does
make its own, whether or not you see it.

Whether or not you see it is not your
business alone/whether or not it tells
you the difference between yourself and
busyness, it does tell whether or not.

In Paul's Room

This is Paul whose habits are
all he has to die of. He
has survived a shooting war,
an auto wreck, two wives, and three
collapses into Bellevue.
Tell me, bottle, tell me true:
do you drink him? does he drink you?

When Paul has seen his final Thing,
twitched his final twitch, and lies
very dead, what radiant wing
will descend out of the skies
to the cold still of his brain
that his rotted soul again
stretch and lift? When Paul has lain

in statistics and a sigh,
tell me bottle, tell me true,
will you lift his soul on high
for all those years he lifted you?
Paul is here but Paul is dead.
There is no one in his head.
All that was Paul has been shed.

I remember, you do not,
what was Paul a thirst ago.
How do good men go to rot?
Is that something I could know?
If I drank you for a clue,
tell me, bottle, tell me true:
could I taste the Paul in you?

As I Would Wish You Birds

Today—because I must not lie to you—
there are no birds but such as I wish
for. There is only my wish to wish you
birds. Catbirds with spatula tails up
jaunty. Jays, gawky as dressed-up toughs.
Humming birds, their toy engines going.
Turkeys with Savanarola heads. Bitchy
Peacocks. The rabble of Hens in their
stinking harems—these three (and
Ostriches and Dodos) a sadness to think
about. But then Gulls—ultimate bird
everywhere everything pure wing and wind
are, there over every strut, flutter, cheep,
coo. At Dover over the pigeon-cliffs.
At Boston over the sparrows. Off tropics
where the lyre-tails and the green-
iridescent heads flash. And gone again.

You never see Gulls in aviaries. Gulls are
distance. Who can put distance in a cage?

Today—and I could never lie to you—
there is no distance equal to what I wish
for. There is only my wish to wish you
a distance full of birds, a thronged air
lifting above us far, lifting us, the sun
bursting in cloud chambers, a choir there
pouring light years of song, its wings
flashing: See this with me. Close your eyes
and see what air can do with more birds in it
than anything but imagination can put there.
There are not enough birds in the eyes we
open. There are too many hens, turkeys, and
that peacock seen always on someone else's

lawn, the air above it wasted unused, songless.
Birds cannot be seen in fact. Not enough
of them at once, not now nor any day. But think
with me what might be, but close your eyes and see.

A Missouri Fable

A man named Finchley once
without thinking much about
it broke into the premises of
Mr. Billy Jo Trant of these
parts, by which felonious
entry he meant to separate
Mr. Billy Jo from various
properties, but stepping on
a noise without thinking
enough about it woke Mr.
Billy Jo who took in hand a
Colt .45 and, improvising the
order of his rebuttal, fired
three times in an entirely
accurate way and then said
"Hands up!" without thinking
that the man named Finchley
once was not listening as
carefully as he might have
had Mr. Billy Jo thought to
disagree with him in a
slightly different order.

Moral: commit yourself to
another man's premises and
you may, in logic, have to
accept his conclusion.

When I Am Not Dead

When I am not dead I
see and can remember
everything. I am able
and well-feasted. I
can go to anything
for it to happen, or
wait for it to come.
I know your name deep
as you wait to know
it. I am there wait-
ing and being your
name. I can say sun
and the shadow of all
names in it. I can
count fishes by rings
on a ripple. I love
and am instantly be-
lievable and can wait
for every instant I
am
     and then I do die
(the telephone rings,
a car stops, a calend-
ar clicks into an air-
plane and fastens its
seat-belt, the host-
ess smiles, I talk to
salesmen and get off)
and do not know I have
died and do not know
even that I am wait-
ing
     until instantly
sometimes I am again

not dead and I see and
can remember every-
thing I am, and your
name, and sun, and our
shadow in it and that
I was always (and did
not know it) waiting.

Are We Through Talking, I Hope?

Why do I have to make
sense? What sense is
there to make unless
our senses make it? I
don't want to make
sense. I want sensibly
to make you because any
thing else is nonsense
and what sense is there
     in that?

Counting on Flowers

Once around a daisy counting
she loves me/she loves me not
and you're left with a golden
button without a petal left to
it. Don't count too much on
what you count on remaining
entirely a flower at the end.

The Tragedy-Maker

Everything you/I/we do in the natural course
she did on tightropes over abysses. Any man/
woman/child, God knows, risks falling. She
made sure of it. Look through your town for
the man most likely to put his head into the
oven: she married him, prodded him into having
six kids before he did take the gas-pipe, and
nearly died of each of them. She fell and
broke her hip when she was five months gone
to the first, but had it. With the second it
was pneumonia, but she had it. With the third
it was second degree burns from the oil heater,
but she had it. She fell downstairs with the
fifth, but she had it. The fourth and sixth
almost killed her with no outside assistance,
but she had them—the sixth in time to nurse
at its father's funeral. Then she killed her-
self for twenty years keeping them fed and
keeping them from killing themselves and one
another, and just keeping them. One way or
another, keeping them. Until she began to
lose them one by one. One got drafted and
killed in training at Fort Bragg (he went on
maneuvers and bedded down in the dark on what
turned out to be a road) and she buried him and
one took a Fourth of July weekend around a curve
too fast and she buried him and one just walked
away and never looked back and she couldn't
bury him and wept maybe because he spoiled her
collection and one took the ancestral gas-pipe
and there of course she was on familiar ground
(in which she buried him) and one—he was a
cop—shook down the wrong Sicilian and they
boxed them separately without being entirely

sure of some of the pieces and she buried hers,
and the last one took a baseball bat to a girl
lovingly and got himself buried alive in State
storage and there was another to spoil her col-
lection until finally morning by morning she
came to one day dimmer than all and could not
wake to it and they buried her and from some-
where a wreath came saying *Mother* and she lay
there, just she and the wreath that no one
came with, not looking at one another, and
then they buried her and whatever it was she
was she finally was not, poor bird, poor husk,
poor sufferer at everything, and at last done.

One Jay at a Time

I have never seen a
generalized blue jay.
I have never heard a
specific one utter a
denial. Blue jays are
one at a time and they
are always screamers
of an assertion. Look
at that stiff dandy on
the sill-box. YES! YES!
YES! He screams forever
on a launching pad in-
side himself. I AM! I AM!
I AM! AND HERE I GO!

I'm No Good for You

I'm no good for you and you'
re no good for me, we'
re no good for this that or
anything unless, even at
the risk of being bump-
tious, we let our skins be
skins and our bellies be
bellies and our lips be for
    giving.

A ghost in the sun so hairy
with light he seems to be a
fire as he comes, seems to be
lanced with rays and aureoled
and with birds mating in and
out of him as he comes, seems to
be naked as light on the dew on the
    grasses,

to be seen through more shining,
to redouble all first green-
light, seems to be walking in
your eyes and my eyes to a
blessing in both of us, seems to be
easily the kindliest and most
    radiant

thought we have of our
selves here naked in our
first green (if we can be for
giving) seems to be our
most sun-up of everything.
And he comes. That ghost (if
rarely) does (now) entirely
    come.

English A

No paraphrase does
between understanding
and understanding.

You are either
that noun beyond
qualification into

whose round fact
I pass unparsed
and into whose eyes

I speak idioms
beyond construction;
or else get up,

fasten your suffixes
and your hyphenations,
buckle your articles,

spray modifiers
and moods
behind your ears

and take the whole
developed discourse
of your thighs to

any damned grammarian
you whatsoever
wish. Period.

Down Narrow Stairs
from a Thin Eye

"If all example is from nature," I thought as I left the apartment of a (particularly) poet, "not all of nature can be imagined to exist in form for convenient reference." He must, my thought ran on, answer to some parable from if not yet quite in nature, but what? So it began:

"Were there," I thought, "in those furry waves of compulsion lemmings form down from their hill-boroughs in their gross seizure to the sea, some particular fur-piece entirely intoxicated by its presence in the race of that tide, yet conditioned to an even more consuming—to an ultimate—dread of salt water, I could (had it a name) cite it in a single neat word as nature's ready equivalence, and I should not need then detail its first far sniff of that sea: how, within one madness, it would wake to find itself raked by another, swept forward within a compulsion to the unbearable: what agonies would contend in it to the wetting of a first toe: and how it would turn then from one sea to be overborne by another: how it would panic backward on that furry-brown tidal conveyor-belt moving forward faster than even panic could outdo itself backward—and lose: until there was nothing left but the one sea in which it frothed and fought another: and how, clenched finally into a spasm like *rigor mortis*, it would float there among particles, lacking all particularity." Nature has specified no such example. Its existence, therefore, may be cited among the uses of the imagination, but with all the inconveniences of having to shape it from inventory, at the risk of boring that suicide who grabs his deaths in gluttonous gulps of his own monologue; and on the other hand of going completely over the head of that exemplar who is navigating his conveyor-belt to incorporated immortalities and who will (quote) be damned if he knows what you're talking about and even (quote) more so if he doesn't. As for that poet from whose apartment I was coming, I have just recalled that I do not know any such person except to go away from and gladly.

Suburban Homecoming

As far as most of what you call people, my darling, are
concerned, I don't care who or what gets into the phone. I
am not home and not expected and I even, considerably, doubt I live here.

I mean this town and its everlasting katzenjammer when-
ever whoever dials again, is going to hell, or to some other
perpetual buffet, in a wheelbarrowful of bad martinis: and you, my

legal sweet, forever in the act of putting your hat on
as I come in the door to be told I have exactly five—
or, on good days, ten—minutes to change in because here we go

again to some collection of never-quite-the-same-but-
always-no-different faces; you, my moth-brained flutter
from bright cup to cup, no matter what nothing is in them; you, my own

brand-named, laboratory-tested, fair-trade-priced, wedded
(as advertised in *Life*) feather-duster, may go jump into
twenty fathoms of Advice to the Lovelorn and pull it in after you—

but I have not arrived, am not it, the phone did not ring
and was not answered, we have not really, I believe, met, and
if we do and if I stay to be (I doubt it) introduced, I'm still not going.

In Some Doubt but Willingly

Nothing is entirely as one
warbler there in the sun-
hazed tree-top invisibly de-
clares it to be.

What an engine this dawn
has going for it on
that limb I cannot find,
there, or in my mind!

Who wouldn't want to be
that glad, had he the
energy to be reckless about it.
I wouldn't be without it,

were there a choice. I'd
find that limb. I'd hide
invisibly in sun. I'd pump up
light to flood every cup.

I can't make it. I'm too used
to want to. But still bemused.
Go it, bird! Sing! I've had
mornings myself. I'm glad

there are still these
invisible tops to trees
from which a bird can break
a piece of the world awake.

Person
to Person

—•—

(1964)

The Size of Song

Some rule of birds kills off the song
in any that begin to grow
much larger than a fist or so.
What happens as they move along
to power and size? Something goes wrong.
Bird music is the tremolo
of the tremulous. Birds let us know
the songsters never are the strong.

One step more on the way of things,
we find a second rule applies
to birds that grow to such a size
they lose, or start to lose, their wings:
they start to lose the very strings
of sound itself. Give up the skies:
you're left your weight. And your last ties
to anything that sings.

Yet Not to Listen to That Sung Nothing

I woke in Florida, late and lazy, my sill
(my few flown hours from winter) a blaze
of tropic, and on it, like a small soul
spilling its echoes of heaven—a fluff of bliss
in full throb—a mockingbird went on and on
in the thrill of itself to itself in that near sun.

Birds have nothing to say. Yet not to listen
to that sung nothing is the death of rapture.
Rapture or loneliness?—the difference is in
what one is reminded of, listening. Only after

reminders can one hear the first, last, and first
again sweet scald of nothing in the bird-burst

godlings that wake, like rose-heads trembling
on their trellises, or hibiscus like a million
butterflies just lighting, or the rambling
trumpets of a vine lifting to blow to Zion
that the time is come of the splitting of the horn
of plenty, that the bird-burst sun is born,

and not heaven, nor earth, nor any waking man
can hold the outpouring of an instant
of nothing, all, and nothing, again and again
on its sill in that sun, where the infant
soul of a bird, its few flown hours
from winter again, sings, and a man, wakened, hears.

Gulls Land and Cease to Be

Spread back across the air, wings wide,
    legs out, the wind delicately
dumped in balance, the gulls ride
    down, down, hang, and exactly
touch, folding not quite at once
    into their gangling weight, but
taking one step, two, wings still askance,
    reluctantly, at last, shut,
        twitch one look around
        and are aground.

At First Flower of the Easy Day

At first flower of the easy day
a buck went wading through the mist.
Legless, he seemed to sail away.
A brown swan with a mythic twist
of antlers to his changeling head.
All that the weaving Greeks referred
to plastic nature's shifting thread

he evidenced. I saw him turn
and dip his head into that pond
and flash the white flag at his stern,
then lift his head and sail beyond
an isle of spruces to the right.
What do we ask of any wraith
but the Greek fact in its first light

that makes of morning's beasts the day
our nights would dream if they knew how?
Starting from this dawn, I could say
sad Io's name to any cow
and have her eyes confirm my guess.
Unless her farmer came like Zeus
and waved me off the premises.

Bees and Morning Glories

Morning glories, pale as a mist drying,
fade from the heat of the day, but already
hunchback bees in pirate pants and with peg-leg
hooks have found and are boarding them.

This could do for the sack of the imaginary
fleet. The raiders loot the galleons even as they
one by one vanish and leave still real
only what has been snatched out of the spell.

I've never seen bees more purposeful except
when the hive is threatened. They know
the good of it must be grabbed and hauled
before the whole feast wisps off.

They swarm in light and, fast, dive in,
then drone out, slow, their pantaloons heavy
with gold and sunlight. The line of them,
like thin smoke, wafts over the hedge.

And back again to find the fleet gone.
Well, they got this day's good of it. Off
they cruise to what stays open longer.
Nothing green gives honey. And by now

you'd have to look twice to see more than green
where all those white sails trembled
when the world was misty and open
and the prize was there to be taken.

One Morning

I remember my littlest one in a field
running so hard at the morning in him
he kicked the heads off daisies. Oh, wild
and windy and spilling over the brim
of his sun-up juices he ran
in the dew of himself. My son.

And the white flower heads
shot like sparks where his knees
pumped, and his hot-shod
feet took off from time, as who knows
when ever again a running morning will be
so light-struck, flower-sparked-full between him and me.

Tree Trimming

There's this to a good day's sweat
high in the branches trimming and down
into the ground rooting—I'm not used to it
any more but it reminds me when I'm done
and sprawl shaky with tiredness, wet
in the sun's wringer. Sweat tells me again
who my people were. And yes, there's more
to it. But without sweat I wouldn't want
it. It takes the whole body to be sure
of what you're remembering. I can't
say my father's or my grandfather's name
a better way than this sog-tired numb
joy of having touched green growing
and the dirt under it and the day going.

Even then I can't really touch them. Not ever
again. They had first things and the power

and the ignorance that go to the receiver
of first things only; that and no more.

I've lost it. I'm my own first. There was never
a man of my blood before
who spoke more than one tongue, or *that*
in a way courts wouldn't laugh at.
My father did read some. But it was
his mountain he came from, not the mind
of man. He had ritual, not ideas. His
world that I cannot find
except as my body aches and sweats hewing,
was holy and dim. But doing
his work, I rest. I remember this:
it is good to be able. To hold axe and saw
and do first things again. I miss
this the desked days I go. I see
him here. I know him. But he is
more than I can teach my children. They
have no first life. *That* is their loss.
I wish we were Jews and could say
the names of what made us.
I could weep by slow waters for my son
who has no history, no name
he knows long, no ritual from which he came,
and no fathers but the forgotten.

He who could sweat down, tree by tree,
a whole wood and touch no memory.

Evensong

In late afternoon, when the light
no longer has a source, but is brushed
like a glowing powder onto leaves
and housefronts, a cock cardinal
in the sconce of a dead treetop
flickers like a wick, and calls his hen
to roost. Or simply calls.
On a wire spanning my lawn
from maples to blue spruce, a dove
repeats its slow broken sound
for some minutes of this world,
then leaves it. One by one
the bright dusts wear off. Trees
and sky enlarge toward one another,
mass into one shadow.

The ardor of this world looked at
in the moving meaninglessness
of light and of the lives
that sing to it, and leave,
is, finally, the grace there is.

Birds, Like Thoughts

Watch a wild turkey come in to land—
(they are rare, but a man can find most
of what he wants if he wants it enough
to look for it)—you see a long slant
out of the air, like the approach of
some queer plane. Its landing gear first
let down, then agitated, it starts to run
before it touches, finishes yards on
from the point of touch down; and only then
folds its wings and is back, a hen again.

Not wrens, warblers, swallows—(I can't even see
what it is swallows do on the air. They
change it, exceed it, make it serve impossibility)—
all smaller (not lesser) birds play
instantly in and out of the air. There are no
parts to their coming, going. A whirl and they light;
a whirl, and they are airborne. Watch a jay go
its long dart through branches. It is too right
to need caution. It lands like an arrow
with no separation of its motions—So!

And there it is, and instantly gone if it feels
like it. Talk about landing on a dime!—
it could land on the edge of one. I've watched
every bird I could find to look at as it wheels,
heaves, whirls, glides. Whatever is hatched
to wings has its own way with them. But I'm
sure of one thing: the more weight you take to air,
the more space you need to get down
the more slowly. Birds are like thoughts: they're
more instant as they stay light. Both come and gone.

Sea Marshes in Winter

Marsh hummocks that were a sabbath hill
for a witches' dance of lives the last weather I looked,
go Christian as Calvary in the stone still
and sackcloth sky. At four, a wind-hooked
glacier of cloud chills a last thought and the snow
starts. And all that night that comes at once
the snow sifts dry as salt, scratching the window.
Then day leaks back from the edge. A half-light hunts
somewhere to settle, a place to begin, but slumps
onto the black-streaked sheet and the dead white humps
between me and the sea. It never quite—
not all that day—makes up to enough light
to see a world by. And still I look at this
world as worlds will be seen—in what light there is.

Aquarium

There is almost no such fish as this which is
the children's awe for a minute, and the world's
glassed from the world. It was another imagination
than anyone's that colored it with minerals
and hung it trembling from the rubber pouch
of its own hanging mouth as from a perfect balance:
the weight of the sac behind it precisely equals
    the weight of the world before it.

A self, I think. Shaped gross and delicate
to its million years of currents out of sight.
A frown like a tragic mask's but drawn in pink
cordage and mottled black. A pig-iron body

the shape of bloat, yet trembling weightless as
burst milkweed. A fantail
drawn from a Chinese dream of fires dancing.
     It is one thing of this world.

What world is there but the world looked at?
I see and am seen. Until all seeing blinds
in the idiot-certain hang of this in-taking, all-taking,
and impossible brine mouth dry children gawk at
by permission of the City of New York
whose glass walls split the world into time and Sunday.
Two utter imaginations at their meeting.
     Seeing and being seen.

Old Man

When the old man who had bought all his wives
ran out of cash, he took to feeding pigeons
in Washington Square. He had never learned
how to summon a meeting except by a bribe.
Now he was down to peanuts. But for once
he was buying responses that really
came to him and then really flew. He hummed
in that cloud, and wished he might scatter
diamonds to his pigeons as he had once to his
various chicks. Luckily for the pigeons,
however, he was beyond diamonds and could strew
only what was useful—a difference that made
the difference, for he grew gentle in the wing-worked
sun about him and learned he would die a lover.

When a Man Dies

When a man dies angels tick.
An alarm of roses rings.
Folded moths on every wick
crack like fine glass, and their wings
slide like powder down the light.
So goodmorning. So goodnight.

Where the pane breaks rain will fall.
Every house turns inside out.
God's the root that tangles all.
What the devil is about
I don't know and I don't care.
But anyone can hear the air

hissing from the things we say
when we stand beside the bed
as the dead man starts away
from the rooftree overhead
to the seepage underfoot.
Where else shall we think to put

Dad and Mother in their time?
Deeper than the judgment waits
beetles click what churches chime.
Eternities of figure-eights
scribble out the face that was
the instant that it leaves the house.

So goodmorning. So goodnight.
So goodlife—if it *was* good.
May great roses ring me bright
my last instant understood
when I hear the air hiss out
of—whatever it was about.

From Adam's Diary

In the planetarium of an apple tree
I shook some spiral nebulae
and sent some systems reeling, just to see
how that might be. Just between time and me,
to see how it might be
to shake a universe—or an apple tree—
and see what fell, and think how it would be
if any of what fell was me.
None of it was—that day. But I could see
it all would be. Some day. Whatever tree.

Two Hours

I. Evening

The low-fi scrapes the phrases from the strings
of something neither of us was listening to.
Whatever it is, the strings grate still, the drums
begin to cough a bronchial bass crack. You,
I, someone, thought a music, but it comes
wrong from the machine. Which brings

me to you-and-me as you start to undress
at last (which brings me to you) and how
frothily from foam-trim perkily your thighs
dimple and your arms reach and grow
till they are elements of the light and the wise
S's of your hips enter the great S
of your languor as, reaching behind,
you unstrap and unribbon and your breasts
go from the advertised to the invincible
first line of mantime, and a last rustle rests

you ungirdled at the bird-sung well
of gardens this twisted music cannot find,

of lights and airs and palpable here-and-now
to confound all Heaven's recorders and amplifiers.
How shall they hear us on any machine of theirs?
—your nakedness is more music than they have wires.
Yet, if it's true that angels watch in pairs,
they still may learn. Come here. We'll *show* them how.

II. Morning

A morning of the life there is
in the house beginning again
its clutters in the sun

babbles and sways and tells
time from its sailing cribs. Enter
three pirate energies to murder sleep:

the bed rocks with their boarding:
a fusilade of blather
sweeps the white decks. We're taken!

—Goodmorning, sweet with chains.
We win all but the fight.
Do as they say—I'll meet you here tonight.

Of Fish and Fishermen

Fish are subtle. Fishermen
are gross and stinking and they lurch
hauling their nets. Which clod of them
could shimmer like a cod or perch
through blue and green and purple spells?
It isn't shimmering grace that tells
in the long run. It's being taught
to track and set and haul and stink.
If stinking's part of it. It's not?
It needn't be? That's what you think.

An Aspect of the Air

Through my hemlocks and the spruce beyond,
mist hangs and closes. What change is this?
Not a bird dares it. Not so much as a frond
stirs in the shadowless absence
of this light I see by, not knowing what I see,
there in the green caves and up into a sky
that isn't there, except as there must be
some source for any light. I don't see, I
conjecture sources. It is too still
not to be thinking out from things, not to feel
a presence of the unreality that *will*
mystify what incloses us. Mist is not real;
not by the handful. And thought is not
fact, nor measurable. It is simply there.
An inclosing condition. A dimension taught
the sourceless light. An aspect of the air.

The Poet's Words

Language ends in the tongue's clay pit.
Say the name of the dead man: he is not there.
Say the name of the dead poet: who hears it?
My friend and teacher, John Holmes, who made air
answer to the words of his name is dead
of everything he knew, understood, said,

and made sayable. A variation of what he was.
A stubborn and a weak man—then, quietly, that hour
of his language forming, a poet, a place of pause
for the thought, the thing, that came and was sure.
He died in agonies his life was too calm to have thought,
yet terrible enough, yet not

too terrible to unform his same mixed self while he had
strength enough to say it. Pain
is the other clay pit, the gray-yellow bad
water that gathers. Life is the rain
that will not stay clean. Language, the wind
that brings all thought to mind.

Pain washed him dirty, made of him the stale
pool original water comes to. The wind
that brought him is over. I loved him. Failed him. Fail
him now, and will, and fail myself. Till we find
failures to love from there will be no
love. His tongueless ruin, mine, go

to one another. Is there more language
than the chiming of our losses? It ends.
This language, and any, ends. What good is rage?
a literary tradition. We were friends
and are not. Barring wreckage of car, plane, train,
and such chances, I think much the same drain

will soil me past words. He lets me dare
say nothing. As all is said. These lines talk
round the clay places. They do not care
to be memorable. We are not. We walk
what health says us, and die used
as run-rain. The silt in us, loosed,

silts out. But the water never clears.
Not wholly. And words are not understood;
they live beyond understanding. What years
language stays to me I shall sing the good
of language that has no cause to mean.
I shall say his name among many—John Holmes—and a clean

rain will seem possible. The best of a man
is what he thought of and could not be.
The best of the rest, what he said, what we all can
say, or think of saying, because we see
the clay-gray gathering of all water, but drink
from what first wells our most thoughts think.

My Father Died Imperfect As a Man

My father died imperfect as a man.
My mother lied him to perfections. I
knew nothing, and had to guess we all mean
our lives in honor of the most possible lie.

She was no more herself than a gull is
its own idea to make on any air
precisions of itself. What instinct does
for the egg in nature, history did for her.

So Italy's dark duplicating spines
bred her precisely herself, instinctual as
peasantry breeds in any Apennines.
Those centuries repeat; they do not pass.

And everywhere at their end which is always again,
always present, and everywhere the same—
as alike as gulls, as grass, bred of the chain
that breeds its likeness back through any name,

the ritual women sweep their Italies,
move step by step from grave to birth to grave,
scrub clothes and speak to God on the same knees,
and take exactly the shape of how they live.

So history lied my father from his death,
she having no history that would let him be
imperfect and worth keeping vigils with.
She made a saint of him. And she made me

kneel to him every night. When I was bad,
he shadowed me. And always knew my lies.
I was too young to know him, but my bed
lay under him and God, and both their eyes

bored through the dark to damn me as I was,
imperfect as a boy and growing worse.
Somehow I loved her in that haunted house
she made of her own flesh. And so, in course,

forgave myself and learned how to forgive.
Love must intend realities. I can
be anything but saintly and still live
my father's love, imperfect as a man.

An Afternoon in the Park

I lived an age that could not be.
Formal and fast to every look
its men stood to each other's eye,
signed in each other's common book.

Nothing but men had changed in this.
Birds were exactly birds. The sea
kept every fold just as it is
in what must pass for memory.

The Lion dozing in the zoo
of that grave Helicon looked out
as much like Zeus as lions do
in any Bronx. It was about

three-thirty of an afternoon
I got that world into my thought.
Would four o'clock have been too soon
to start back from it? I had not

meant to come back at all. But then
some worlds are good enough to mean,
some only good enough for men.
And, yes, I knew which I had seen.

I Remember the House That Was

I remember the terraces down from Portland Road
to the Shrewsbury River, and the lyre-shaped gray
tulip tree trunks above, and the holly below
the house where Fletcher Pratt lived. I don't know
who lives there now. A doctor, I've heard say,
who raises Great Danes, some of which have showed.

Well, I myself have bought a dead man's house
and live in it. A nameplate on the door
becomes a calendar. A letter sent
comes back unknown. Perhaps a doggy scent
clings to it. Probably not. But truth is more
imaginable than proven. Fletcher was

the keeper of great doorways. When he died
some part of all doors warped—imagined doors.
What we call real of real estate still stood.
Was salable. Was sold. But if the wood
stayed to the house's sills and steps and floors
the house went from itself, its walls blown wide,

its unconveyable entrances all shut,
or gaping in on nothing. Doors must lead
to presences. Walls must be built around.
They still are, I suppose. Someone has found
and bought a house he likes. And Fletcher, dead,
is out of tenancy. And that's about

the gist of it. The trees and terraces
still ride to the Atlantic, and the sun
rises from water in a doubled blaze
to what was Fletcher's great house those salt days
and windy gabled nights when everyone
was at the party in the house that was.

Instances

Walt Whitman took the Earth to bed.
Insatiate man! He felt her stir
and advertised it as a love.
She let him. And by reason of
the unadvertised, when he was dead
she took him back to bed with her.

Millay, too, did her best to take
the whole thing in her arms. Her reach
fell short, and so she sang of that.
Sometimes she sang a little flat.
More usually her voice would break
and her high-C come out a screech.

Emily as a general thing
kept things to scale. At least by day.
In wild nights she was harder pressed.
Not the whole moon clutched to her breast
could stay her. May our late thanks bring
this lady gardens that *will* stay.

Poets are mad. Perhaps the act
of singing addles any brain.
Perhaps the best of anything
is wanting it enough to sing
the madness up from any fact.
Poets are mad. Are bankers sane?

Reality and Willie Yeats

Reality and Yeats were two.
He even told it what to do—
where to enter, what to say,
and when to turn and go away
and let the ectoplasms take
his hand and write. And, writing, make
realities Reality
could not outstare. At least not while
he held it in the trance of style.

There the style is—speech and song.
Long as Reality is long.
It is the stylist lost his tongue,
and lost his texture and his tone,
and vapored off. Now, skin and bone,
styleless as mud caked into stone,
Reality and Yeats are one.

—•—

Mme. Blavatsky, who was part
of Willie's vapors (not his art),
arranged with friends before she died
sure signals from the Other Side.
Some of her friends insist she tried
to send them back but none came through.
That same Reality you and you
(and I) are never sure of, must
(I conclude) include such dust
as chokes off signals. What we hear
is: poets die, their poems appear
still to transmit, and still to be
signals from some Reality.

Lines

I did not have exactly a way of life
but the bee amazed me and the wind's plenty
was almost believable. Hearing a magpie laugh

through a ghost town in Wyoming, saying Hello
in Cambridge, eating cheese by the frothy Rhine,
leaning from plexiglass over Tokyo,

I was not able to make one life of all
the presences I haunted. Still the bee
amazed me, and I did not care to call

accounts from the wind. Once only, at Pompeii,
I fell into a sleep I understood,
and woke to find I had not lost my way.

Tenzone

Soul to Body

That affable, vital, inspired even, and well-paid
        persuader of sensibility with the witty asides
but, at core, lucent and unswayed—
        a gem of serenest ray—besides
    being the well-known poet, critic, editor, and middle-high
    aesthete of the circuit is, alas, I.

Some weep for him: a waster of talent. Some
        snicker at the thought of talent in him. He leaves
in a Cadillac, has his home away from home
        where the dolls are, and likes it. What weaves
    vine leaves in the hair weaves no laurel for the head.
    The greedy pig, he might as well be dead—

to art at least—for wanting it all and more—
        cash, bourbon, his whim away from whom.
He's a belly, a wallet, a suit, a no-score
        of the soul. Sure, he looks like a boom
     coming, but whatever he comes to, sits to, tries
     to sit still to and say, is a bust. It's booby prize

time at the last dance whenever he
        lets a silence into himself. It grinds
against the jitter in him and dies. Poetry
        is what he gabs at, then dabbles in when he finds
     hobby time for it between serious pitches
     for cash, free-loading, and the more expensive bitches.

I give him up, say I. (And so say I.)
        There are no tears in him. If he does feel,
he's busier at Chateaubriand than at asking why.
        He lives the way he lives as if it were real.
     A con man. A half truth. A swindler in the clear.
     Look at him guzzle. He actually likes it here!

Body to Soul

That grave, secretive, aspirant even, and bang-kneed
        eternalist of boneyards with the swallowed tongue
but, at dream source, flaming and fire-freed—
        a monk of dark-celled rays—along
     with being heretic, ignorant, Jesuit, and who-
     knows-what skeleton, is, alas, not wholly you.

I've watched you: a scratcher of scabs that are not
        there. An ectoplasmic jitter. Who was it spent
those twenty years and more in the polyglot
        of nightmares talking to Pa! If I went
     over your head to God, it *was* over your head.
     Whose butt grew stiff in the chair the nights you read

whose eyes blind and wrote whose nerves to a dither?
        And who got up in the cold to revise you by light?
You're a glowworm. A spook. A half-strung zither
       with a warped sounding box: you pluck all right
    but if what whines out is music, an alley cat
    in moon-heat on a trashcan is Kirsten Flagstadt.

Yes, I like it here. Make it twenty times worse
        and I'd still do it over again, even with you
like a monkey on my back. You dried-out wet-nurse,
       think you're the poet, do you? You're wind that blew
    on ashes that wouldn't catch. You were gone
    the instant I learned the poem is belly and bone.

I gave *you* up. Like a burp. For a better weather
        inside my guts. And, *yes*, I want it all—
grab, gaggle, and rut—as sure as death's no breather.
        Though you wouldn't know, being dead as yesterday's squall
    where the sea's a diamond-spilling toss in the bright brace
    of today's air, to glitter me time and place.

On Flunking a Nice Boy out of School

I wish I could teach you how ugly
decency and humility can be when they are not
the election of a contained mind but only
the defenses of an incompetent. Were you taught
meekness as a weapon? Or did you discover,
by chance maybe, that it worked on mother
and was generally a good thing—
at least when all else failed—to get you over
the worst of what was coming. Is that why you bring
these sheepfaces to Tuesday?
                                    They won't do.
It's three months work I want, and I'd sooner have it
from the brassiest lumpkin in pimpledom, but have it,
than all these martyred repentances from you.

Autobiography of a Comedian

Years long in the insanities of adolescence—
because my father had died but still
spoke to me, because my mother was mad,
because the cross was bloody on the One Hill—

I wrestled God gaunt on my knees and wet
in the sizzle of nightmare wakings till
there was nothing to do but die or embrace
a more comic spirit. Which, being hard to kill,

I did. I told jokes my family fled from.
My friends knew me through cracks in the door.
Father Ryan black-sheeped me from the pulpit.
—God knows he had more than enough to deplore.

Then suddenly my jokes became lucrative.
My wallet acquired a vocabulary. My four
thumbs and twelve toes turned jugglers.
I learned to dance loose. And the more

I shuffled the more money, cars, houses
I got for it. I grew rich grinning.
Bankers learned to pronounce my name.
I even won at Harold's Club. I'm still winning

what I have no real use for but
might as well take. In my beginning
was no end of a wry humor. I am my broker's
keeper. Not even my hair is thinning.

I tell you this world's as crazy as I was once.
Even scholars take me seriously. And why
complain, you say? Friend, I am trying
as simple and as marvelous a thing as honesty.

As I might say I love my wife, enjoy
playing with my children, expect to die
and not to profit by the experience—
I think we are of some Stone Age, you and I.

How do we make sense of ourselves?
I do not understand presidents, popes, kings,
ministers, marshals, or policemen
except as I see the ritual featherings

of the tribes in their hair. What do I know
of the invisible people I killed for wings
when I was a gunner for our tribe?
I remember the fires we started, not the things

we burned in them. I think Harold,
crazy as he is for God now, has our real
mystery in his spinning department store.
What we all pray to is the dice, the wheel,

and the holy jackpot. Have you *seen*
the grandmothers praying at those steel
altars where the heaven-eyes blink and wink
fruit, bells, and dominion? It's God they feel

coming at the next click. But Harold
keeps the books for his three per cent. Another
comic spirit, except that he believes it
and works at it. As once my grandmother

in *her* tribe's dark, kept herbs and spells
and studied signs and dreams. Why bother
to believe what there is a sure three per cent of?
Somehow we must keep our brother

by what will not be kept. Between
our slapstick successes and our wry
confessions, there is the day the sun starts.
The low sea to the west of Reno and the high

desert to the east. This world. And in it
the mercy that sees and knows why
we must not love ourselves too much—
though, having no other, we must, somehow, try.

Elegy

I. As I hear the family thinking it

This is the body of my good gray practical dead
uncle. We are going to bury it today. We are
not going to bury it because it is good gray
or practical, but because it is dead. We are
observing, I submit, the proper proprieties.

Were he good gray practical and not dead, we
certainly would not bury him. Not today.
We would let him go on burying himself in
his good gray practical way. It is because
he can no longer bury himself that we

do it for him. We are a family and we observe
our observances. We have even chosen a
good gray practical day. For, more or less
inevitably, he is dead, and we know how to
put two and two together and get it all

buried. What else is a family for? Do you think
we would let our uncle bury himself all
these years and not finish the job for him?
Besides, he is unusably dead. Which, even
as a matter of practicality, changes things:

What good would it do to keep him? He
could only grow more noticeable than
we have ever allowed him to be, or than
would entirely fit his character, or
what we took to be his character, what

the bottle had left of it. He did try us. But
he is dead. This is his body under a good
gray sky with all the practical arrangements
arranged. And the family here, practically mourning.
But a family. And one that knows what to do.

II. As I find myself remembering

But because he bought me my first puppy (a brownsilk
ears nose and tail all going with a red ribbon
around its neck) and gave me (on another birthday) my
first .22 (with which I walked whole continents any
afternoon) I don't care what rumpot he bloated into
and floated out of mushy. He is dead. As dead
as if he had turned into a magnolia and decayed
open. But by all the sick flowers of this world,
I remember a gorgeous and a boozy man with
hairy arms and neat hands and an eye that never
missed a quail or a pheasant (as I believe my dream).
And because he was made to hide even his ruin, I kiss
his stone forehead and leave him my tear openly, for
myself, perhaps, but openly—who was a dream I had
young and lived glad in. I did him no good ever
and I am ashamed to remember how he could laugh once.

Coq au Vin

In Paris once, just as the waiter
in his priesthood laid before me
a silver-capped ritual steam
which he uncovered in the certainty
of the body and the blood and the
fragrance of attended art, summoning
me as his parishioner to bend
my head into the steam and inhale
the holiness of his intention—and as
I did bow in homage to his office
(hearing God say, "Qu'est-ce que tu fais?"
to which I replied, "Je m'amuse")—just
then, through the sacred vapors
of our toy altar, I saw black before me
the unuttered scream of a ruined presence.

It was a woman. Or not a woman. A
residue that was to the idea of woman
what excretion was to my priest's
holy viand—an animated rot
of the flesh, a face gnawed by syphilis,
eyes webbed red in their filthy gashes,
a nose grated like the Sphinx's
but to blood, a mouth like a spoiled
fruit. She stood gibbering and
cursing. A beggar, but too sure of her
horror to need beg. She accused.
Destroying us with her reality. Her
ruin gloating at us.
                    I emptied
my pockets blindly and bowed to her
cursing. I would have stripped
and given her my clothes and the
hair of my body had not the waiter

and the owner and the owner's wife
rushed her, herding her, not daring
to touch, parsing small money into
her cupped claw as she stalked, still
gibbering and cursing, back into
whatever unmentionable hole she had
come from like pus to infect our
novena of sauces in the stinking
abbey of God-the-Tourist, who said
in Midwestern, "Living it up, son?"

And I flung down my napkin and fled
with a sound in me like ripped cloth.

Possibilities

A week ago on longer clocks than ours
a supernova in Orion lit
the sky like a full moon. The dinosaurs
might have looked up and made a note of it
but didn't, and the next night it blinked out.
The next day from a metaphoric tree
my father's father's beetle brow and snout
poked through the leaves. Just yesterday at three
he spoke his first word. And an hour ago
invented God. And, in the last hour, Doubt.

I, because my only clock's too slow
for less than hope, hope he will not fall out
of time and space at least for one more week
of the long clock. Think, given time enough,
what languages he might yet learn to speak
when the last hairs have withered from his scruff,
when his dark brows unknit and he looks out,
when the last ape has grunted from his throat.

"Nothing Is Really Hard but to Be Real—"

—Now let me tell you why I said that.
Try to put yourself into an experimental mood.
Stop right here and try to review everything
you felt about that line. Did you accept it
as wisdom? as perception? as a gem, maybe,
for your private anthology of Telling Truths?

My point is that the line is fraudulent.
A blurb. It is also relevant that I know
at least a dozen devoutly intellectual
journals that will gladly buy any fourteen
such lines plus a tinny rhyme scheme and
compound the felony by calling that a sonnet.

—Very well, then, I am a cynic. Though, for
the record, let me add that I am a cynic with
one wife, three children, and other invest-
ments. Whoever heard of a cynic carrying a
pack for the fun of it? It won't really do
I'm something else.
                              Were I to dramatize myself,
I'd say I am a theologian who keeps meeting
the devil as a master of make-up, and that
among his favorite impersonations he appears,
often as not, as the avuncular old ham who winks,
tugs his ear, and utters such gnomic garbage
as: "Nothing is really hard but to be real."

I guess what the devil gets out of this—if he is
the fool he seems to be—is the illusion of
imitating heaven. If, on the other hand, he is no
fool, then his deceptions are carefully practiced
and we are all damned. For all of us, unless
we are carefully warned, will accept such noises
as examples of the sound an actual mind makes.

Why are we damned then?—I am glad you asked that.
It is, as we say to flatter oafs, a good question.
(Meaning, usually, the one we were fishing for. Good.)
In any case. I may now pretend to think out the answer
I have memorized:

                    We are damned for accepting as
the sound a man makes, the sound of something else,
thereby losing the truth of our own sound.

                              How do we
learn our own sound? (Another good question. Thank you.)
—by listening to what men there have been and are
—by reading more poets than jurists (without scorning
Law)—and by reading what we read not for its
oration, but for its resemblance to that sound in which
we best hear most of what a man is. Get that sound into
your heads and you will know what tones to exclude.

—*if* there is enough exclusion in you to keep the
pie plates out of the cymbals, the tin horns out of
the brass section, the baling wire out of the strings,
and thereby to let the notes roll full to the ear
that has listened enough to be a listener.

As for the devil—when he has finished every imp-
ersonation, the best he will have been able to accomplish
is only that sound which is exactly *not* the music.

Styles

Assuming, in some dreamscape, some
stylist past the domeless dome
whose metaphors, asprawl, include
the dark in which first gases brood
and hatch the star-shower billion years
between what blinks and disappears—

and then, assuming that this dust
on one fleck of the outer crust
of one arm of one galaxy
gets up and walks—like you, like me—
and in, perhaps, the millions years
before it blinks and disappears

develops some style of its own
beginning with light, water, stone.
And, now, say that first stylist chose
to write a universe—there it is.
Can we, as stylists, read that style
but from ourselves, and for a while,

before there is no style like ours
to read at all, and the star showers
fall on unread, their text asprawl
on everything and after all,
when no one's left to try to spell
what none of us read very well

to start with?
               Well, enough of this.
A universe is a lot to miss.
But our not missing it won't be missed.
While there is time, it's time we kissed.
What time's left over drifts asprawl
on really nothing after all.

What *Was* Her Name?

Someone must make out the cards
for the funeral of the filing clerk.
Poor bony rack with her buzzard's
jowled eyes bare as a dirk
and as sharp for dead fact, she
could have done it better than anyone
will do it for her. It will be,
to be sure, done.
And the flowers sent. And the office closed
for the half day it takes
for whatever we are supposed
to make of the difference it makes
to file the filing clerk
where we can forget her.

Someone will do the work
she used to do better.

The Starry Heavens, the Moral Law

Kant saw them as the two eternal sources of awe:
the starry heavens above, the moral law within.
Both of which it is possible to doubt, but, all in all,
impossible not to have thought about. Stated as Law:
everyone would like Heaven as a second skin.

We know we are here and small at the outskirts of
some fabulous system we sense above and far off,
we of this grainy planet of this pebbly sun
at the pelagic fringe, who dreamed ourselves once
the size and center, and called it Father and Love.

And we sense we are related to one another
by some compact whose terms we all forever
puzzle at, wander from, but return to, and must again,
from every loss of phrasing and abdication
of ourselves. And think to call that, Man.

Take it for awe if you like. Whatever we mean *is*
in a dimension like truth, as we dream it. But awe
is the invention of ourselves. Call the compact Law;
call those lights Heaven; but add this:
they are themselves nothing. They imagine *us.*

No, not even that. It is we who imagine them
imagining us. Another species might have been born
blind and found its awe in the unseen edges of stone,
or in the endless peeling and reunion of a stream
around a dipped hand. Anything can find its dream

in anything: it is there to be found. What made
stars more than rock and water? Whatever we are born to,
a mystery will follow. We do
need one another. The rest we adapt to. Mud
is heaven enough for crocodiles. Suppose we grew

senses for the motion of roots under us? heard waves
of one another's thoughts? or the breaking of flesh in graves?
We should build ourselves then to such hearkenings,
live in them, find our mysteries and imaginings
in them. And still we should need those things

and one another. Separation is the one death. As life is
the fitting and refitting of what we shall never quite
join. We are—and what are we? Found wrong. Lost right.
Floundering and in love. All of us, somewhere. Meaningless?
No. Only—unsayable to ourselves. Though I might

say most of it for myself if you would carve it
over my head at the speaking time: *Thank you*
for the experience which I, lovingly, did not
understand. And not to waste good stone, a usable plot,
nor any love, let me beg that if you do

honor my wish, you make my stone a bench. Anyone
who will stop by another man's life may need to sit down.

The Colossus in Quicksand

One night I read philosophy.
When Plato went to sleep on me
I made this dream up willfully:

I saw a stone colossus rise
from Libyan sands through the Nine Skies.
Someone's idea of something's size—

man's of a man, I seemed to know.
I couldn't force the dream to go
so close that a whole truth might show.

Still it went near enough to guess
it wasn't some high mightiness.
No emperor or emperess

ever had slaves enough or stones
breaking each other from the bones
of time enough, though it were aeons,

to haul so much of earth so high.
The figure stretched from sand to sky.
Its very height, at first, was why

no one had noticed it was sinking.
Only a dream could see it shrinking—
or so I dreamed the dream was thinking.

One sky after another cleared
to nothing as the great head neared.
Skins, then kneecaps disappeared.

It slid like weather from the skies.
Thighs, the great sex in the thighs,
the first rib—then I saw its eyes.

Whatever the thing was meant to be,
all Greece and Rome intended me
to look into its eyes and see.

I watched the chest and then the chin
go under, and the sands begin
to rim the mouth and trickle in.

Then it was eye to eye, and then
the desert was all sand again,
a nothing where a dream had been.

And what I saw as it went by
was its own image in its eye
still standing higher than the sky.

This
Strangest
Everything

—•—

(1966)

Talking Myself to Sleep at One More Hilton

I have a country but no town.
Home ran away from me. My trees
ripped up their white roots and lay down.
Bulldozers cut my lawn. All these
are data toward some sentiment
like money: God knows where it went.

There was a house as sure as time.
Sure as my father's name and grave.
Sure as trees for me to climb.
Sure as behave and misbehave.
Sure as lamb stew. Sure as sin.
As warts. As games. As a scraped shin.

There was a house, a chicken run,
a garden, guilt, a rocking chair.
I had six dogs and every one
was killed in traffic. I knew where
their bones were once. Now I'm not sure.
Roses used them for manure.

There was a house early and late.
One day there came an overpass.
It snatched the stew right off my plate.
It snatched the plate. A whiff of gas
blew up the house like a freak wind.
I wonder if I really mind.

My father died. My father's house
fell out of any real estate.
My dogs lie buried where time was
when time still flowed, where now a slate
stiff river loops, called Exit Nine.
Why should I mind? It isn't mine.

I have the way I think I live.
The doors of my expense account
open like arms when I arrive.
There is no cloud I cannot mount
and sip good bourbon as I ride.
My father's house is Hilton-wide.

What are old dog bones? Were my trees
still standing would I really care?
What's the right name for this disease
of wishing they might still be there
if I went back, though I will not
and never meant to?—Smash the pot,

knock in the windows, blow the doors.
I am not and mean not to be
what I was once. I have two shores
five hours apart, soon to be three.
And home is anywhere between.
Sure as the airport limousine,

sure as credit, sure as a drink,
as the best steak you ever had,
as thinking—when there's time to think—
it's good enough. At least not bad.
Better than dog bones and lamb stew.
It does. Or it will have to do.

Back through the Looking Glass
to This Side

Yesterday, in a big market, I made seven thousand dollars
while I was flying to Dallas to speak to some lunch group
and back for a nightcap with my wife. A man from Dallas
sat by me both ways, the first from Campbell's Soup,
the other from some labeled can of his own, mostly water,
and Goldwater at that. Capt. J.J. Slaughter

of Untied Airlines kept us all in smooth air and well
and insistently informed of our progress. Miss G. Klaus
brought us bourbon on ice, and snacks. At the hotel
the lunch grouped and the group lunched. I was,
if I may say so, perceptive, eloquent, sincere.
Then back to the airport with seventeen minutes to spare.

Capt. T.V. Ringo took over with Miss P. Simbus
and that Goldwater oaf. We made it to Newark at nine
plus a few minutes lost in skirting cumulo-nimbus
in our descent at the Maryland-Delaware line.
"Ticker runs late," said the horoscope page. "New highs
posted on a broad front."—So the good guys

had won again! Fat, complacent, a check
for more than my father's estate in my inside pocket,
with the launched group's thanks for a good day's work,
I found my car in the lot and poked it
into the lunatic aisles of U.S. 1,
a good guy coming home, the long day done.

Daemons

I pass enough savages on the street
to credit the daemon in things. But they
have forgotten how the soul breathes
from plant, beast, and man and must
be propitiated. They do avoid thirteenths,
walk wide of ladders and black cats,
make the sign of the cross for hearses.
But shabbily. Ritualists without conviction.

My mother, at bone and breath, was the savage
I learned from. When we poured
concrete for a new house, she leaned over
the half-filled forms muttering,
and dropped in a penny, a crucifix, a key,
then pricked her finger and shook out
a drop of blood. Then stood there,
waiting. Giving, had she given enough?

Because she meant to take no chances,
I thumbed a bean pod open and gave her
the beans, saying nothing, and she threw those
in. That started her going again. Off
she went to her kitchen and brought back
oil, wine, a sliver of meat, snippets
of all the food we had. In they went. Then
she thought a minute and told me to spit.

She was using everything she knew anything
about, and she knew she was using it. That
is my kind of savage. She was living at
the ghost of all she lived by.
Now suppose I say again I do
credit daemons? Suppose I pick up
a conch and blow it and ask if it hears
itself making music?—the idea loses you.

But there go the savages in and out of
Tiffany's, the Waldorf, the Cathedral,
the Subway. They take place; they do not
know themselves. They do, I suppose, move
to the music they think they hear. But
what I mean is—you have to hear your self
making the music you didn't know was
in you, living at what you live by.

Was a Man

Ted Roethke was a tearing man,
    a slam-bang wham-damn tantrum O
from Saginaw in Michigan
    where the ladies sneeze at ten below
but any man that's half a man
    can keep a sweat up till the freeze
    gets down to ninety-nine degrees.
    For the hair on their chests it hangs down to their knees
        in Saginaw, in Michigan.

Ted Roethke was a drinking man,
    a brandy and a bubbly O.
He wore a roll of fat that ran
    six times around his belly O,
then tucked back in where it began.
    And every ounce of every pound
    of that great lard was built around
    the very best hooch that could be found
        in Saginaw, in Michigan

Ted Roethke was an ath-a-lete.
    (So it's pronounced in Michigan.)
He played to win and was hard to beat.
    And he'd scream like an orangutan

and claw the air and stamp his feet
    at every shot he couldn't make
    and every point he couldn't take.
    And when he lost he'd hold a wake,
        or damn you for a cheat.

Sometimes he was a friend of mine
    with the empties on the floor O.
And, God, it's fun to be feeling fine
    and to pour and pour and pour O.
But just to show we were not swine
    we kept a clock that was stopped at ten,
    and never started before then.
    And just to prove we were gentlemen
        we quit when it got to nine.

Ted Roethke was a roaring man,
    a ring-tailed whing-ding yippee O.
He could outyell all Michigan
    and half the Mississippi O.
But once he sat still and began
    to listen for the lifting word,
    it hovered round him like a bird.
    And oh, sweet Christ, the things he heard
        in Saginaw, in Michigan!

Now Roethke's dead. If there's a man,
    a waking lost and wanting O,
in Saginaw, in Michigan,
    he could hear all his haunting O
in the same wind where it began
    the terrors it could not outface,
    but found the words of, and by grace
    of what words are, found time and place
        in Saginaw, in Michigan.

Epithalamium at
St. Michael's Cemetery

My father lay fifty years in St. Michael's bed
till we laid back the covers and bundled in
the hag end of his lost bride, her wits shed
some years before her light. O, bones, begin
with one gold-banded bone. The bride is dressed
in tissue, ten claws folded on no breast.

Man and woman made he them, but gave
dominion to Dominion. Does He know
how deep the whale goes to its grave,
its hull of ribs still trembling in the flow
under the dark he makes there, or that is
unmade? If every deep is His,

then all bounds are abysses, as they were
when the set eyes of Sphinxes still stared through
their gilded doors to a green delta's stir
of rayed and hovering dynasts, while the Jew,
back at his interrupted captivity
in the ashes of lamentation, sang "Eli! Eli!"

What loss is this when nothing's left to lose?
She waited and she came, and he is there,
whether or not he waited. Can we choose
what we shall wait for? Can I find a tear
for what this is? I have none left. I see
a twice unfinished bridal. The chivaree

has been rescheduled. The Capuchin suite—
a grotto off the Via Veneto—
has been reserved for this first night, complete
with its two skeletal cupids flying low.
A crypt of the dead sea. There, side by side,
the sodden groom, the driftwood bride,

begin again forever what they began
in God's will, or the sand-blast through no door,
or the wind in the Jew's ashes, or as this man
and woman crossed their sea once, through whose floor
Capuchin birds silt into the abyss
He sets His bounds by. Or that simply is.

Boy

For Jonnel

He is in his room sulked shut. The small
pouts of his face clenched. His tears
as close to holy water as I recall
any first font shining. A boy, and fierce
in his sacrament, father-forced this two-
faced way love has. And I, who

am chain-chafed and galled as any son,
his jailor: my will, his cell;
his hot eyes, mine. "Whose will be done?"
I think, wrong as a man.—Oh, very well:
I make too much of nothing much. My
will a while. A boy's tears dry

into the smudge of any jam. Time hurts,
but I am not much destiny. I am,
at best, what cries with him; at worst,
a smallest God, the keeper of one lamb
that must be made to follow.—Where?
That takes more God than I am to make clear.

I'm wrong as a man is. But right as love,
and father of the man whose tears I bless
in this bud boy. May he have cried enough
when he has cried this little. I confess
I don't know my own reasons or own way.
May sons forgive the fathers they obey.

Incident

Not that it matters, or not much, and not
to the children now, but it was
Spring as a daisy chain and not yet hot
but skin-prickle new and the grass
all lazy-breeze lolly when
the madman came up from his wrong roots
and played horrors with the children
who had been playing all sorts
of nothing really, or all, and who died
so hard even one of the cops cried.

Who, for that matter, has cried enough
for what feeds madness? This
small boy and this small girl unwove
their daisies and did not miss
what they had been loving, or just being glad in,
which must be the same thing.
It could have been rock-Winter and no garden.
It did happen to be Spring.
But Spring came to Dachau, too, and not one
corpse there chose his season.

This is a note on stagecraft. Soft days
darken most. Imagination
seizes contrasts. Horror dies
of horror. This could have been done
in a bitter time. Still the soft moon
most calls the wolf; bright sky, the hawk.
Madness wakens beyond intention,
buzzes to soft airs, goes for a walk,
and finds children playing. We are all
dangerous till our fears grow thoughtful.

No death is an invention. They were small bright,
are hugely dark, and everything does matter,

yes, but not to them now. Do stones see light?
winds keep diaries?—a leaf, a child, tatter;
a cause flows. There are
madmen, but horror must first be made.
The cop dried his eyes and swore war,
his tears instantly wasted. Three dogs bayed.
The madman was shot running over the same flowers
the children had dropped. His. Ours.

The Catalpa

The catalpa's white week is ending there
in its corner of my yard. It has its arms full
of its own flowering now, but the least air
spins off a petal and a breeze lets fall
whole coronations. There is not much more
of what this is. Is every gladness quick?
That tree's a nuisance, really. Long before
the summer's out, its beans, long as a stick,
will start to shed. And every year one limb
cracks without falling off and hangs there dead
till I get up and risk my neck to trim
what it knows how to lose but not to shed.
I keep it only for this one white pass.
The end of June's its garden; July, its Fall;
all else, the world remembering what it was
in the seven days of its visible miracle.

What should I keep if averages were all?

Small Elegy

I saw a bird pasted to muck.
His death, already part of it,
was half a clod and half a shuck.
Still feathered, but as far from flight
as luck can drag down any wing.
As far as time drags everything.

It is, perhaps, a trifling mood
that solemnizes by small death.
It lay beside a country road,
And I was strolling out such health
as I have not yet quite destroyed
enjoying the diet I have enjoyed.

It was—had been—I still could see
by one small flaunt not yet put by
a red-winged blackbird. Obviously
not much to lose from a whole sky
that, for that matter, once outsoared,
barely begins the mass of God.

—Could I, that is, believe such mass
describes itself to fear or love.
I strolled the only road there was
and guessed a law: there is enough
wayside for every sparrow's fall.
And time enough for all of all.

A bird must be a heavy cause
to change to mud. A man must be
a heavier yet. Then what's that mass
all cause falls to? I think I see!—
How intricate is the world we live!
How simple is the world we leave!

Think it and change! Oh, could I think
this bird back to its weightlessness!
Or that bird, soul! Then I could thank
my father for a massive guess.
And, myself lightened into flight,
soar to some singing Infinite.

Well, then, it is a trifling mood
that solemnizes by small death.
But where's a larger? Have Popes made
their way into a greater earth
than this fluff comes to? All death's small,
into whatever mass we fall.

How large is life? Once on a shelf
a candle lit a plaster saint
and I knelt in a blaze of self.
The reek of guilt would leave me faint
where my mad mother stretched my soul.
Let this bird have the beads I told.

Is it my failure or my luck
that, since then, I have found no death
I could not pause by for a look
and then stroll on—above, beneath,
within this mass that we, outrun,
fall from and to, barely begun?

Have I lost most by wanting less?
I have not happened anywhere
on more regret than I could lose,
nor on more love than I could bear,
nor on more pity than I could give
the small sad days to which we live.

As small as this unfeathering clod
in country muck. Which, who shall mark?
I'd like a mass I could call God.
—I'd like a cruise on Noah's ark:
imagine being there to see
the lives from which all life would be!—

I'm here instead to see one fluff
weighed down into the mass there is.
Any stroll is long enough
to stop a man by elegies
so small they almost lack a cause,
yet leave him guessing out first laws.

Fragment

To the laboratory then I went. What little
right men they were exactly! Magicians
of the microsecond precisely wired
to what they cared to ask no questions of
but such as their computers clicked and hummed.

It was a white-smocked, glass, and lighted Hell.
And their St. Particle the Septic sat
lost in his horn-rimmed thoughts. A gentlest pose.
But in the frame of one lens as I passed
I saw an ogre's eye leap from his face.

Why Don't You Write for Me?

For you, or of you? It can't be
both. If you must ask that
question, you are not ready for
yourself. If I write for
you, I must write about someone
else: someone dead, though you
haven't heard of that death. If of
you, you haven't heard that
news either. Then what can I tell you?

You see there are few customers
in this business. Not that it matters.
I live by eating up the profits.
There is that to be said for it as
a business: check the books any way
you like; there is always a profit,
and it can always be eaten. . . . Scorn
you? Never. Customers are
always welcome. Cherished even.

I mean I have learned to stock
only what I can live by
when no customers come. When one
does come, therefore, it follows
that he can buy only what I have my
own appetite for. A black-bread
store, if you like. Stiff crusts and
garlicky cores. But learn to like it
and nothing can feed you better.

Galileo and the Laws

Galileo thought he saw
the spinning center of the Law
radiating pure equations.
He did, too. But the coruscations
of that center left him blind
to the dark rims of man's mind.

The legal center! How it shone!
But soon the man of laws was gone
into exile with a pack
of legal Jesuits at his back.
So, for eighteen chained years, he
wandered a loose periphery.

Then, by a law outside the Law
Galileo thought he saw,
chance blurred its wheel and he was free:
Cosimo, Grand Duke of Tuscany,
gave him a post, a salary,
the aegis of a Medici.

Back came the center, all ablaze.
In a few months and a few days
this Doctor, safe now from the Pope,
constructed his first telescope.
And there it was! He saw! He saw!
The spinning center of the Law

opened its radiant arms! What then?
He saw beyond but not through men.
Beyond the tower, beyond the Dome,
he saw the eye of Kingdom Come,
its First Equations burning wide
and absolute. Then the Duke died.

A Duke died and a Duke was made.
But there the sky began to fade.
In his old age he knelt and lied
the Law away. Before he died,
Milton called, and wept to find
Galileo had gone blind.

—•—

Blind, but no longer blinded, did
the old man see what his sight hid:
the spinning center of that buzz
that crazes all man is and does
and is no less Law than the Law
Galileo thought he saw?

Advertisement for a Reader

This itch to sit at paper and to say
a midnight into fact, a flesh to rhyme,
is what I do instead of doing. May
the life I do not live in the still time
I sit here scratching, by some grace
there is in words, be justified. At best
nothing does better by the untold race
than its own tongues. So have all men been blest
by deeds of words from dead men who took time
they have no longer, but were glad to take
when they were rich, to make into a rhyme
they have forgotten, what they itched to make.

Some Sort of Game

Toy-maker Ptolemy
made up a universe.
Nine crystal yo-yos he

spun on one string. It was
something to see it go,
half sad to see it pass.

Why won't the things we do
describe reality?
What if it isn't so?—

Why must there always be
some Galileo there
poking his Q.E.D.

into the spinning air
until the spinners break,
the string hangs scrawled nowhere?

Must it be a mistake
to guess a heaven wrong?
Some sort of heaven-quake

and end of song
roared down that telescope.
Somewhere among

such angels as men hope
are there, but do not know,
a dark began to grope.

So toys and angels go.
Not that it's much to me.
I have been reading Poe

and take this liberty
of bumping into rhyme
touched by some irony

what he set to the chime
of Gothic bing and bong
to knell for time

that proves our pretties wrong
with its damned Q.E.D.
End of whatever song,

if any, this may be.

Tommy's Pond

Frogs' eggs in globular clusters
cloud a jellied universe. A light-bending
Magellanic scum seeded with black lusters.
Has God said this sending?

In the pomegranate of Mother Church, saints
are such seed. Their ruby blood-beat—
cloud-bent, and again in the telling—taints
light as life does. It is no feat

to misunderstand a universe: all man-time
fables great possibility wrong.
Yet seed does burn. Slime
is a sure fire. Its puddle-hung

plenum will burst, these periods
become commas in a heartbeat beyond
pleroma, their myriad myriads
unsaid as galaxies. In any pond.

The Formalities

On September 2, 1945,
the battleship *Missouri*
flagged like a parade
lay anchored in Tokyo Bay and

the Japanese brass with swords
and the frock-coat detail in
silk toppers briefcases and
horn-rims like wine-bottle bottoms

walked aboard on tightropes
they had stretched inside themselves,
and pushing a separate button
for each part of each bow,

rendered unto Douglas MacArthur
what was MacArthur's, and
what was God's too, MacArthur
ignoring the difference, and in

the skeletal witness of Jonathan
Wainwright come from prison, and of
A. E. Percival, British Army,
wherever *he* had come from,

and of a choir of misc available
native and allied brass in open-collar
suntans assigned by the cameras,
and of the cameras themselves—

still and moving and by flash and
previously arranged floodlighting and
with full sound equipment—the
signatures fell-to and it was

done there on God's deck there
in Tokyo Bay into which I had
watched Hewie splash burning less
than two months before with Doc

dead in the nose and O'Dell
probably blubbering a prayer and
Frankie, poor bastard, blind in his
coop di-dahing no message to Whom

and T.J. waving from the top dome
and Chico and Coxie—whoever if any
they were who wanted their medals
getting them all at last—

which is to say boys at bad luck
in their tribe and wings melting
and the photographer come. And had
fish had time in two months

to pick clean Coxie's little go-to-hell
moustache like the one I shaved off,
and Chico's tattoo and the mole on
Frankie's shin and the scapular from

O'Dell's neck and so for each in (or
out of) himself there under the keel
of the battleship *Missouri* on which
the representatives of the nations

stood witnessing how much like God
Douglas MacArthur was and what a
candidate He would make
if only He were a civilian?

The Week That Was

The pet shops were advertising non-rabid bats
for air-raid shelters. ("For that natural touch.")
LBJ and Mao were placing bets.
("The sky's the limit.") Overkill held her torch
high over the harbor. ("Give me your weak, your poor.")
England asked to be mentioned as a world power
and France said, *"Comment?"* (Transmitted as "No comment"
by the wire services, and botched by a lino-hack
to read "Con meant"—at which Parliament
took qualified umbrage until Nelson gets back.)

After that there was no more direct quotation.
It goes better in paraphrase. Evade the question:
you need no answer. And why speak
what's already in the junk mail?—Those bats sold.
And Norman Rockwell did a cover that week
of a boy and his pet hyena, both oddly soiled,
digging up an old sunset by a charred road.
Comment? No comment. This is pure mood.

A Magus

A missionary from the Mau Mau told me.
There are spores blowing from space.
He has himself seen an amazing botany
springing the crust. Fruit with a bearded face
that howls at the picker. Mushrooms that bleed.
A tree of enormous roots that sends no trace
above ground; not a leaf. And he showed me the seed
of thorned lettuces that induce
languages. The Jungle has come loose,
is changing purpose.
Nor are the vegetations
of the new continuum the only sign.

New eyes have observed the constellations.
And what does not change when looked at?—coastline?
sea? sky? The propaganda of the wind reaches.
Set watches on your gardens. What spring teaches
seed shall make new verbs. A root is a tongue.

I repeat it as he spoke it. I do not interpret
    what I do not understand. He comes among
    many who have come to us. He speaks and we forget
    and are slow to be reminded. But he does come,
    signs do appear.
                There are poisoned islands far over:
    fish from their reefs come to table and some
    glow in the dark not of candlelight. A windhover
    chatters in the counters of our polar camps.
    A lectern burns. Geese jam the radar. The red phone
    rings. Is there an answer? Planes from black ramps
    howl to the edge of sound. The unknown
    air breaks from them. They crash through.
    What time is it in orbit? Israeli teams
    report they have found the body, but Easter seems
    symbolically secure. Is a fact true?

How many megatons of idea is a man? What island
    lies beyond his saying? I have heard, and say
    what I heard said and believe. I do not understand.
    But I have seen him change water to blood, and call away
    the Lion from its Empire. He speaks that tongue.
    I have seen white bird and black bird follow him, hung
    like one cloud over his head. His hand,
    when he wills it, bursts into flame. The white bird
    and the black divide and circle it. At his word
    they enter the fire and glow like metal. A ray
    reaches from him to the top of the air,
    and in it the figures of a vision play
    these things I believe whose meaning I cannot say.

Then he closes his fist and there is nothing there.

On the Poet As a Damned Poor Thing

I adored her and she giggled and I adored her.

It was entirely summer in her fleshdom
and she her own breeze through it, tittering leaves
that trembled round her bearing. Lemons glowed
on reaches of her tousling. Honeydews
bent light rays round her like a gravity.
She shucked like new corn. Was it to bed or table
she let me spill her, giggling as I nibbled
cherries and flesh of pears and bursting grapes?

I wrote gold reams of nothing that could say
how she lay by me, sleeping as I watched
what Raphael forgot the light could do
when he ran out of angels to stand in it.
Hers was the face of the most stupid angel,
too lost in its own bliss to think of being,
apart from all but its own representation.

That child-head lay adrift above her body
like a small separate soul above the Spheres
of Dante's walk across the universe.
"Beatrice!" I thought nights when I sweated to write her.
But when I crossed at last the swollen Eden
where she stood lit in her gold choruses,
that face of floating heaven knit its brows:
"Alighieri?" it said. "Ah, yes, you're Gemma's husband.
—What's all this you've been writing about me?"

It should have been vision enough to warn off visions,
but pens are hypodermic, and she was the drug
addiction is the dream of. I heard her giggle
floating above us like a face in a cloud,
or blind and separate as a *putta* smirking
from a gilt cornice over a Roman bed

where a boy-cardinal knelt, burning in prayer
to all of her sprawled summer in his arms.

Nothing could save his soul from incoherence.
He swore to make her shudder as he had
for wasting visions, but a vision came:
she was a peach tree, an Ovidian soul
trapped in a golden bearing all might eat
and none might change a leaf of but the wind
that tittered through her. Rising in a rage,
he leaped into her branches to shake down
one fruit of her locked soul. But though he hurled
whole tempests at her, not one gold globe fell. . . .

I was the only windfall in that dream,
a lump among the stubble at her roots,
hearing that other breeze her green sprays toyed with
in their own climate, above the death of mind.

She giggled and I died and still she giggled.

Twice, Away from Jack,
I Thought of Him

Once in snowed-in winter I was caught
on a Utah mountain till a blower plow
slammed head-down through the drifts and shot
a creeping ten-mile howl of rainbow snow.
I followed it down the gap, all roar and light,
until it came to where the road was black,
and it turned around frustrated, its loud bite
still gnashing, empty—and I thought of Jack.

And again in no known season at Waikiki.
I had taken the elevator to the nothingth floor
of the Surfing Hilton for some chivaree
at a pots and pans convention, and the door
slid open on the waterfall roar of Hell
dive-bombing its own turbines while a flak
of gaggle broke in the acoustic shell
of its own carved canyon—and I thought of Jack.

L'Inglese

Walpole, traveling in the Alps,
talked of goat trails and abysses.
Powdered wigs make prickly scalps
in a chaise above a crisis.

"The *least* step"—so he wrote to West,
would have tumbled wig and all
into such fog and sudden rest
that—well, he had no wish to fall.

"But is it possible," he thought,
"the next step is not one too many?"
While the sweating peasants sought
footholds for their daily penny.

One man's terror, one man's trade.
With milord upon their shoulders
and a long way back to bed
the porters edged around the boulders.

Came "a cruel accident."
Next day Walpole still bemoans:
when the trail at last had bent
to an almost-road of stones,

he lets his little spaniel out
("the prettiest, fattest, dearest creature!")
—for its creature-needs, no doubt,
or to admire some Alpine feature.

"When from a wood"—he wept and wrote—
"a young wolf sprang at once and seized
poor, dear Tory by the throat"—
and vanished, one must guess, well pleased.

"I saw it but I screamed in vain!"
—the prey was seized, the wolf was gone.
What seemed, above all else, to pain
Walpole, once the thing was done,

was that it happened in full day—
"but two o'clock and broad sunshine!"
His "Alpine savages"—for pay,
and full, he wrote, of "sour wine"—

made such commotion as seemed due,
but had their Englishman to bear.
In three leagues Turin came in view.
And they could rest once they were there.

Envoi

Sensibility better suits
the man inside the chaise
than the bearers—ugly brutes—
of those Alpine ways.

Yet the weight falls on all mankind
the day the wolf attacks.
Milord had great griefs on his mind;
they, milord upon their backs.

Sermon Notes

It's easy to walk out of Hell. But there
Hell starts again. Another channel but
the same damned show. Hell's what we are, not where.
It's easy to walk out of Hell? To what?
To exactly nothing nowhere and unemployed.
The Anti-Hell's not Heaven but the Void.

An Evening of the Private Eye

"I live, therefore I love," said the Excerpt-Lifter
and Skimmer of Beatitudes, paying no
attention whatever to Plagiary. "Ach, so?"
crouped the Teutonic Monocle, the Brandy Snifter,
and the Iron Cross for Continental Manners,
"I live, therefore I follow Particular Banners."

"Boys," said the Advanced American Female who
had learned her Languages, married Breeding,
and renounced Mere Nakedness for Wider Reading,
"I love, therefore I live." And splitting in two,
she gave her Vowels and Aspirates to the Civilian
and her Consonants to the Thoroughly Charming Villain.

"I live, therefore I live—in some bemusement,"
said the Prosodic Eavesdropper at his Key-Hole
into the Obvious Infinite. "This See-Hole
is good at least for Relative Amusement."
—"Arrest that man!" cried all those Coupling Parts
of Speech, ajabber at their Lively Arts.

"Judgment!" called Monumental Momus. "Hear me!
I pronounce one a Frappé. Two a Bore.
I pronounce three a Particle on No Shore.
I pronounce four Unborn until he fear Me,
Uncock his Eyeballs and Rewrite his Face
in Characters legible to Prevenient Grace."

"Goodbye," said the Private Eye as it Withdrew.
"I leave, therefore you lose." And they were Gone.
Then the First Impulse that he Came Upon
shrugged off Habituation and Away they Flew,
Entasseling every Twig with Lints of Spring,
Including Airs, and Summoning Bones to Sing.

Pencil Stub Journals

On an Exalted Nonentity

Must we believe that what ascends aspires?
That altitudes are measures of desires?
That nothing mounts until the holy fires
of self have dreamed a height? So Dante taught.
And though it makes some difference who inquires,
and how, this world suggests a counter-thought,
suggested, maybe, by the Prince of Liars,
our Adversary, whose prompting never tires:
the eagle's ticks are airborne but no flyers.

Parenthood

My son was insolent to me.
I blessed him: love is liberty.
My son was insolent to my friend.
I hit him: liberty is to defend.

Choices

George says he chooses poverty. That's rash.
It's bad enough just learning to live through it.
Name any substitute you like for cash:
I've an experienced aversion to it.

For Clavia on a Rejection Slip

Your soul is full of yearning? So is this prose
you set to tick and rhyme under my nose.

On Evolution

Pithecanthropus erectus,
could he see us, would reject us.

An Alphabestiary

⁓•⁓

(1967)

A is for ANT.

No one knows
how many Ants have stayed busy
how many years since the first
went into busyness, but any
estimate would produce a figure
something like a one followed
by pages and pages of
zeroes.

Whatever you do with
a figure like a one, it should
be clear, certainly, that zeroes
can go on accomplishing nothing
thereafter

practically

forever.

—.—

B is for BOMBERS, our national pride.
And also for BOYS who like Bombers to ride.
And also for BLESS in "God Bless Our Side."

B is for BAD (the Enemy) whom
we Bless our Boys' Bombers Bravely to Bomb.
And for BELLS we ring out when we welcome them home.

B is for BANNER, which proudly we hail.
For BLAST and for BRASS and for BURIAL-DETAIL.
And for BILLY and BUCK, who are studying BRAILLE.

—.—

C is for CAMEL, a very right beast.

So perfectly adapted is the Camel
that it endures with equal ease
the desert griddle and the mountain glacier.
Its dense lashes keep any speck
of sand or snow from its eyes.
It stores its own water. Its great
splay feet do not sink in sand,
and they grip securely on stone
and ice. The Camel can be ridden
or pack-trained. And it is practically
tireless.
       As a result of such
perfect adaptation, it provides man
with transport, water (in an emergency),
hair, milk, and (eventually) meat.

Now, children: what is a Camel right for?
and for whom?
           Once you have stated
your own thoughts, try to answer
from the Camel's point of view.

—•—

G, also inevitably, is for the GNU,
or Wildebeest, technically an antelope,
but more like a horse in the rear end,
and more like an ox in the head and horns.

There is always some likelihood of confusion
in the animal kingdom, or in what we
expect of it. Considered either way,

you can always write to your Senator
for further information.

Who is more likely
to know how an ox-like mind may move
with the speed of an antelope leaving
to final view the rear end of a horse?

—•—

H is, reluctantly, for HUMAN, a word
derived from Latin *homo,* signifying "man,"
and, more aptly, from *humus,* signifying
"soil/earth," hence "of clay," but
more recently an adjective involving
a distinction that in turn involves
a slander of the higher apes, implying,
as it does, that Human primates
have evolved a more enviable position
than their cousins by shedding their tails
in order to be followed around
by a less visible conclusion.

—•—

I is, naturally enough, any author.

"I"
we say, employing the same character
for "Number One," and always capitalizing it
when we mean ourselves.

(The consequences
of which have been made clear.)

It might
have been well, perhaps, to let I stand for
Iguana, a creature of great antiquity, which,

having been spared the concept of I-ness,
has already been here some aeons before us,
and seems likely to be here at least as many
after.

    (In whatever I-dea time is.)

—•—

J is, splendidly, for JOHN, my—
I repeat—*my* name.
               Others, to be sure,
have attached themselves to the same
sound and have insisted on being
identified by it. None, however,
has plumbed the infinite-true-secret
identity of John-ness in quite
the way I know all about.
               John
(can you fail to see?) is I. Begins
with, is the name of essential I-ness.

In Italian, in fact, J is I-lungo,
as Y is *I-greco*.
           It is exactly
that long I my name is, as you must
finally be made to understand
if you mean ever to have your own
name. I mean *truly* have it.

—•—

M is for MOTHERS, who are, above all,
useful. Preferably, to be sure, married,
but in any case indispensable.
Motherhood can, we understand, be carried
too far. As can the attitudes
toward it. Some Mothers are harried.
Some are placid. Some beget feuds.
Some, harmonies. Some could
be called loose. Some are prudes.
Mothers, that is, are various. It is good
to have a Mother; to have had one,
inescapable. Motherhood would,
I daresay, command the respect of many
more clinicians were the prerequisites higher.
(It can, after all, happen to almost any
girl.) It is reasonable, I suggest, to admire
individual merit as it occurs
rather than the category. Inquire
of Eve, in reason, what is truly hers,
and of Lilith, hers. And so on.
Then, in proportion, as love measures,
love a bit more, and gladly.
Mothers are good to have, but if everyone
kept his, things would go badly.

— • —

N is for NANNYGOAT—the silly
who finds her loved one in a Billy;
while he, poor fool, without demur
finds all his dream of love in her.

With this much said, my fable ends.
Go look at your own married friends,
or look at your own wife at home,
and write your own end to my poem.

—•—

O is for OX, by which word we
signify what was meant to be
a bull, but suffered alteration.
Husbands, in late meditation,
may find some parable in this
all-hauling beast that does not miss
what it is missing.
                    The real joke
played on the Ox is not its yoke,
nor yet the spiking of its spoke,
but its name, which comes, we learn,
from German *ochse*, drawn in turn
from root words meaning "to make wet
[the female]"—that is—"to beget."
—What? Humor in the alphabet?

Words betray us. But the ox
is safe in this: it seldom talks.
A mercy—should it learn its name,
even it would blush for shame.

—•—

Q may as well be for QUEEN,
the feminine of King, and sometimes
of Prince.
There have been many Queens
in history, and some of them
have been anything you care to
imagine.
There are fewer now,
and they require much less imagination.

Some are still profiled on money
but all have suffered some devaluation.

Time is inflationary.
It is easier
to put one's face on money
than to keep money up to face value.

— • —

R is for RAT, the noise in man's wall.
Wherever man goes, in no time at all
his Rat will be heard at work in the dark.
It is written that Noah took on his ark
two beasts of each kind to Mount Ararat.
But surely genetics knows better than that:
though Noah took no more than two Rats aboard,
it's certain that what came ashore was a horde.

The moral of which is—with all due respect—
don't start saving worlds till you learn to select.

— • —

T, the TURTLE, has been a long time coming
through everything, including fablers and
logicians. Aesop had him outrunning rabbits
(a likely story), and Zeno proved that Hercules
could not overtake him because however fast
the hero ran, by the time he came to where
the turtle had been, it would have moved on.

What is this professional passion to speed him up?
Do we resent what sets its own pace? Wise Hercules,
unable to catch him by logic, simply overtook
him, and class was dismissed.
                                        The fact is
that even with logic on his side, he *is*
slow. He *means* to be overtaken.
Then he stops being and becomes a box.
It's a trick he learned from the egg:
hatched from a shell, he returns to it.
There is less to fear in not being born.

Nevertheless there is no reason
for taking him too lightly.
What if he does go nowhere?—he travels
without leaving home. He is ugly,
certainly—but how long has it been
since your last beauty prize? Remember, too,
the turtle takes revenge: when savage boys
carve their initials on his back, he waits,
goes off, then waddles in fifty years later.
"Look at you now," he says. And there you are.
Mock the turtle if you will:
armor is its own species and survives.

Lives of X

—•—

(1971)

The Shaft

At first light in the shadow, over the roach
like topaz on the sill, over the roofs,
the Old North Church spire took its time to heaven
where God took His to answer.
                                        I took my drink
at clammy soapstone round a drain of stinks
and slid back into bed, my toes still curled
from the cold lick of linoleum. Ma was first,
shaking the dead stove up. Then Pa,
a rumble hocking phlegm. When the cups clattered
I could get up and climb him and beg *biscotti*
while Ma sipped cups of steam and scolded love.

The shaft went down four darks from light to light,
through smells that scurried, from the sky-lit top
where I built cities of kindling, to cobbly streets
that curved away as men go, round their corners,
to what they do after they kiss their sons.
Where *did* he go? He kissed me and went down,
a step at a time, his derby like a bob.
And then pulled under. And the day begun.

Later, when days were something that had names,
I went there with her, out of my sky-lit first
on the top landing, to the falling streets.
The stores were cellars and they smelled of cheese,
salami, and olive brine. Dark rows of crates,
stacked back to damp brick where the scurries were,
made tunnels in whose sides the one-eyed beans
were binned so deep I could lose all my arm
into their sliding buttons. In a while
I got my cookie and knew I had behaved.
Then up the shaft again, through its four darks
to the top landing where we lived in light.
A latched-on fence playpenned a world I made

of slant and falling towns. Until his derby
rose from the shaft and all the kitchen steamed.

God's cellar was one more dark. A tallow deep
where nickels clinked at racks of burning flowers.
Black shawls kneeled there whispering to the dead,
and left the prayer still burning when they rose.
He had such gold saints by Him in His dark:
why was God so dusty? Was He making
the dead from dust again because she prayed
and made me pray? Would all the dead be made
back to the shawls draped on those altar rails,
and come home singing up their shafts of dark?

I kissed the stone he changed to in his flowers.
But when he stayed away she would not waste
the prayers she lit but got him back in me.
His letters came. From God and Metropolitan.
A piecemeal every week. And he had bought us
half a house in Medford—out of the shaft
and into green that had a river through it.

And still he would not come back, the garden summer
nothing to him, the fruit with nothing to say.
My aunt and uncle bought the other half.

God had a house there, too, but would not speak
His first Italian to her. She came home
and spoke the rest to Pa, hissing all night
how much she was afraid. Or a dream rattled
and speared her to a scream, and the girls woke crying,
and ran to fetch her water, while I lay
guilty of happiness, half-deep in books,
learning to guess how much hysteria
could be a style of acting, and how much
have its own twisted face, and how much more
could be the actress acting what she was,

panting and faint but gripping the glass of water
they always ran to fetch and watch her drink
till she sank back exhausted by medication
and let herself be fussed to sleep again,
satisfied as long as she was feared for.

So all was well. And if a glass of water
and the girls' fears were medicine enough,
why the girls would wake, the pipes would not run dry.

I lost her, and I lost them, shutting out
more night-rattling and more day-squalls
than I had sky for, there behind my books.
I made a cave of them and crept inside
and let the weather blow away unheard.

They had to run those weathers of the dark
forked day and night by lightnings of her nerves.
Not they, nor I, guessed half those howling years
the lightnings were her staff and they her sheep
to frighten close, all madness being fear.

And still they grew away because they grew.
And she came stalking after like a witch
when they strolled after supper. They found her out,
flitting from tree to tree with the black cat
of sniffed suspicion sliding at her feet,
a shadow in a shadow, and they led her
foot-blistering hikes through nowhere and back home,
slowing to let the shadow flit away
around the corner, slide into the house,
be dumped in a back closet, and not be there
to mar her innocence when she looked up
from sorting sorted socks at the kitchen table,
or sweeping the swept floor, and breathing hard,
but half believing their straight-faced innocence

as they clacked by to shut a bedroom door
on gales of whispering with giggly showers.

I read my book and guessed and didn't care.
An oaf in a madhouse. Keeping my escape
but staying on for meals. She learned at last
suspicion makes sore feet. But she wasn't finished.
Not while she still could faint and not come to
till everyone was crying in a circle
of guilt and glasses of water and grand opera.
I didn't know she was crazy. That we all were.

Nor that I dropped my book and lost my place.
I knew she had fainted and we were to blame.

Then, one night when the girls had invitations
her black cat hissed at, she stood in the doorway
ranting to turn them back, and when they argued,
she turned her eyes up, started breathing hard
and settled to the floor across the sill.
She had her act so polished by that time
she could sink like a dropped sheet, all one motion
and down without a thud. It was well done—
It took me in and sent me running for water—
but by whatever tells truth to the badgered,
it was too well done. When I came running back,
the girls had clucked her gently to one side,
pillowed her head, smoothed on a comforter,
and bent to kiss her cheek, cooing, "Poor Ma.
A nap will do her good." And off they clattered,
squeezing their giggles tight. Then even I—
the oaf of the litter—got it. I found the glass
still in my hand, started to put it down,
then drank it off. And, having watched that much,
sat down to watch the rest.

Were her eyes closed?
The girls' heels clicked across the porch and off it.
The last click jerked her upright in a rage,
but to one side, in case the girls looked back.
She hadn't seen me and I guessed she meant
to be found lying there when the girls came home.
God, what a weapon! I could *hear* her glower,
her lips grimacing vows to kill a saint.
"Have a good nap?" I said.
                              She snapped around,
head and body together in one shriek.
My skin crawled on a rasp of shame too late.
Then she was on me like her blackest cat,
its claws turned into fists. She beat so hard
it hurt me not to hurt. She'd hurt herself
unless I stopped her. Well, I'm an actor, too,
from a family of actors, I told myself,
and tried to clown it away. "Hey, Ma, lay off.
You'll hurt your wrist again. Come on, let's dance!"
The thing was to catch her mood and turn it around.
I picked her up—she weighed about ten pounds—
waltzed her across the room, her fists still going,
then settled her soft as dandelion fuzz on cushions.
"Just like your father, pig!" she tried to scold,
but her glower was out.
                              "So what? So it didn't work.
So now you can stop fainting. So what's lost?—
your stage career? It was a lousy act."

I'd kept my head just far enough above books
to guess my best chance was to play her husband.
"Just like your father," she scowled, but her grimace
quivered halfway to a smile. I thought I'd won.
But it slipped past a smile, turned into a giggle,
and out through a mad laughter to a scream

that had no actress in it but the fear
I was no husband to, and could not be.

—And gasped at last, since comedy is all,
to hiccups that went on until she lay
where comedy is nothing, strewn like lint
blown down into the bottom of a well
I could remember like the smell of tallow
inside a dark where racks of burning flowers
swallowed black shawls to altar rails of bone
down every turn and landing of the shaft.

If God still spoke her language there, I hope
she heard enough to promise her the light
I didn't know how to light her when I tried.

She did ease into age with half a smile
mending inside her. But her eighties raveled.
Her wits went back to muttering, and she sat
hugging a raggedy doll that would not light back
husband or son. And never saw us again
although we came and stood there in the shaft
bringing her pastries that oozed down her chin,
candies we had to wash out of her fist,
and jokes she did not hear the nurses laugh at.
She hugged her final dark to a rag God
who spoke in broken weathers to no wits.
And then we turned my father's grave and laid her
to take her time to Heaven in her last faint.

And there's a life, God knows, no soul would choose.
And if I send love after it, what's that
but one more scurry sounding down the shaft?

A Knothole in Spent Time

I have to believe it's a limited society
that remembers the Craddock School on Summer Street
where the tennis courts are now. Still, everyone
is local to his own ghosts. The one-room school
my wife rode spavined Josh to in Haw Creek
hid itself in a thicket for twenty years
after the school bus came, and then was sold
to Mr. Buster Robinson, who moved it
onto his place to house the hired man's family,
and let the thicket back over the well,
the two caved-in outhouses, the skip-rope yard,
the knocked-in stones no memory could sit long on,
though we strolled back for one that wasn't there.

A week before we were married we went down
and found the thicket onyx'd with blackberries,
went back again with a pail and picked it full,
ate them in cream so thick it wouldn't pour
but had to be spooned off the top of the pail.
Alas, the jewel thickets had been threaded
with poison ivy. Judith's arms went scaly.
She had to add long gloves to her wedding gown.
Then, when we took the Pullman to Chicago
the air conditioner quit and we lay sweltering
in a Black Hole of Calcutta. I caught a cold.
And all our honeymoon she scratched, I sniffled.
Our gem days in a sweet too thick to pour.

Are tennis courts a better end than thickets
that poison with their sweets? The elms came down
to let a pavement in. All change unghosts
something we change in leaving. Imagine Wordsworth
revisiting Yarrow—or Tennyson, Locksley Hall—
tourists to a nostalgia (why else go back?)

finding the place scrubbed out to Super Mkts,
cloverleaf ramps, and ten Drive-In Self-Service
Omnimats—they'd suffer a change of style
before they got the poem out of their dendrites
and into itself. I'm doing what they'd have done
at some last elmtop down from heaven's first
not for nostalgia but for nostalgia rebuffed.
My own, but a condition of us all
at the gates of lost infinities.
                              Craddock School
was hardly an infinity, but could spell one.
As anything begins. My mother took me
my first day gone into its creaking ark;
the huger, I have to guess, for my being small,
but huger again for all Ma's sermoning
on the sanctity and omniscience of school teachers,
as witness their salaries—almost as much as a cop's.
They were born in enormous palaces called "college"
and came to earth in kindness, that small boys
might "get an education" and "get ahead"
as nobody's parents had been able to,
which is why they were "sacrificing." At least why she was.

Which meant she'd strap me if I didn't behave.

Which meant, in the sad nonsense that speaks dearest,
she loved me and feared for me.
                              In I went.
It's out of focus now. I remember the elms,
a whispering sky that spattered sunlight through,
walls like the sides of a ship, and the ark roof
riding the elms in a sunlight of its own.
It must have been built soon after the Civil War
when lumber still grew on trees and was meant to be used
a tree to the ridge, a half tree to the joist.

It must have taken a forest for the studs.
Even on brightest days the hallway ceilings
were lost in their own dusk. It smelled of chalk,
the furnace room, and sneakers. It creaked and breathed
as if there were giants sleeping in its attics.
If heaven needed a barn for better beasts
than any of us were, the Craddock School
would have done for Apollo's cattle.
                           I sat down,
pure in worship, ready to be saved,
and even to earn salvation. Miss Matron-Column
(I don't remember her name but she stood pillared
over our heads like a corseted caryatid
spilling out of her corsets on a scale
of two of anyone's mother) said what she said,
I don't remember what. I was having trouble.

Ma meant the day to be ritual, and had made me
a jumper-something called a Buster Brown,
and bought me new school shoes, and long white stockings
that buttoned, or tabbed, into my underwear.
I wasn't exactly comfortable but I took it
until a pug-nosed Irish snot behind me
—Tom something-or-other—got his needle in
to let me know white stockings were for girls
and that I was not only a Dago but a sissy.

I had set out to worship and be saved.
Now I'd have to fight when school was out.
The fight wouldn't be much, but it meant ripped buttons,
probably grass stains, maybe a red-lined nose,
and that meant Ma and the strap. I was better off
when I ran into trouble on troubled days.
But when the day began in a fuss of love

and then went sour, that meant I had betrayed her.
Which meant our opera played with the volume up
screaming to extra whacks with that damned strap.

While I was thinking that, I was looking around:
most of the girls, alas, had on white stockings
and none of the boys. The stinker saw me looking,
knew he had me, and began recruiting
more of the boys. Why did God have to waste
good schools on the lousy Irish?
                                        —I heard a name.
"John Sea-YARD-i," Miss Matron-Column said,
"are you sure you are paying attention?"
                                        I sat up
and tried to manage the look I guessed she wanted,
but I had forgotten even the stink behind me:
Omniscience had changed my name! I was John Sea-YARD-i
—and not even allowed to argue! What's a teacher
if she can't say a name right? . . . John Sea-YARD-i . . .
That was no sound of mine. I was John CHAR-di.
I knew that. And Ma knew it . . . well, what *did* Ma know?
House things, yes. And things about Italy.
But nothing about what went on out of the house,
such as how to say an American name in America.

I had been rechristened. All the way through high school
and my little while at Bates and my time at Tufts
—at both of which there were kids I'd started school with—
I was Sea-YARD-i. It took me seventeen years
and a bus ride out to Michigan—out past Canada—
to make my escape. And the first thing I did, free,
was to get rid forever of Matron-Column's
last ghost upon me and get my own ghost back
the way it sounded when its ghost began.

Meanwhile, to keep insanity in sequence,
we had our fight. I bloodied my jumper a fleck,

lost the buttons I expected to lose,
got grass stains on my knees. We tried our cuss words,
then backed off trading sneers and started home.

Ma would be waiting with that strap. My tail
would come away from it ridged. Then *she'd* cry,
and I would have to stop bawling to comfort *her.*
I've never thought far enough back—not for not trying—
to understand how we came to that arrangement.
I know it had something to do with my being ghosted
into her husband and he into her son.
Sometimes I think she was beating him for dying,
and me for not being enough of what she'd lost.

Something like fifty years later, when she'd faded
almost past touch and hearing in the Home,
but was still half remembering who we were
when we went to visit, and then forgetting again—
her long ghosts out, back in her ghosts again,
I sat beside her and she called me "'Ndo."
("'Ndo" was her way of shortening "Antonio.")
What visitation in what mist was that?
Not he. Not I. A ghost halfway to black.
Then she drew back through mists I could not enter
even as a ghost.

                      Which year of what came first?
Time's all one once it's by. The ghost I walked in
was scheming its small way out of a ridged butt.
"Look what you did!" I yelled when I slammed in.
—If I could stake my claim as the offended
before she staked her own, I had a chance.
"These are GIRL stockings! I had to fight ALL the boys!"
(I never was stingy with flourishes. This was opera.)
"They called me a GIRL and tried to rip my stockings!"

I doubt it would have worked, all else being equal,
but my sister Edie came home just then from her school

full of hot news. "Ma, Johnny had a fight!"
she yelled, and waited around to see me get it.

Ma shut her up. *"Fati i cazzi tui!"*
—that's mountain barnyard Billingsgate, southern style,
for "mind your own phallic business." When Ma got earthy
she never was one to mind a little manure.
Except in recollection, those nine lives back,
I wouldn't even have noticed, except to know
I was off the hook once she shut Edie up.
"Take off the stockings," she sighed her martyrdom.
And when I had them off she tossed them to Edie.

"Somebody has to wear them," she said. "Go wash them.
—And you: get out of those clothes so I can fix them."

I changed to overalls and went back to the kitchen.
"Ma, the teacher said I was John Sea-YARD-i.
That's not our name."
                              "Che nomi! First your sisters—
now you. *Chi ne capisce?* Say what you like."
Then she caught herself: "You do what the teacher says."
I shrugged and started out. She called me back.
"I'm sorry about the stockings. I didn't know.
You want a *tarallo?"* (That's a hard shell bagel.)
"That's all right," I said. But I took the *tarallo.*

That did for my first day into omniscience.
I settled down to worship as I was told,
and wouldn't have thought not to. I learned to write "Squirrel"
with a bushy tall on the "q," "Look" with two eyes,
"Cat" with a whiskery "C"—proofs of a heaven
where things were locked forever in their names
as Nona and every Old Wife knew already
and could mumble charms for; as my Uncle Alec
could lay *tarrochi* pictures out of the deck
and read the next thing coming, that always turned out

to be something else, that on re-examination
turned out to be what the cards had really said
except that he'd read them wrong. The cards and teachers
(and, later, Mussolini) were always right.

I doubted the cards, and never took Mussolini
for heaven's hope, but of the omniscience of teachers
I was God-certified and rebaptized
in perfect faith—at least for one more year.
Then I found my first knothole in spent time.

I had been passed along from Miss Matron-Column,
Sea-YARD-i'd and still in awe, to Miss Absolute Void.
Don't take that name for disparagement: I was still
ready to play *cherubino* to all God's virgins
in our first age of innocence, but the fact is
I haven't a shred of her in my memory
except that she was the first chink in the wall
of heavens I had been schooled to as a faith,
though she didn't know it, and couldn't have been told.
I doubt she could have guessed the wall was there.

I droned fly-drowsy sun its leafy day
down through the elm's own daydream into mine.
The class was reading something, each in turn
rising to take a page—some Henny-Penny
or Puss in Boots. I'd read it twenty times,
and was off somewhere through elmtops in a float
when green clouds split to thunder. "John Sea-YARD-i,"
she called, her voice a judgment waiting to fall.
The book was on my desk but I'd lost the page.
I got to my feet. Somewhere in a separate haze
I remembered a girl reading and her last words
still floating in the elmtops. I held the book
and said from memory whatever Blind Mice
or Chicken-Little came next, pretending to read,
and knowing I'd make a slip, and read forever,

and DIDN'T make one! I must have been twelve years old,
having begun at six, before I heard,
"Very well, then. You may sit. And pay attention!"

I sat, relieved at first. Then burst inside:
I'd fooled her! She thought I had been reading! She was a Teacher
and *I* had fooled *her!* I started to tell the kid
ahead or behind or beside me or all at once.
Then hit on a truth as if I'd cracked my skull—
they wouldn't believe me! Ma wouldn't understand.
My sisters wouldn't care. Miss Absolute Void—
well, how could I tell her? I was alone
my first time into the world, at an edge of light
that dizzied like a dark; my gloat, half fear,
my eye at its first peephole into heavens
where Teachers were only people and could be wrong,
and all Ma's stations and candles could be rounded
by a truth I'd caught and held, and couldn't tell!

Thirty years later I did tell Merrill Moore,
though it was half a joke then. A slick squad
of thugs had cracked the Brink's Express in Boston
for the biggest haul in history, and over lunch
Merrill was theorizing they had to be caught
in spite of what seemed to be the perfect crime.

"Give them a year—or two—or three," he said.
"They're sitting on a world's record and can't claim it.
The money's cached: they wouldn't dare start spending.
Meanwhile they have to act as if nothing had happened.
Which is to say they're still bums among bums.
How long can a hero play at being a bum?
Some tart will give a man his walking papers,
a bar will shut off credit, a drunk will laugh.
Can a champion's ego hide in rags forever?
Ego's a king, and kings must claim their crowns."

"Maybe," I told him, "but what if you know to start with
no one will believe you while it still matters?"
And I told him how I'd found my hole in heaven
and seen Miss Absolute Void take off her wings
and soak her feet in a bucket of steaming water,
and never found a heaven whole again
nor anyone to tell about what I'd found.

"Well," Merrill said, "the Brink's Boys have the cash
to prove their story, wherever they have it hidden."

And so they had. I hadn't even the building
I could go back to and say, for whatever good
nostalgia of place might do me, "This is the room.
The first place in the world where I was alone
with more than I could tell of what was true.
Here something-nothing happened, and I remember
the day, the place, its ghost of elm-light falling,
and that I went through a door that wasn't there,
except that it once was real, and now it isn't."

And what is, but this lingering back of ghosts?

Feasts

My Uncle Alec's friend, Dominic Cataldo,
was straw boss of the treetop monkey gang
at Forest Hills, the woodpark cemetery
just at the edge of Boston. Across the street,
the North End's dead were tenemented tight
right to St. Michael's fence, stone crowding stone
and four names to a slab, but at Forest Hills,
down maple-dappled rhododendron drives,
the dead kept their suburbias lawned and sloped
to birdy hedges, brooklets, squirrel chatter,
and pheasant dells where dawn mist looked like snow.

St. Mike's looked like Pompeii on market day,
which must have looked like Prince Street excavated
after the stalls and pushcarts turned to stone
around the soot-streaked angels who froze there
in the act of reaching down to feel a melon
they never would pick up to bargain for.

The dead, like the Etruscans, kept their houses,
their neighborhoods, and their uses whole to God,
still zoned by ordinance. On Memorial Day,
a slope down from the villas of still money,
St. Mike's was at death's rush hour, the commuters
all carrying lunch and stiff wax wreaths to stone
past red-hot ice-cold hawkers. I planted pansies
I brought from home to border a last house,
prayed, ate my lunch, and spilled an orange tonic
that wet Pa's granite name, and prayed for that,
though it couldn't be a sin. I hadn't meant it.
I didn't even have another nickel
and had to drink tap water, iron-flavored.

Ma drank her tears awhile, then stilled to prayer,
then stood me by her in the receiving line,
her husband's name to her right, and sighed through neighbors,

cousins, *paesani,* and the delegation
from the Sons of Italy with its three-foot wreath
slant-ribboned *Presidente e fratello*—
Eterno in noi il santissimo ricordo.

It was her last of matronage, the one house
where she could stand, her husband at her side,
and welcome in the man's guests. All year long
she waited for that afternoon of graces,
once more a wife and ritual to his name
and presence. And all the loud hour on the El
and the half more on the trolley back to Medford
she sat carved straight to a found etiquette
she hadn't meant to lose, though late that night
I'd wake to hear her fear hiss through its dreams.

Still I passed Pa's grave more times than I stopped.
I spent more Sunday mornings at Forest Hills
than at St. Mike's. Which brings me to Cataldo,
to Uncle Alec, and to being bird dog
for the last organized gang of pheasant poachers
to operate within the city limits
of Boston, Mass; a gang led by Cataldo,
a long-armed, bow-legged, broken-toothed gorilla
with a chest of hair that coiled up like black smoke
from open collar to jawbone, and who was known
through all the bellowed treetops as Sputasangue,
which means "Spitblood," and was the heave-ho cry
he gave his sweaty gangs when backs were breaking
at crowbars and at peaveys and needed a lash
to break the boulder from the sucking till
or start the felled log over.
                            I rang with joy
whenever Cataldo, halfway down his gallon,
turned into Sputasangue, the one artist
I ever knew to stretch a roaring curse
a full ten minutes and not run out of figures
nor use the same one twice. Religious poetry

lost a fountain the day he was kept from school
to weed his first dry ledge. The man could start
at the triune top and work the hagiography
down to St. Fish by strict anatomizings,
to frottery, battery, buggery, rape, plain mayhem,
and on to atrocious-assault-with-intent, compounded
twelve generations back and twenty forward.

He made me a bull-roarer once and showed me
how I could whirl the thing till the air shook—
Cataldo did. But Sunday nights in the kitchen
when Sputasangue smoked up from the jug,
I sat my corner and heard the vault of glory
split its stone arches and spin heaven and hell
in the avalanche of rhetoric, while Ma shook,
helpless in admiration, and Uncle Alec
bravoed the rhapsode at the root of man,
his flowering tongues.
                        Cataldo died of the shakes
a dry ghost later, but while he was a man,
the goatiest Greek down from the mountaintops
could not outhowl him on God's axletree,
nor chop it down so sighted to a line
that it would crack a walnut but not mash it.

Being half a Greek himself, he was a thief,
which is to say, a mountain fox. Forest Hills
was stocked with ring-neck pheasants that did so badly
in what seemed perfect cover, the hatcheries
had to ship crate on crate, month after month.
Something kept getting at them. Sputasangue
would go to the headman's office with a sack
of feathers, heads, and legs found in the bottoms
where skunks had left them, and would volunteer
to gun the varmints by the Trinity,
the twelve Apostles' crooks, and Lucifer's tail,
if he had to twist it off himself.

                    That got him
the keys to iron gates. Sundays at dawn,
a throbbing touring car—a rusty Moon
that belonged to my Uncle Alec's friend Joe Pipe-dreams—
coughed through the gates. Uncle and Sputasangue
sat in the back, one shotgun left, one right.
Joe Pipe-dreams drove. I rode in front, cocked ready
whenever I got the signal, to jump out
and stuff the haul into a burlap sack.

Down in the dell, mist dreamed among the grasses
in the first light, and then a pheasant's head
would twitch up from no body like a snake
swimming but head high, half as Milton dreamed
Old Scaleskin for his cakewalk up to Eve
before God, Calvin, and William Jennings Bryan
condemned him to go crawling for the sins
he was already damned for in Tennessee
and the one-book farms of glory.
                            The old Moon
crawled at two miles an hour, Joe Pipe-dreams working
the spark and choke to make the thing backfire.
That flushed the birds. Then shotguns and backfiring
made one blur, till my uncle gave the word
and I went running with the burlap sack.

Our least haul was sixteen before the mist
drained to full day-ray. Later, Sputasangue
would walk his traps, finish a skunk or two,
and drop it behind the greenhouse for the headman.
Then he would empty the bird sack and twist off
heads, feet, and plucks of feathers in evidence.
He didn't have to be so foxy about it,
but man's the artist of his means. Art served,
we all drove back to Medford and gluttony.

Pipe-dreams and Sputasangue didn't want birds.
Not to take home. If they had a home, and I doubt it.

They played at hen-house fox as an act of nature.
Had the headman kept chickens, they'd as soon
have saved the shotgun shells. Why waste good money?
We didn't hunt: we harvested God's hand
and lived well out of it. As for those two,
they were both bachelors married to sour wine
they reeked of, and Uncle Alec, who made his own
(in the Aladdin's cave of barrels, bottles,
Mason jars, pickled peppers, crocks of lard
with half-fried liver balls layered in to keep,
apple chests drying under hanging herbs,
sausage, and drying grapes, the stacked squashes
by sand bins for potatoes, beets, and carrots,
under the footsteps sounding from the kitchen)
drew off a bottle of his best to start them,
and another when that went dry, and then another,
while Sputasangue made it up to rhetoric,
and Ma and Aunt Cristina, back from the fields
with dandelions and mushrooms, plucked the pheasants,
worked up the ovens to roasting, and started sauces
we gorged on for two hours in steams of heaven,
then slept off like a drunk, then woke again
to gorge again the last feast not to die.

Food was the flaming altar of the house.
All Hunger's tribesmen praise God as a feast,
fear him as famine, live as they can between.
Those birds were free grace and our week-long meat.
Hens cost money and were needed to lay,
and killing one cut into capital.
But free birds and free mushrooms sent a steam
up to the holy ghost that shines on harvests.

The stinking hen house and its morning bulbs,
green-smeared by droppings, was another bin.
Another was the garden where I sweated
my spring shame at manure I scooped from streets
and hauled home in a barrow while the fiends

who were my friends leered from the fence, and Riley,
the iceman, stopped his wagon to work me over
and offer me the next plop from his nag
if I would follow him.
                        But the Great Bin
was Albert's farm in Marlboro, twenty miles off
on pavement and ten in ruts, though that Joe Pipe-dreams
would have driven to Anchorage for the gas plus wine.

Every crop in, or when new mushrooms sprouted,
Albert would phone, and while Uncle Alec potted,
in or out of season, God's great day
of squirrels, rabbits, and anything with wings
(a robin in spaghetti sauce was a meatball
that didn't have to be bought) I dug potatoes,
or filled my sacks with apples, pears, and corn,
while Ma and Aunt Cristina worked moss bottoms
of rotten trunks for mushrooms. We drove back
with sacks lashed to the fenders, milk cans rattling
the cheeses Ma would make late, Uncle Alec's
bloodstained knapsack tucked under my feet—
and that was food and faith and holiday
high mounded home in incense of oregano,
basil, parsley, bay, mint, tarragon,
and oils that crisped the body and the blood
of rabbit, squirrel, and of whole small birds
whose skulls we nut-cracked for the brain's sweetmeat
when every bone was picked. Then the house clinked
its dishes and the innocent sat glad,
leftovers shelving a next day's gift of grace
from open-handed heaven, whose clenched fist
had starved the mountain hamlets back to stone
deeper than Pompeii's, whose forgotten tongue
they twisted and still spoke for Heaven's
unanswering name; till sweating at their sacks
stuffed with the last of nothing, they went steerage
to heavens whose last gate was St. Michael's slum—
itself a heaven to which no man went starved.

I diet in suburbias past the dead
on checkbook lo-cal, or, a jet away,
pick at my sirloin among signing angels
who skip potatoes for a third martini.
Poor Alec's 94 and has religion
in both bad legs. He lives on the third floor
of what God left him, where he prays to God
to call him in before his legs give out.
I offered to pay the first-floor rent to spare him
those flights of stairs. He gummed a dunked *biscotto*
and shook his head too late a world away.
Those stairs were the one challenge time had left him.
His whined prayers were the tendons of his climb,
his diet of last dusts before the dead,
half dead already.
                              And still I had had my first
hound pup and shotgun from his living hand,
who lived beyond himself, locked forty years
in the shop under the El on Causeway Street,
but climbed his foxy Sundays to the feast
of God's permission to man's appetite,
and cheered on the bull-roarer in his power.

And were I God, and he back in My dust,
and I, in the infinity of My whim,
could give him back his prayers or appetites,
but not both—oh, as foxy as the foxes
I made of My own nature, I'd rig his answer
against the palsied maunder of his end
and send him back to Sunday in his power
over the gift-wrapped morning of the world
to its daylong feast and night-roar up from wine—
My man of plenty, ritual to his friends,
and honored home and hale, safe in the garden
that flowered forever, till it wasn't there.

The Benefits of an Education:

Boston, 1931

A hulk, three masted once, three stubbed now,
carried away by any history, and dumped
in a mud ballast of low tide, heeled over
and a third swallowed in a black suck
south of the *Nixie's Mate*—itself going—
gave me a seal of memory for a wax
I wouldn't find for years yet: this was Boston.
Men with nothing to do plovered the sand-edge
with clam rakes that raked nothing. I walked home
over the drawbridge, skirting, on my right,
Charlestown ramshackled over Bunker Hill
and waiting for hopped-up kids to ride The Loop
and die in a tin rumple against the girders
of Sullivan Square, or dodge away toward Everett
and ditch the car; then walk home and be heroes
to ingrown boyos, poor as the streets they prowled.

There, house to house, the auctioneer's red flag
drooped its torn foreclosure to no buyer.
Now and then a blind man who could see,
and his squat wife who could stare out at nothing,
sat on the curb by the stacked furniture
and put the babies to sleep in dresser drawers
till charity came, or rain made pulp of all.
The rest lived in, guarding their limp red flags.
The bank was the new owner and that was all.
Why evict nothing much to make room for nothing?
Some sort of man is better than no man,
and might scrounge crates to keep the pipes from freezing
until the Water Co turned off the meter.
Or come Election, when men got their dole,
the bank might get the trickle of a rent
that wasn't there.
                              I'd walked those seven miles

from Medford to T Wharf to get my job
on the *King Philip*. Well, not quite a job,
but work, free passage, and a chance to scrounge
nickels and fish all summer till school opened
Miss Bates and Washington Irving.

                      The *King Philip*
rose sheer, three river-boat-decks top heavy;
but she could ride an inner-harbor swell
and not quite capsize, though, God knows, she'd try.

Excursion fishing. She put out at nine
from the creaking stink of Sicilian fishing boats
praying for gasoline they sometimes got.
And came back in at five—in any weather
that might turn up a dollar-a-head half deck-load
doling four quarters into the first mate's hand
as if the fish they meant to eat were in it
and not still on a bottom out past luck.
Sometimes a hundred or more, but of them all
not twenty would turn up with a dollar bill.
It was all change. We called the first mate Jingles,
waiting for him to walk across the wharf
and spill his pockets into the tin box
in the Fish Mkt safe. When he came back
his name was Dixon and we could cast off.
Your dollar bought you eight hours on the water,
free lines, free bait, your catch, and—noon to one—
all the fish chowder you could eat.

                            Good days,
the decks were slimed with pollock, cod, hake, haddock,
a flounder or two, and now and then a skate.
(A sharp man with a saw-toothed small tin can
can punch out Foolish Scallops from a skate's wing.
A Foolish Scallop is a scallop for fools
who eat it and don't know better.) I made a scraper
by screwing bottle caps to an oak paddle

and went my rounds, cleaning the catch for pennies,
or grabbing a gaff to help haul in the big ones.

Dixon, jingling again, took up a pool—
a dollar for the biggest cod or haddock,
a half for the largest fish of any kind.
No house cut but the little he could steal
and not be caught or, being caught, pass off
as an honest man's mistake in a ripped pocket.
The deal was winner-take-all. And the man that gaffed
the winning fish aboard was down for a tip.

One Sunday, with over a hundred in the pool,
I gaffed a skate we couldn't get aboard.
Dixon boathooked it dead still in the water,
then rigged a sling and tackle from rotten gear
and I went over the side and punched two holes
behind its head. Then we payed out the hooks
the fireman used for hauling cans of ashes
to dump them overboard, and I hooked it on,
and all hands hauled it clear to hang like a mat
from the main to the lower deck. We couldn't weigh it,
but it was no contest. Dixon paid on the spot.
He counted it out to fifty-seven dollars,
and I got two.
       We took it in to the wharf
and let it hang—a flag—till the next day
when we cut it loose with half a ceremony,
mostly of flies, just as we cleared Deer Island.
The Captain didn't want that shadow floating
over his treasury of likely bottoms,
so we let the current have it.
       After five,
the fireman rigged the hose, turned on the pressure,
and I washed down, flying the fish and fish guts
out of the scuppers in a rainbow spray
to a congregation of God-maddened gulls

screaming their witness over the stinking slip.
For leavings.

     Fishermen are no keepers. One to eat,
a few to give away, and that's enough.
The scuppers might spill over, and the deck
on both sides of a walkway might be littered
with blue-backed and white-bellied gapers staring.

I cleaned the best to haul home. Or I did
when I had carfare, or thought I could climb the fence
into the El and ride free. Now and then,
Gillis, who ran a market next to ruin,
would buy a cod or haddock for nothing a pound
and throw in a pack of Camels.

       And half the time
an old clutch of black shawl with a face inside it
and a nickel in its fist would flutter aboard
like something blown from a clothesline near a freight yard,
and squeeze a split accordion in her lungs
to wheeze for a bit of "any old fish left over,"
flashing her nickel like a badge, and singing
widowed beatitudes when I picked a good one
and wrapped it in newspaper and passed it over
and refused her ritual nickel the third time.

"I can afford to pay, son."

      "Sure you can."
"Here, now, it's honest money."

       "Sure it is."
"Well, take it then."

     "Compliments of the house."
"God bless you and your proud mother,"
she'd end, and take the wind back to her line.
Then the Fish Mkt man got after Dixon
for letting me steal his customers. Nickels are nickels:
for all he knew, I might be stealing from him
out of that pocket of nothing. But I foxed him.

Next time the old shawl came I sent her off
to wait by Atlantic Avenue. (And I'm damned
if the Fish Mkt man didn't call to her
waving a flipper of old bloat, calling "Cheap!
Just right for a pot of chowder!") After that,
I made an extra bundle every night,
cleaned and filet'd, and when she wasn't there
I fed the cats, or anything else of God's
that didn't run a market.
                   Then five nights running
she didn't come. Which, in God's proper market
might be more mercy than all nickels are,
whoever keeps the register, whoever
folds old shawls for burial.

                   Some nights—
once, twice a week, or some weeks not, the ship
was chartered for a stag by the VFW,
(we used to call them the Victims of Foreign Whores)
or some lodge, or some club, though the promoter
was always the same stink in tired tout's tweed.
He rigged a rigged wheel forward on the lower deck.
Sold bootleg by the men's room. Used the Ladies'
as an undressing room for the girlie show
that squeezed its naked pinched companionway
to the main deck "salon" to do the split
or sun itself in leers, clutching a stanchion,
or, when the hat was passed, to mount the table
and play house, if not home, two at a time,
with a gorilla stinking of pomade
who came on in a bathrobe from the Ladies'.
Two shows a night, prompt as mind's death could make them
while it still had a body. And on the top deck,
for an extra quarter, Tillie the Artist's Model
undid her flickering all on a canvas screen
lashed to the back of the wheelhouse, where the Captain
kept a sharp Yankee watch for the Harbor Cruiser.

He was a good gray stick of salt, hull down
in some lost boyhood that had put to sea
with the last whales still running into myth.
And down to this, or be beached flat, keeled over
like Boston, or that hulk off the *Nixie's Mate*,
to stink in the mud for nothing.
                                        Nevertheless,
It was some education in some school.
I panted at those desks of flesh flung open,
did mountains of dream homework with willing Tillie,
and, mornings, ran a cloth and a feather duster
(God knows where it came from—I'd guess Mrs. Madden
who cooked the daily chowder of leftovers
in her throbbing galley) over the counters, chairs,
and the great ark-built table, still flesh-haunted.

If it wasn't an education, it was lessons
in something I had to know before I could learn
what I was learning. Whatever there was to learn
in the stinking slips and cat-and-rat wet alleys
off the black girders and the slatted shadow
of the Atlantic Avenue El in Boston
where the edge-grinding wheels of nothing screeched
something from Hell at every sooty bend
of the oil-grimed and horse-dolloped cobbles
from Federal Street to the West End's garlic ghetto,
where black-toothed whores asked sailors for a buck
but took them for a quarter, in the freight yards,
or on the loading platforms behind North Station,
or in any alley where the kids had stoned
the street lights to permission.
                                        I took home
more than I brought with me of all Miss Blake
and Washington Irving knew of Sleepy Hollow.
(It had stayed clean and leafy I discovered
years later—like the Captain's boyhood
waiting its fo'c'sle south of Marblehead—

yet, a day further on the same road West,
the hollows had turned grimy, and the hills
fell through tipped crowns of slag—like Beacon Hill
stumbling through trash-can alleys to Scollay Square.)

Still, I got one thing from my education.
One stag-night when the tired tout's bootleg sold
too well for what it was, four poisoned drunks
lay writhing in the stern on the lower deck
in their own spew. And one, half dead but groaning,
green in his sweat, lay choking and dry-heaving,
his pump broken. While from the deck above
girls clattered, the pimp spieled, and the crowd raved.

Dixon came after me with the tout. "Hey, kid,
got a good stomach?" Dixon said. "Yeah, sure,"
I told him, honored.
                        "It's a dirty job."
"What isn't?"
                        "Five bucks!" said the tout. "Five bucks!
Here, Johnny. Five bucks cash and you can hold it!
My God, the guy could *die*!"—and passed the five
to Dixon who spread it open with both hands
to let me see it before he put it away.
"And a deuce from me if you'll do it," he tacked on,
taking my greedy silence for resistance.

"Who do I kill?" I said, taking the line
from George Raft, probably.
                        "Look, kid, it's legal.
You *save* a guy!" the tout said in a spout.

"Lay off," said Dixon, and putting his hand on my shoulder,
he walked me off two paces. "It's like this.
The guy's choked full of rotgut and can't heave it.
I tried to stick my fingers down his throat

to get him started, but I just can't make it.
Kid," he said, "it takes guts I ain't got.
You got the guts to try?"

                      And there I was
with a chance to have more guts than a first mate,
and seven dollars to boot!

                    "Which guy?" I said—
only for something to say: I knew already.

"The groaner by the winch. I got a fid
to jam between his teeth if you'll reach in
and stick your fingers down his throat."

                      We raised him,
half-sitting, with his head back on the chains,
and Dixon got the thick end of the fid
jammed into his teeth on one side. "LET'S GO, KID!"
he screamed, almost as green as the half-corpse
that had begun to tremble like a fish
thrown on the deck, not dead yet, though too dead
to buck again.

               But when I touched the slime
that might have been his tongue, I couldn't make it.
"Dixon, I can't do it!"

                  "Well, damn your eyes,
you *said* you would. Now put up, or by God
I'll heave you over!"

                  "Wait a minute," I said,
catching my education by the tail.
"Can you hold him there a minute?"

                       "If he lives.
Now where the Hell you going?"

                    "I'll be right back,"
I called, already going, "I'll be right back."

I ran for the locker, grabbed the feather duster,
and ran back, snatching out the grimiest feather,
took out my knife, peeled off all but the tip,

then fished his throat with it, twirling the stem
till I felt him knotting up. "Evoe!" I shouted
for Bacchus to remember I remembered,
not knowing till later that I mispronounced it.
"EE-VO," not giving Bacchus all his syllables.

"Heave-ho it is!" roared Dixon and ducked aside
as the corpse spouted. "There, by God, she blows!"
And blow she did. I've never seen a man
that dirty and still alive. Except maybe the tout
clapping me on the shoulder. "You did it, kid!
By God, you did it! Johnny, didn't he do it!"

Dixon wiped his hands on the drunk's back
where he had twisted and sprawled over the winch-drum
(what reflex is it turns a dead man over
to let him retch facedown?) and fished the five
out of his pocket. "Where'd you learn that trick?"
he said as I took the money and waited for more.

I could have told him, "Dmitri Merezhkovsky,
Julian the Apostate," but it wasn't
on Miss Blake's list, and certainly not on his.
"How about the other deuce?" I said instead.

He was holding the feather duster by the handle
and turning his wrist to inspect it from all sides
and looking down into its head of fuzz.
"What's this thing doing on a ship?" he said.

"Waiting for Romans," I told him, guessing his game
but hoping to play him off. "That's history, Dixon.
When a man went to a banquet and stuffed himself,
he'd head for a men's room called a *vomitorium,*
tickle his throat with a feather, do an upchuck,
and then start over. How about that deuce?"

"If you're so smart, then you can figure out
I said if you used your fingers."

                      "Hey," said the tout,
"If you ain't paying up, get back my fin!
If you can welch on this punk kid, then I can!"

"Go peddle your sewer sweat," Dixon said. "Here, kid.
You earned it right enough. Go buy yourself
more education." And stuffed into my pocket
a crumple I unfolded into—one bill,
while he went forward, shoving the tout away.

Six dollars, then. One short. But the first cash
my education ever paid, and that
from off the reading list, though of the Empire,
if not the Kingdom.

                 Meanwhile, the hat passed,
the crowd's roar signalling, the pomade gorilla
came from the Ladies' and pushed up the stairs
from his own *vomitorium* to the orgy
where low sisters of *meretrices honestae*
waited to mount their table through lit smoke
into my nose-to-the-window education
one deck below the Captain's Yankee eye
on watch for the Harbor Cruiser and the tide,
bearing off Thompson Island to the left,
Deer Island to the right, and dead ahead
Boston's night-glow spindled like two mists:
one on the floodlit needle of Bunker Hill,
one on the Custom House, both shimmering out
to sit the waters of Babylon off Boston,
whose dented cup—an original Paul Revere
fallen from hand to hand—I drained like the kings
of fornication, mad for dirty wine.
And for the kingdoms opening like a book.

The Little
That Is All

—·—

(1974)

Addio

The corpse my mother made
panted all one afternoon
till her father called down, "Oh, stop that!"

I saw her hear and obey
and almost smile
to lie down good again.

Then that blinked gone.
She gaped, her face
a run wax she ran from.

I kissed her forehead and thought,
"It will never be warm again."
Oh, daughter, if *I* could call!

Minus One

Of seven sparrows on a country wire
        and off in the instant ruffle
of hawk shadow, one was no flyer,
        or not enough, or was lost in the shuffle,
six stunted their little panics one spin
        around a pasture and an oak, and spun
back to whatever they had been
        in much the same row minus one.

        Is there a kismet
    the size of one of seven
        sparrows? Is it
    written before heaven,
        swami, in the mystic
            billion ungiven

Names? Is there a loving statistic
     we are motes of?
Whatever remembers us, finally, is enough.
If anything remembers, something is love.

Meanwhile a shadow comes to a point,
    to beak and talons. Seven surprises
start and one stops. Six joint
    excursions circle a crisis
they return forgetting. And what am I
    remembering? It was not on me
the shadow dove. I can sit by
    noting statistically.

     Is there an average
the size of one? of any?
     Is there no rage
against numbers? Of many
motes, mathematician,
     shall none be
more than decided? for once its own decision?
     I have spun loose
again and again with your sparrows, father, and whose
hawk is this now? unchosen? come to choose?

A Conversation with Leonardo

It was a stew of a night. The power failed,
killing the air conditioner. And the windows sealed.
I flailed off the one sheet and lay spread-eagled.

The instant I wilted to sleep Leonardo pounced,
drew his circle round me on the sheet,
tried fitting hands, feet, head to one turned ratio.

Ah, the greatness of lost causes! "I could have told you,"
I said, "if what you're after is ideal proportion,
you're sketching the wrong times." He frowned.

"A collector," he said, "can always use deformity
among examples, but only if lost within it
there hides a memory of man to illustrate."

"You are thinking," I said, "of Praxiteles, and beyond,
to that business of God's image, which is harmony
as measured by the famous scholastic hole

in Plato's head, where nothing is really real
but the abstraction of nothing—of the idea
of the abstraction of nothing—to an absolute.

After you, blessed maestro, came genre—the thing
measured not by absolutes but by other examples
of the same school. I am, alas, *that* man."

"Forgive me," he said, "I seem to hear you claim
an absolute irrelevance as a poor excuse
for what there's no excuse for." "None," I said,

"but a reverence for what was never there.
God measures perfection and crock measures pot."
—"You make me grateful I died in God's formed day."

"Master," I answered, "do you imagine God
is thinking you in this sequence? I'm
thinking you, more reverently, I daresay,

than He would be inclined to, were He inclined."
He looked away. "If I sense what you mean,
I am obliged to add that the thought disturbs me."

"Great Soul," I said, "how else could we have fallen
out of your circle but in that same disturbance
no man asked for and none yet has welcomed?"

"Thank you for a theme," he said. "I shall try
a drawing of it. If it lives on paper—
if I can make it live—I may understand."

"I wish I could hold to this same dream," I told him,
"Until it contains that drawing." "Perhaps," he said,
"it will be in one that comes later." "I will live for that,"

I said. But woke. The air was soup. The power still off.
It was pointless to try for sleep again in nature.
I went down and opened a bottle and sat to the dark.

Ugliness

The windows I see into
when the El stops
are my hunchback cousin Sal
dead there
        the paint flaking

his pretty good tenor
gone under curve-screech
when he starts again being
one of the big kids
I was small to and always
glad faster
to see him come laughing.

When we had to find jobs
he couldn't lift anything
and ran numbers
darkened by cops
but went to night school
till he lit himself
a bookkeeper and a desk
to come from easy
again.

      And moved to New York
and nothing, the firm folding
and times tough those
years I hadn't seen him
and needed work and wrote me
—Sal, my goddamn beautiful
twisted own big brother cousin—
"Dear Mr. Ciardi. . . ."

                    And if I do not
cry into one of these
dead alley windows once,
what tear shall I ever
be some of a man to?

A Man Came Tuesday

A man came Tuesday.
Wanted what I didn't owe yet.
"By Friday you will. Pay now
and I'll discount 10%." That
made sense . . . would have . . .
except. . . . "Anything off
for good intentions?" I asked.
"I," he said, "am not
the Parole Board. I'm your
nonnegotiable future
come to a take it or leave it."
"If I had the price of a choice."
"Exactly." "But if I had,
I'd have a different future."
"That," he said, "is what I'm trying
to get you to." "Who the devil
are you?" He shrugged:
"I have no contract with the truth
but I like to be persuasive—
what are you prepared to believe?"

Washing Your Feet

Washing your feet is hard when you get fat.

—·—

In lither times the act was unstrained and pleasurable.

—·—

You spread the toes for signs of athlete's foot.

—·—

You used creams, and rubbing alcohol, and you powdered.

—·—

You bent over, all in order, and did everything.

—·—

Mary Magdalene made a prayer meeting of it.

—·—

She, of course, was washing not her feet but God's.

—·—

Degas painted ladies washing their own feet.

—·—

Somehow they also seem to be washing God's feet.

—·—

To touch any body anywhere should be ritual.

—·—

To touch one's own body anywhere should be ritual.

—·—

Fat makes the ritual wheezy and a bit ridiculous.

—·—

Ritual and its idea should breathe easy.

—·—

They are memorial, meditative, immortal.

—·—

Toenails keep growing after one is dead.

—·—

Washing my feet, I think of immortal toenails.

—·—

What are they doing on these ten crimped polyps?

—·—

I reach to wash them and begin to wheeze.

—·—

I wish I could paint like Degas or believe like Mary.

It is sad to be naked and to lack talent.

It is sad to be fat and to have dirty feet.

One Wet Iota

I could see God once when I believed telling
look into a mud and His eye
start one wet iota swelling.

An untold later toward some when and why
come to no answer, I put
a lesson to a lens and saw the jelly

webbed to bone-spars of a live frog's foot
flow like blips across a radar screen.
And that was all blood circling in and out.

Told or untold, I saw nothing mean
but small looking. I can look home
to the size God was, seeing the thing seen

start like that wet iota and become.

Small

Swatted a custardy small thing.
A stain with a shell center.
Ugh where its eyes were. This
I must dawdle at. What was it?
All of itself. Not much
of what I am. How much
of what I am not will stop
at my eyeholes leaking after?

Why dawdle at nothing left?
Ask God later. His last word
unsays the first. I am. This was.
What else have I to do
but watch what I can—
and while—asking it?
What's small enough
to stay wholly outside of?

And inside? In the eye
of custardy small things
is the universe other raisins
than heroes munch? What grades
the sensations of protein?
I'm ego and think questions;
dread, and guess answers
at stains of myself.

If I can be situation comedy
at last eyeholes,
let me speak good ironic lines
going from compassionate
disinterest to what small

cleaning problem will not
be there long enough
for much notice.

If it is a passion play
I must sink through, flailing
nerve ends like wires of a blown
still spinning computer,
tears of solder melting me
from connection, good lines lost
in the stink and peel of burning
till even fire's out—

then pity me, dawdlers, for your own sake,
that I was a man at the edge
of your interest, and within mine,
wanted no more than to go
toward custard from firm eyes,
quipping a final style
for what shapeless small wonder
we could have loved through.

East Sixty-seventh Street

Wondering what to take seriously
without going as far as Fire Island,
I sit with Jamie to suffer his fourth bar.

Frank O'Hara died there, X'd out
by a beach buggy, its tire-tread scrawled
like a moustache on a poster. Let it not be

Fire Island. There could be another cause
not to die of. Maybe a liberation
from too much fretting. "We are so damned worthless!"

sighs Jamie the assessor. The universe
owes him a meaning. His mother, a Jewish princess
with an ark in her cleft, taught him to expect:

See my apple? It's from the Hesperides.
You could never imagine such fruit!
—No, nor distinguish it from another.

Now, having bitten it and found it mealy,
he can't get through the night on less than six
bars to his grief, some of which could be real,

maybe enough to mourn a meaning for handsome
Frank O'Hara, my student and friend once,
his headfull leaking into a tire track

on the sands of the gay. Whatever it comes to.
As Jamie might be suffering not to suffer
but because we are what we are and some of it hurts.

An Apology for Not Invoking the Muse

Erato popped in. What a talent for suspicion!
"Now what?" she said. I thought I knew.
"I am writing an unimportant poem," I told her.

She slammed her lute down on my desk.
Slammed it so hard it shook the air forever.
Even in anger she gives off such sounds

I cannot summon an adequate emotion
except in sensing how all loss belittles
what's left to make a truth of.

"Who authorized that?" she wanted to know.
"Honey," I said, "do I have to check with you
before I scratch an itch? This was a small one

in a minor crease I needn't specify
except to say we all have some—I mean
we mortals—and they do burn."

Was I being unreasonable? She chose to wail.
"Four thousand years of lute lessons in those crags
in a suffered dream of tuning types like you,

and you show your gratitude by scratching creases!"
—Nothing is more demanding than a woman
who has given everything. Yet, how she glowed!

"Darling," I said, "you were born to natural grandeur.
I worship you for it. Gratefully. I've prayed
to be worthy of you. It's no use:

"I am small, dull, subject to gravity, and locked
in these creases that itch and must be scratched
by those who haven't had your advantages.

"Besides—may I add?—this unimportant poem
is outbulging Doric proportion. Less
would be better than more, being more to the fact."

She glared nobility. "Are you one of mine,
and still dare to speak of unimportant poems?
The least song, clod, consumes the singer!"

"Angel," I pleaded, "not everything's an *Aeneid*—
which would make it Calliope's business, to begin with. . . ."
She flatted: "You leave my sister out of this!"

"I mean, I love you most for the sweet small
that trembles to a silence it awakens
and echoes back a ghost, when you let me say it."

"*I* let you say it! You didn't even invoke me!
You haven't invoked me in over forty years!"
I recalled my first trembling toward her and burned with shame.

"Beloved," I said, "I didn't want to bother you.
I thought I could say this little on my own,
the way it happens to us in our smallness."

She touched a chord and was herself again—
I have never seen her more glorious—then leaned down
to read what I had written, then stood tall.

"See for yourself what comes of that!" she said,
and struck her lute and was gone wherever she goes
to the silence trembling after her. In silence

I read what I had written, and despaired.
How had I dared imagine I might dare
be only what I am?
                    and yet . . .

                              and yet . . . .

A Thanks to a Botanist

Setting his camera to blink a frame
every X minutes, his lights to a forcing pace,
he shot a reel of growth from seed to sere.
The Half Hour of the Zinnia. Up it rode,
slippering toward light, sliding from swelling pockets,
unfurling flowering hands from ends of thread,
holding them up to light, then letting fall,
and threads fall: a river system fled backward
to no system. Has God seen this
His distance from all fact? A man and camera
passed the miracle of the raised usual
and brought this near-weed to motion
and countermotion. As music is—
an ecology of emotion in balance.

Could a tree grow in thirty
held minutes of such blinking, that
would be a visible symphony.

On the Orthodoxy
and Creed of My Power Mower

All summer in power, outroaring the bull fiend,
      it raves on my lawn, spewing
   into the dirty lung hung on its side.
      Myself maddened by power, I ride
the howl of how new-mown sacks-full,
      the powder bursts of gnashed mole runs,
till in one sweaty half day of the beast
      my lawn is lined to tidy passages. So

neatness from lunacy, the orderliness of rage,
      Bedlam's Eden, all calm now,
the dead beast washed in cool light and stalled.

Again and again, all summer in power at a touch,
      it frenzies. At fall's dry last
I kneel to the manual, to the word, touch,
      and pour extreme unctions that the locked life
waken when called. And do call, year after year
      in season, to the lunacy of power and am not answered.
I probe, prime, pump, and might as well pray
      to headless stone gods. Nothing—
nothing I know—wakens the power blast
      hidden in it, which is no cause of protestant
conscience to be worked out between me and the source
      but a priest-held power of maintenance.

Always at last defeated, I call, and its priest comes
      with cups, knowledge, and the anointed touch
that does reach power and mystery. The beast
      gasps, shakes, wavers deep in itself, then
roars full to resurrection, and here we come
      to cure green again, our triumph of faith!
Which is, of course, that even the powerless
      and inept may ride fit power once wakened
by the anointed man believed in
      deeper than conscience and defeat;
whole in his knowledge given, his touch charged,
      the dangerous blind beast tame in service.

To a Lovely Lady Gone to Theory

You could be the beginning of treated birds
that have changed their migration patterns.

Doctor Tinker has found the code written
on the inner wall of the egg and transcribed it.

Now he can read it, but the birds can't.
Some of them start south again every Tuesday.

When I come home too fast then, my scrambler
jamming the State Police radar,

they hear my wavelength as a mating signal
and light on my roof, drunk with a wrong nisus.

You wouldn't entirely believe what happens
in the jungle gym of my TV antenna.

Then, in a week, the weighted egg yet to come,
their new signal scrambles them south again.

Some of them. Many, I know, do not make it.
Some no longer balance on the air.

I find bodies in the driveway. Or my mower
sprays them. I no longer drive on Tuesdays

for fear of calling them or the State Cops.
I depend on cabs and on having nowhere to go.

On Wednesday, when I find you there, we are both
littered with dead birds. Is there no end to them?

They keep on coming faster than they die.
Then they keep dying almost as fast as they come.

Sometimes they sing as if all were well again.
I am tempted to doubt what I know about them. And us.

Always then it comes Tuesday again and it starts;
Wednesday, and once more I know what I know.

Sooner or later, I see, I must give you up
to the tireless Doctor who meddles with everything.

Go to him: finish building your faith around him.
I have had enough of watching us go random,

everything responding but in no sequence.

Exit Line

Love should intend realities. Goodbye.

In the Hole

I had time and a shovel. I began to dig.
There is always something a man can use a hole for.
Everyone on the street stopped by. My neighbors
are purposeful about the holes in their lives.
All of them wanted to know what mine was *for*.

Briggs asked me at ten when it was for the smell
of new-turned sod. Ponti asked at eleven
when it was for the sweat I was working up.
Billy LaDue came by from school at one
when it was for the fishing worms he harvested.

My wife sniffed in from the Protestant ethic at four
when the hole was for finding out if I could make
a yard an hour. A little after five
a squad car stopped and Brewster Diffenbach,
pink and ridiculous in his policeman suit,

asked if I had a building permit. I told him
to run along till he saw me building something.
He told me I wasn't being cooperative.
I thanked him for noticing and invited him
to try holding his breath till he saw me change.

I ate dinner sitting on its edge. My wife
sniffed it out to me and sniffed away.
She has her ways but qualifies—how shall I say?—
alternatively. I'd make it up to her later.
At the moment I had caught the rhythm of digging.

I rigged lights and went on with it. It smelled
like the cellar of the dew factory. Astonishing
how much sky good soil swallows. By ten-thirty
I was thinking of making a bed of boughs at the bottom
and sleeping there. I think I might have wakened

as whatever I had really meant to be once.
I could have slept that close to it. But my wife
came out to say nothing whatever, so I showered
and slept at her side after making it up to her
as best I could, and not at all bad either.

By morning the hole had shut. It had even
sodded itself over. I suspect my neighbors.
I suspect Diffenbach and law and order.
I suspect most purposes and everyone's
forever insistence I keep mine explainable.

I wish now I had slept in my hole when I had it.
I would have made it up to my wife later.
Had I climbed out as I had meant to be—
really meant to be—I might have really
made it up to her. I might have unsniffed her

clear back to dew line, back to how it was
when the earth opened by itself and we
were bared roots.—Well, I'd had the exercise.
God knows I needed it and the ache after
to sing my body to sleep where I remembered.

And there *was* a purpose. This is my last house.
If all goes well, it's here I mean to die.
I want to know what's under it. One foot more
might have hit stone and stopped me, but I doubt it.
Sand from an old sea bottom is more likely.

Or my fossil father. Or a mud rosary.
Or the eyes of the dog I buried south of Jerusalem
to hide its bones from the Romans. Purpose
is what a man uncovers by digging for it.
Damn my neighbors. Damn Brewster Diffenbach.

Note: In Selected Poems, *two small changes in punctuation and typography
were made, and the last line was changed as follows: Forgive me my neighbors.
Forgive me Brewster Diffenbach.*

Keeping

Put a dog in a bottle. It won't bark.
Not long. A scuba diver can't. He'll
swim up to the cork and try knifing it.
He has about thirty minutes to knife through.
Sometimes, for the strongest, that's enough.
If, therefore, you really mean
to keep things bottled, do not fill to the top.
It may be better to use no liquids at all.
Some ferment and blow the cork.
Any of them makes the bottle heavy
and the act of bottling up is itself
heavy enough. Suppose you were to spend
all your nights for years building a ghost ship
or a replica of your nervous system
inside the bottle, then filled it with water:
unless you used some nonbiodegradable
plastic junk, the thing would waterlog
and turn to bloat. If it didn't disintegrate
it would run, leaving you a dirty bottle.
It is a nuisance enough to carry the thing around
without having to watch it go dirty.
Not that you can manage without one.
You have yours. I have mine. We all
have something to put into it. Does it matter
what? We aren't given much choice.
Often, as I sense it, we have nothing to do
with actually doing it. We look,
and there is the bottle with things in it—
the dog, for example, that stopped barking
instantly its forty years ago
but starts again unstopped the instant we look
and remember there is the bottle, and what's in it.

Blue Movie

There is no cause for love in such a script,
nor even for much transition. Two girls come
mincing in crinoline to a pool. Stripped
as if on truant impulse, frolicsome
(the camera zooming in on clefts and hair),
they wet a toe and show the water's cold
by hugging one another in play, till bare
touch to bare touch tingles, and they fold

together on the moss bank and lie panting.
Their white hams, like their hamming, twitch and tremble
till teasing teases something like true wanting.
Not all of even this flesh can dissemble.
Some part of false touch touches. Thighs outflung
to camera angles, they squirm public meat
till they are tongue to crotch and crotch to tongue,
their bellies beaded wet in a made heat.

Cut to two lordly hunters in the wings,
a camera on their flies, which they unzip
with that same cueing from the first of things
that says, "No introductions, boys. Just strip."
And *ooh* and *aah*, the maidens (only started
by girlish mere contrivance) flit away
behind a bush. (No, they have not departed:
they run to show the cameras what will stay.)

The hunters and their finger-beckoned bunnies
wet one another. For such juices once
the gods came down. Now, retold in the funnies,
Leda and Europa, two coy cunts,

having been spread and had, work up to tricks.
Drooling at the boys' crotches all a-wiggle,
they beg the unwilted gods, and those rock pricks
pump their assholes while the humped girls giggle.

There, while mythologies teach them their Greek,
they French kiss like two chums at boarding school.
The camera, in a high artistic streak
flashes a hot montage of ass, tit, tool,
the kissing girls, and their ooh-la-la eyes.
Enter, of course, two other hunters then—
it's the quail season. Still quick to surprise,
the girls, still bashful, hug and cry, "Ooh—men!"

The rest is variations of no art
at easy orifices, one by one,
and two by two. A shock of flesh to start,
then bald redundancy. In tireless fun
the flesh assembles, joins, and then untangles
to start again, stretched skins of pure intent.
Their one lie is that nothing ever dangles
but outyearns Keats, in spending still unspent.

Till the director, bored to the point of wit,
works up a last touch. When the hunters go,
still cocky after twelve dives in the pit,
he shows the broads arranged in a tableau
of innocence undone by bestial rape.
Strewn like husks and separate on their bed
of swallowing moss, they sink to dark and gape
the disassembled gestures of the dead.

Differences

Choose your own difference between surgery
and knifing. Both cut. One
thinks to rejoin. Can something be made
of this difference? Defend your answer.

Now think of a surgery without intention:
here the scalpels, there the body.
Everyone is some doctor. You, too,
may as well be employed. Cut.

Is this something like a soft version
of a machine built to do nothing?
We are experimenting in the new art:
by contradicting purpose we explore,

possibly nothing, but explore,
possibly a reality, possibly a way
of inventing what a reality might be
had we some way of inventing it.

The first incision is hardest, but look
closely: you will find it already made,
inherent. Put the alarm clock inside it
and stitch. You now have a TV commercial

someone could be born to or die of.
And you? Are you my murderer
or my healer? You do know. Why else
did you set the alarm without being told?

Remember, however: distinctions
are never made wholly for their own sake.
You are doomed to decide not only
what you do but what you have done.

Yes, we chose what was already open,
putting into it what came to hand.
We must still take what attitude we can
toward what will already have been done

by the time we have time to think about it.
Were we successful killers or failed
surgeons? We will come to that difference.
And what difference will it make?

Letter from a Pander

Nothing, the cross-haired sky tells lenses,
is long. A flare behind Arcturus
reaches how far? It's over. There is
this while of days, eras, species
between novas. And that guessed
machine of bursts—does it burst, too?
Sooner ask doctoral gnats
their theory of evolution:
no scale speaks another.

"Eternal City," says the myth-nerve:
a twinge of self, long to that scale
invisible to another. "Immortal Homer,"
says Liberal Arts: a cultural eternity,
two shelves of the fissionable library.
And the infinities of the Etruscans?
—who speaks them on what scale?
what did those lovers do
to be forgotten in a lost tongue?

"Countless as stars in the sky,"
sang the rhapsode, whose naked eye
never saw more than fifteen hundred at once
had he thought to count them
the clearest night of his evanescence.
What liars poets are! Toward,
I suppose, some nerve-truth,
could they find it to say, as some—
all the good ones—have.

                  Yet fogged.
One squirt of mother's milk in the eye
and we're blinded. We suck
nonsense with love, then defend

love *and* nonsense. And say
we endure millennia—will we have learned?

Do not hurry the answer.
We are newer than newts here.
Could the race learn its scale,
a greatness—something like
a greatness on some
scale we might agree on our while—
seems possible. Remember
love itself may be madness.
But where then is the child's milk?
and the man? and millennium come to?

We may also blow ourselves out of whiles
this reasoned step by step we go blam.

Now then, toward neither nonsense
nor always, and on no scale
we are finally sure of, can you
in the soft transience and girl-dusk
of what could be instantly
your nakedness, think better access
to this moon's rising?
                              Off
with propositions, darling. I speak
a fathering disinterest. I set these lines
for a boy to say to you
toward his Now and yours
on their own scale.
                              Answer softly.
It is gentleness forgives us.
Refuse him if he is dull, but not
because he will not love you always.
Nor you, him.
                              If authorities
question you later, tell them
a dead man was your pander,
and loved you as God should.

Notes

I found myself at the conceptual tomb
of Saint Theresa with no particular
intention. I had been browsing
and it caught my attention.

At once I began to develop attitudes,
expectations. "Here I am,"
I said to myself on p. 1,
"approaching the conceptual tomb."

I sensed I might be about to enter
some centralizing experience. The presence of even
conceived absolutes is rare and powerful.
It was, I found, the absolute that shifted.

"God-rayed, god-blinded, god-taken
sub-Immaculata of the direct experience,"
I noted in the margin of p. 32,
"I feel you turning into observed data."

"Epitome," I concluded on p. 402,
"something is forever red-kneed kneeling
in chosen gravels I have no cartilage for.
Thank you for the notes I have taken."

"What's at the bottom of one pecking order
could, with intelligence, fantasize another,"
I wrote on p. 77 of a later notebook
on the behavior of lesser apes I was

imitating for data in the crotch-cramping saddle
of a tree of patience, the replacement batteries
in my left cheek pocket martyring
my unadapted metaphysical ass.

Is it purposeful, I wonder, to endure this
stumped straddle of observation posts,
the gouging of what equips us,
the banality of recorded impressions?

Hanged (experimentally) from the same tree
I held my breath to watch the snorting ecstasy
of mating hippopotami. I would have exhaled
saeculi saeculorum but for the rope

and the thought that I might hang there
unannotated—which moved me to seize the branch,
climb back to my notebook, and slip off
the parachute harness I had been faking it with.

They had plowed the ground under me. There was blood
on the female's back—even for hippos
it is a tearing weight. They have gone off
in different directions. If something

is born of this, it will repeat itself
to extinction, or to mutation and then extinction.
Between itself and whatever comes last
there will be experiences and they should be noted.

Driving across the American Desert and Thinking of the Sahara

I hang the cloth water bag from the door mirror.
A seepage evaporates. By wasting a little,
and having a wind to my going, I cool—
almost to freshness—what I live by.

I cross bone dusts to rimrock,
leaving a storm of dust in my rear vision.
I breathe some million molecules of argon
breathed by Christ once. Part of His pronunciation.

The dust of saints' brain cells is also a matter of fact.
I rinse it from my throat, let the water bag swing to the wind,
its strap tilting the mirror to sky. I adjust it
back to the storm I make and forever leave.

At sundown in an oasis of green money
girls silvery as frost on pewter goblets
smile me from passage to a made air,
time and space filtered from it.

I pay gladly for absolution
from saints' grit, rimrock, the sucking sun
burning the storm I stirred and outran
the other side of this filter we change through

from what lies open, where any man
can feel his immortalities sucked like water
to gather and fall again—and who knows where?—
till even the sun we can bear some of

gasps; and it, unchangeable argon, bone dust,
saint dust, dust of the last idea,
drift wide gravities that will—somewhere
outside dens we come to—form again.

Requisitioning

I needed 800 dozen golf balls.
I got 1700 basketball hoops.

—From an advertisement by Western Electric

There are no imperfect answers from perfect data.

Spec numbers, state of Inventory-Now,
urgency of requirement as crosshatched
from orders outstanding, credit substantiation,
promised delivery plus days of grace,
seasonal-demand configuration
adjusted for such variables as weather,
shifts in population, inductive events
(the sales effect, for example, of opening day
of the baseball season), duration of induction,
disposable income, demographic doctrine
—all must be weighed where all things balance true.

The answers are beyond us, not the method.
We describe our need, submitting it as we know it,
laboring always for the perfected input.

The Circuits then decide. We may think, at first,
they ignore our need. In time we understand
they scan that total universe of data
that is not visible to us at our stations.

We think we need 800 dozen golf balls:
good faith has been tendered, the customer confirmed,
we get back 1700 basketball hoops
and the customer phones for redemption: rains
have flooded the courses, the play has moved indoors,
gyms are under construction everywhere:

the need is for 3000 basketball hoops
with nets, backboards, brackets.
                                    We absolve him
and send up the conversion. We get back
5000 pairs of water skis—regular, slalom,
trick, a few with hydroplanes.—Of course!
the flooding has been calculated. Seepage
has warped the gym floors. Cancel basketball.

We learn to answer as we are willed to answer
where all our needs are known before we know them
and ministered to our good.

                                    There are, to be sure,
those 1700 basketball hoops, now surplus,
but before we can remainder them, Public Works
sends in an order for them as mooring rings.

That, too, as we see backwards, was foreseen.

There in the total universe of data
all things are parts and harmonies of one plan
that calls us to Itself, demanding only
our faith and our vocation to describe
fallibly, but laboring for perfection,
the need that shall be given perfect answers.

Dialogue with Outer Space

Do you?
> Yes.

> > *Do you what?*

> > > Whatever—

to the unqualified question the unqualified answer:
I do.

> *Everything?*

> > Yes.

> > > Every*thing?*

> > > > I do.

In the fact or the thought of it—everything.
What is done in fact without thought, in place of
thought. What is done thoughtfully, premeditatively
in fact. Or in thought only, to escape fact,
to make it bearable, to seduce it—everything.

And do you now confess?

> > > To myself, everything.

To the world in practical fact what is in its own terms
convenient. Except that in an anger like an assault
of honesty I do now and then not care and do openly
admit being and having been and meaning to be everything,
and to relive it.

> > *You have lied?*

> > > I recall that life.

Cheated?

> And that one,

> > *Stolen?*

> > > Negligently.

What has there been that would have been worth the time
it would have taken to steal it?

> > > *But you have?*

Sometimes there was something?

> > > At times. A trifle.

And always instantly not worth keeping.
You have killed?

Always alas for the wrong reasons.
For what reasons?

For duty. For my captain's approval.
Not for survival?

Survival lay with my captain,
the controls his. I killed because I could.
You were proud?

For no reason I have not survived.
Envious?

At times, but I have admired many.
Wrathful?

In bursts from the sperm center. A screeing
of sensation like Morse Code drowned in a cosmic whine.
Slothful?

Yawningly when that was my mood's pleasure.
Avaricious?

No.
Gluttonous?

Hungry.
Lustful?

Gladly.
What then do you believe should be done with your soul?
Erase its name and make way for another experience.
Why?

First, because it is completed and time is not.
And second?

Because it will in any case be erased.
And third?

Because, though it does not matter, eternity
would be the one experience beyond mercy.
And you claim mercy?

I do.
Why?

Because I was born.

A Prayer to the Mountain

Of the electric guitar as a percussion instrument
and of my son who wails twelve hours an animal day
in the stoned cellar of my house I sing, oh pothead baby
from the rock rolled Nine Sisters classic crag group
hit album featuring The Body Counts in "I'm Blowing it Now"
from "Don't Have to Have a Reason till I Stop."

And pray to you, Apollo, first of indulgent fathers
to weep a thunderstruck son down from the high hots
on more horsepower than God could let run
and not fear. And also as the angel who backed
The Nine Sisters to all-time superstardom
on warehouses full of gold millionth albums
and a tax structure that could have saved England.

As you watched Daedalus once watch his boy down
from a high beyond warning, watched and remembered Phaeton
trailing a sky-scar, watched the man watch,
his eyes wind-watered but holding himself to flight-trim,
balancing slow cold turns down the hot shaft
the boy plunged, and hover at last too late
over the placeless water that had taken and closed . . .

Grant us, father, not a denial of energy,
its space-trip spree above environment,
but a rest of purposes after the seized seizure,
the silence after the plunge without the plunge,
a fulfillment not necessarily final,
an excursion not from but to one another.
—I ask as a son in thy son's name for my son.

A Poem for Benn's Graduation
from High School

Whenever I have an appointment to see the assistant
principal about my son again, if they will keep
him (which no one wants to and sometimes I)
it is always at 9:00 impossible o'clock A.M.

It is at least twenty years since I made it to
9:00 unbearable o'clock A.M. from the south side of sleep.
My one way there is the polar route over the Late Late
hump of the swozzled world's chain-smoking fog.

I do not seek these differences between me and
assistant whomevers. I am confined to them. Bit
by bit the original wiring of my nervous system
has been converted to solid state insomnia.

It does no good now to reverse the leads or to try
reprinting the circuits. At 9:00 paralyzed o'clock
A.M., in the name of what can despair and still
attend, I nod to the repetitions of the assistant

whomness. We are both dull as the Mudville choir
flatting platitudes. I could by now have been drunk,
enough possibly to doze. I do not need
to be stoned sleepless to know this boy is

difficult but more possible than this assistant
who-bah brisking me to ideal endeavor, community
cooperation, and the general detritus of the white
man's burden after the wreck of the Hesperus and

the spread of the Dutch Elm Beetle, which floated
ashore in logs ordered to be the ridge beams of
Wiley's Cozy Corner Sunset Rest Motel (local
residents only after previous indentification)—

or as the bus driver between Victoria and Russell
(Kansas) ritualized at the end of the line:
"Last stop. Kindly let all those going out first."
(I have been free-associating past the assistant whom

and the blanks thereof. I might as well have been
inhaling Richard M. Nixon, the elephant's
capo dei capi, or some other maunder.) My son
is bored incommunicado. I am drafted to boredom

and must answer by name, rank, and serial number. It
ends. He, still sinus-smelling last night's pot,
goes off to his American-Dream-and-After
Seminar. I go for two eggs-up with bacon at Joe's,

garden for two hours, stir and reject the mail, and
doze off just in time for the 4:30 P.M. Great-Great-
Master-Marvel-Universe-Premiere (no Reruns ever)
Movie, which is all about carefully covered crotches.

When I wake to the trembling of the last, symbolized,
plagiarized, living-color veil, I find my son half
asleep in the other polar route chair to 9:00 inedible
o'clock A.M. "Well?" I say. "Hello, you old bastard,"

he says. So ends the trial of all assistant
whomnesses. Ours is no summary justice. We have
deliberated and found them guilty of being
exactly themselves. It does not, finally,

take much saying. There has even been time
to imagine we have said "Goddamn it, I love you,"
and to hear ourselves saying it, and to pause
to be terrified by *that* thought and its possibilities.

An Emeritus Addresses the School

No one can wish nothing.
Even that death wish sophomores
are nouveau-glib about
reaches for a change of notice.

"I'll have you know," it will say
thirty years later to its son,
"I was once widely recognized
for the quality of my death wish."

That was before three years
of navel-reading with a guru
who reluctantly concluded
some souls are bank tellers;

perhaps more than one would think
at the altitude of Intro. Psych.,
or turned on to a first raga,
or joining Polyglots Anonymous.

One trouble with this year's
avant-garde is that it has already
taken it fifty years to be behind
the avant-garde of the twenties

with the Crash yet to come.
And even free souls buy wives,
fall in love with automobiles,
and marry a mortgage.

At fifty, semisustained by bourbon,
you wonder what the kids see
in that Galactic Twang
they dance the Cosmic Konk to.

You will have forgotten such energy,
its illusion of violent freedoms.
You must suffer memory
to understanding in the blare

of a music that tires you.
There does come a death wish,
but you will be trapped by your
begetting, love what you have given,

be left waiting in a noise
for the word that must be whispered.
No one can wish nothing. You can
learn to wish for so little

a word might turn you
all the bent ways to love, its mercies
practiced, its one day at a time
begun and lived and slept on and begun.

Generation Gap

He parted a beard where his mouth might be—
an anatomical hypothetical—and said:
"Remember me, professor?"

                      "Smith," I told him,
"I forgot you the day you flunked
Freshman English for not meeting assignments
and you showed up for Soph Survey
where I forgot you with another F
and you showed up for Elizabethan Minors
and ditto and then for Remedial Illiteracy
which you did pass but with no reason
for keeping you anywhere in mind
except as so notably forgettable
that I made a note of it.
What are you doing in that shrubbery—
ambushing yourself?"

                   "How could I?"
he said. "I happen to know I'm here—
which rules out surprise, doesn't it?
I am a volunteer observer with instructions
to keep looking until someone asks
for my report."

               "All right, Smith. Report."
"Thank God, sir! I was afraid it might all
be wasted."

          "What?"

                  "My endless observation."
"You have seen?"

                "As through a glass darkly."
"Try removing your sunglasses."
"I did. It makes no difference

except that what's dark gets clearer
not brighter but deeper."
                              "You mean their eyes?"
"I mean behind them."
                        "Like looking
into a microscope?"
"How did you know?"
"And seeing your own eyelashes?"
"My own . . . ! My god, is that what I saw?"
"You realize, Smith, you have flunked again."
He shrugged. "My fate. I hadn't even known
I was taking the course."
                              "And mine," I told him.
"I hadn't known till now I was giving it."

Encounter

"We," said my young radical neighbor, smashing my window,
"speak the essential conscience of mankind."

"If it comes to no more than small breakage," I said, "speak away.
But tell me, isn't smashing some fun for its own sake."

"We will not be dismissed as frivolous," he said,
grabbing my crowbar and starting to climb to the roof.

"You are seriously taken," I said, raising my shotgun.
"Please weigh seriously how close the range is."

"Fascist!" he said, climbing down. "Or are you a liberal
trying to fake me with no shells in that thing?"

"I'm a lamb at windows, a lion on roofs," I told him.
"You'll more or less have to guess for yourself what's loaded

until you decide to call what may be a bluff.
Meanwhile, you are also my neighbor's son:

if you'll drop that crowbar and help me pick up this glass,
I could squeeze a ham-on-rye from my tax structure,

and coffee to wash it down while we sit and talk
about my need of windows and yours to smash them."

"Not with a lumpen-liberal pseudo-fascist!"
he sneered, and jumped the fence to his own yard.

There's that about essential consciences:
given young legs, they have no trouble at fences.

Memo: Preliminary Draft
of a Prayer to God the Father

Sir, it is raining tonight in Towson, Maryland.
It rained all the way from Atlanta, the road steaming
slicks and blindnesses, almost enough to slow for.
Thank you for the expensive car, its weight and sure tread
that make it reasonable to go reasonably fast.

My wife is in Missouri. She flew there yesterday
because her parents are eighty, terminal,
and no longer sure of what they were always sure of.
Thank you for airline tickets, rental cars,
the basic credit cards, a checking balance.

We doubt they can live much longer and not well.
I, too, have learned to love them. Thank you
for the wet roads to mercy on which I buy
the daughter home to the last of mother and father.
I wish I had such destinations left me.

I phoned my son at home tonight, the younger.
He has been busted for pot again. His fourth time.
There is, however, a lawyer, a reliable fixer.
He will cost me only another three days on this road.
Thank you for the road, the bad lunches, and the pleasant ladies.

I phoned my older son in Boston. He has wrecked his car
and has not learned to walk. His apartment, you see,
is almost a mile from school. He will miss classes.
Thank you for the classes he will not miss
if I ask my agent to book me a tour in April.

I phoned my daughter in New York. She is happy
but needs more voice lessons, and a piano.
She could make do with her guitar, but less well.
Thank you for everything she is dreaming of dreaming
and for the unanswered letter from California.

I will answer yes when I get home. The lessons
will come from pocket money. The piano
is waiting there in Claremont in February.
Thank you for Claremont and choices and for this daughter
and for the road I go well enough as things go.

I mean, sir, it does lead on, and I thank you.
It is not what I imagined. It may be better.
Better, certainly, than what I remember from starting.
At times, I confess, it is slightly depressing. The ladies
who are only slightly brittle and slightly silly,

but on any reasonable scale bright and admirable,
depress me slightly. But so do my own bad habits
when I am left to them freely. I do not complain:
I describe. I am grateful but imperfect and, therefore,
imperfectly grateful. It is all good enough

and I thank you, sir. If you are ever in Towson,
I can recommend the high level mediocrity
of the Quality Inn Motel just off the Beltway.
It is only slightly embalmed. It is clean and quiet.
With the TV on you do not hear the rain.

For Instance

—•—

(1979)

Machine

It goes, all inside itself. It keeps touching
itself and stinks of it. The stink
moves a wheel that moves an arm that moves everything.

Or it hunches like a fetus and spins
its own umbilicus till it sparks.
Hands off, or it sizzles your hair straight!

Sometimes it turns its back, clicks,
and spits things down a chute.
It has many ways to its own kind.

Sometimes it breaks, battering itself
and must be stopped or we shall all
be saved. But it is always stopped. There is

no salvation. When it dies, we melt it
and make another that looks different
no better but does more of the same faster.

It can disguise itself as anything
but fools no one. There is always that look
of being inside itself, always that stink.

Bicentennial

This official bicentennial arts person programming
state-wide culturals for the up and coming
year-long Fourth of July, made an appointment,
and came, and I said I would (what I could),
and she said, "Are there any other New Jersey
poets we should mention?" And I said,

"Well, William Carlos Williams to start." And she:
"Has he published books?"

                          And I saw hall on hall
of stone glass buildings, a million offices
with labels on glass doors. And at the first desk
in every office, nothing. And beyond, in the inner
office, nothing. And a lost wind going, and doors
all swinging bang in the wind and swinging bang.
And at the end of every corridor
a wall of buttons blinking data dead.

For Instance

A boy came up the street and there was a girl.
"Hello," they said in passing, then didn't pass.
They began to imagine. They imagined all night
and woke imagining what the other imagined.
Later they woke with no need to imagine.
They were together. They kept waking together.
Once they woke a daughter who got up
and went looking for something without looking back.
But they had one another. Then one of them died.
It makes no difference which. Either. The other
tried to imagine dying, and couldn't really,
but died later, maybe to find out,
though probably not. Not everything that happens
is a learning experience. Maybe nothing is.

Alec

At ninety-seven my uncle found God heavy.
"My legs," he sighed, "May I go before they do."
So small an ambition: could it be asking too much
even from a universe? It or luck

spun him the answer he wanted. Sometimes we win.
I was in Asia and missed the funeral,
all but a postcard C/O AM. EX., BANGKOK.
I bought gold leaf and rubbed a Buddha for him,

my shoes at the door, with feet left to put in them.
His name was di Simone, which is "of Simon."
He could not read, but his family legend whispered
of a turned Jew centuries back. He married

my mother's sister and passed as Alec the Barber,
though really Alessio. The gold leaf crumbles.
It makes sparks on the floor like lathe-curlings.
But some of it sticks. In time the God turns gold

and we are all one family. Back in my shoes,
I fed beggars in his name for the plains-wide days
he walked me for quail or pheasant or what comes
in or out of season. "God," he would say,

"sends birds, not calendars." He was right a while,
but calendars come, too. I must have loved him,
and did not know it till I fed beggars for him
and gilded an unfinished god in its vault.

Two for Gertrude Kasle

The trouble with the avant-garde of the Seventies is that it has
taken it fifty years to be behind the avant-garde of the Twenties.

I. The Abstract Calorie

A doughnut is no sculpture.
Or anything is, and art is

theory, the assertion of theory,
the performance of the assertion.

Theoretical doughnuts (to assert)
are conceptually edible:

to the abstract gut
the abstract calorie.

A ten ton concrete doughnut
is not a ten ton concrete doughnut.

It is an assertion about doughnutry
as a condition of the human condition,

especially that of people who assert
ten ton concrete doughnuts.

II. The Title of the Last Poem Was Wrong Again

Put a dot in an infinite plain:
it is nowhere. Frame any part
of that plain and put your dot
inside the frame: you have placed it.

Now place a second dot inside:
you have drawn the invisible line
connecting your two dots. The rest
must be learned slowly, but now

it can be—*if* you are a learner
—and *if* you are not only willing
to live it as if it made a
difference, but helpless not to.

The Sorrow of Obedience

The lieutenant ordered me to ask Abdhul
    if he would sell one of the speckled puppies
    his mongrel bitch was mothering.

As I waited for Abdhul to finish cleaning his rifle
    —he is known to be testy—I reviewed the difference
    between "puppy/son of a dog" and "bitch/mother."

Obedience, as even generals must understand,
    is no substitute for idiom. I translated,
    praying to get it right once. When, however,

Abdhul first shot the lieutenant, then slit his throat,
    then lopped his sex and threw the mess to the mongrel,
    I was once more left to grieve for my imperfections.

On Passion As a Literary Tradition

Asked by a reporter out of questions
to name the one thing most important to art,
Lytton Strachey, an old man with the voice
of an uncracked boy soprano, trebled, "Passion!"

It *can* treble. There's no one place on the scale
where burning starts. It can sound silly
and still be what it is. But what is it?
Housman said he had to be careful while shaving

not to think of poetry. A line
could shake him till he nicked himself.
If it cuts, it must be something. Not-much
can be enough to bleed for.

                       Foghorn Odysseus
(he *had* to be gravel throated) nocking arrows
like check marks down the guest list, did what he did
and said nothing about it. He growled instructions
to have the mess cleaned up, and took a bath.

Nikos Kazantzakis, in his version,
had a lot to say about his hair, like fire
up from the crotch to a black smoke in the armpits.
But Odysseus only grunted and reached for a towel.

Whatever passion is, it needn't tremble.
It slashes more than it nicks, can tear the guts
out of the nothing said. If you could say it,
it wouldn't be what you meant. It's a fire

that curls like hair on ape-man. It's mostly tiresome.
You need it like adrenalin when you need it
for getting up the tree ahead of the bear
who sniffs and decides you wouldn't be worth the climb.

—Or so you hope. Once then the beast is gone,
the sooner you stop pumping the stuff, the better
you'll find your bearings out of the fangy woods,
and go home to nick yourself on poetry.

Suburban

Yesterday Mrs. Friar phoned. "Mr. Ciardi,
    how do you do?" she said. "I am sorry to say
this isn't exactly a social call. The fact is
    your dog has just deposited—forgive me—
a large repulsive object in my petunias."

I thought to ask, "Have you checked the rectal grooving
    for a positive I.D.?" My dog, as it happened,
was in Vermont with my son, who had gone fishing—
    if that's what one does with a girl, two cases of beer,
and a borrowed camper. I guessed I'd get no trout.

But why lose out on organic gold for a wise crack?
    "Yes, Mrs. Friar," I said, "I understand."
"Most kind of you," she said. "Not at all," I said.
    I went with a spade. She pointed, looking away.
"I always have loved dogs," she said, "but really!"

I scooped it up and bowed. "The animal of it.
    I hope this hasn't upset you, Mrs. Friar."
"Not really," she said, "but really!" I bore the turd
    across the line to my own petunias
and buried it till the glorious resurrection

when even these suburbs shall give up their dead.

Birthday

A fat sixty-year-old man woke me. "Hello,
Ugly," he said. I nodded. Ugly's easy.
"Why don't you punch yourself in the nose?" I said,
"You look like someone who would look better bloody."
"—And cantankerous," he said. "But just try it:
it's you will bleed." I shrugged. What difference
would that make? Everyone's bleeding something.

He saw me duck out the other side of the shrug.
"Where are you going?"—"Not far enough: I'll be back."
I climbed the maple that grew through our sidewalk once,
and looked at the river with Willy Crosby in it.
A man was diving. Two were in the boat:
one rowing, one working the hooks. The hooker shouted.
I was out of the tree and on the bank—where I'd been

before I remembered wrong. Willy was paler
than all the time I had taken to remember,
but I put on my Scout shirt and went to the wake.
It was better than the Senior Class Play later.
I got the part as the dead boy's best friend.
When his mother and father got tired of keening for Willy,
they turned and keened for me. "Oh, John," they wailed,

"your best friend's gone! Oh, Willy, poor John's here!
Come out and play!" I could have been with Willy,
as pale as he. And when he wouldn't come out,
they sang me to him. "Oh, Willy, we bought you a suit!
Oh, Willy, we bought you a bed with new silk sheets!
Oh, Willy, we bought you a house to put the bed in!
The house is too small! Come out and play with John!"

—"Why?" said the fat ugly sixty-year-old man.
"Not that I mind dramatics, but what's the point
of hamming it up without a line to tatter?"
"Goodbye," I said. He smirked. "Well, it's a start:
at least it's a speaking part. But it's not that easy.
I won't be said goodbye to. Not by you."
"No?" I said. "Just wait a little and see

how little it costs to kiss you off, friend. Meanwhile
—hello, Ugly." He nodded. "Ugly's easy.
Easier than climbing a tree that isn't there."
"It's there," I said. "Everything's always there."
"Your lines get better," he said, "but they stay pointless."
I shrugged: "You live by points. . . ." But he stopped me.
"Don't shrug away," he said, "There's nowhere to go."

Between

I threw a stick. The dog
ran to fetch, but dropped it
and began to dig, right there
in mid-lawn, clawing up
four half-curled baby rabbits
the size of Italian sausage,
two gulps apiece to him. Then
found the stick and fetched,
and I threw, and he fetched.

Being Called

A breakfast reverie in Key West

The Resident Dispenser of Bromides
being included in the general call
after yesterday's train wreck,
packed his bags and went running
with pink pills for the maimed.

What can I offer, doctors, but the will
to be included when the call comes?
Perhaps to assist at triage? At least
to pronounce the dead?—As the one-armed
surgeon still advises at transplants.

He could not bring himself to retire
after his accident. As God
stayed on after His to advise Tillich
on the good it does to do good
after it no longer matters

to Heaven or concept. It is not
not caring, but only that we are
futile. Like the movie queen
who lost her looks but kept old reels
for private viewing (it still runs on TV),

we try to remember as if we still were
what we remember. There is, of course,
power in a name. Once up in lights
it never dims entirely. The old
glow back in it. Late-Lates return it

to the young, who call it "funky," meaning
"hey, wow!" (but at root, "mildewed, earthy").
—Always that next jargon for saying again,
half-lively, what turns futile.
Would it be better not to say? not

to refuse the offered no-help
of good intention?—Not that I hurt,
or only a little, of some imagined
honesty. I am in Florida,
a February rose nodding

over my toast and coffee in a soft
expensive breeze I can afford,
in a sun I buy daily, gladly,
on a patio under a lime tree.
There is a pleasantness. With luck

it is a kindly long trip down
from cramming winter to this basking
knowledge of nothing. And from Miami
on the make-do transistor, a cracked
wrong quaver that began as Mozart.

On the Patio

The rose at the edge of my tax structure
    sways in the breeze before twilight.
Ribbons of a scent that snares me
    whorl from it. I imagine I see them.
Like spirals flowing from Venetian glass.
    It is an air like glass I sit to.
Need it be real to be real enough?
    How real are angels?—yet Vaticans
have bedrocked on an air they stirred. As I
    have ground my hands black, even bled a little,
to turn a fantasy of a sort: the bed
    is weeded, pruned, mulched, watered.
I have paid the taxes on it. Roses
    are not for nothing. I have done
what pleased me painfully. Now I sit
    happy to look at what I look at.

When has a rose been looked at enough?
    A petal can be a shell of lemon
marked at the hinges like a pitted peach
    thumbed open warm from the tree,
but veined paler. What an intricate
    precision it takes to call a bee,
another and another intricacy veining
    to the heart of the rose—the "yellow"
as Dante knew it before hybridizers
    stained some strains red to the core
(though pinks and whites still wash to a yellow center).
    In being intricate nature is pliable.
By growing intricate enough I may yet
    come to see what I look at.
It is not easy. It is better than easy:
    it is joyously difficult. It is never

what one expected before looking. Tomorrow
    I must spray for aphids before they come,
and pay the Lawn Shop something on account.

Are accounts an offense to nature? With my hand
    I can reach six inches into the soil of that bed.
That is not nature, but makes roses. By frost time
    the tree rose must be burlapped and laid flat,
half its roots folded, the other half let loose
    then buried again in moss and old compost,
hay, if I can find it (which I doubt),
    and then more burlap (which I have not yet paid for).
But the grafts have taken. They should bear next year
    four-colored from one stem. If that,
as I believe, is a loveliness, and not
    mere ingenuity of contrivance
(which it is, of course, but still lovely)
    it is budgeted for a grafting knife, tape, wax,
cans of Miracle-Gro, a sprayer, sprays.
    Add what the root stock cost me: a time ago
I ate for a semester on something less
    than a rose comes to. Not that price matters.
Until you haven't got it. I still have,
    and note it to pay gladly for what I buy,
wanting it more than what I spend.
    As I read catalogues for their complications.
It is not simplicity I am waiting to see
    but the rose that will not come easy
and must be painstaken beyond nature.

Knowing Bitches

I was spading a flower bed while the old dog
inspected the lawn for memories of rabbits.
We used to have them till he hunted them out.

He walks the way I spade: it gets done
if there isn't much to do, but keeps pausing
to look back, or to look at anything.

I hadn't been listening to the bitch next door.
Her rave had become a background noise. It changed.
She had wormed under the fence and was coming mean

and meaning to be heard. I threw a clod
that spun her into circles. One of them
cut twice through my peonies. I gave a shout.

Ponti and his boys came running and shouting.
My boys came running and shouting. It would have done
for a race riot: *death to peonies!*

—Except for the old dog. He went on sniffing.
People and bitches are noisy but the earth's
to sniff and think about. When she broke through

he didn't even look up till she tried a nip.
Then, with no parts to his motion, he knocked her over
and stood astride her belly, his jaws at her throat,

not biting, then walked away stiff-legged
while she crawled after, belly to the grass,
till Ponti caught her collar and hauled her back

ravening at the leash. We waved "that's that."
I finished spading and sat on the patio.
The old dog finished sniffing and sprawled by me.

The boys found something else to shout about.
With luck and staking the peonies might come through.
The thing about bitches is knowing who *you* are.

Craft

A cherry red chrome dazzle
with white racing stripes
screams into my drive spilling
hard-rock enough to storm Heaven,
and young insolence sits there
honking for Benn, who's not in.

I put down my book
and press the crafty button
that works the black paint spray,
and press the crafty button
that jabs spikes through the drive
into all four wheels at once,

and press the crafty button
that blows his radio circuits.
Then move the crafty lever
that works the axle snips.
I am happy in my craft;
glad to learn ways to live.

Why does the blare not stop?
He does stop honking.
He slams into the house:
"Couldn't you hear me?"
"I have tried not to," I say, "is that
your radio or the fire siren?"

He beams. "Great sound, huh?"
Then: "Where's Benn?" "In earshot,"
I tell him. "Everything must be."
"Well, is he here or not?"
"He left for Boston this morning."
"Boston, huh? Well, tell him I was here."

"He knows," I say. "It's only
two hundred and fifty miles.
That's within earshot."
"Huh?" he says, wrinkling his nose.
I press my last craftiest button,
but the servo-genie

has shorted out. The trap door
does not open. There is no oil
in the kettle under the floor
and it is not boiling. He does
leave—in a four wheel drift
that smokes the turn-around—

without killing himself,
nor skidding into my arbor again.
That's as near a good as craft
could have worked it. It takes none
to know he'll work it out himself
some loud night on the Interstate.

11:02 A.M. The Bird Disappeared

A humming bird darning the trumpet vine
pokes in, pokes out, pauses to look at the work.
What holds it up? Yes, wings—if this is a test
for the Civil Service and "wings" is one of the choices.
But shouldn't wings leave some blur? A hue—
as propellors darken a circle of air? This
leaves no trace. It is. And now it's gone.
And somewhere an Examiner shakes his head.

Bashing the Babies

Easter, 1968

Sometimes you have hardly been born
when a king starts having dreams about you.
His troops get drunk then—they have to—
and a baby-crop sub-generation is torn
out of its mothers' screams and bashed:
orders are orders.
                    You yourself were rushed
out of the kingdom and lived to become a reader.
(I am a poet, and talk poetry. A man,
and talk chances. A son, and live as I can.
And was a soldier, killing for my leader.
And was taken by wrong parents, though their flight
is proof they could be sometimes, someways, right.)

I submit we should do or at least say
something deliberate and reasoned now
about the bashed babies. That it was they,
not we. That the feast is ours, you
its superintendent. I?—no one comes through
that infantry untouched. I am in this, too—
a father, a son, where every day
half-masted smokes wave masses, and the press
wires back body counts to the nearest guess.

It is Easter. I rise fat, rich,
hand out chocolate eggs, later drink coffee,
smoke. My dog gulps the poverty
of India heaped in an aluminum dish:
meat, egg, milk, cereal, bone meal,
cod liver oil.
                    How shall we not feel
something for the babies who could not leave town?
who were not German Shepherds? who were hit
by their eggs and burned?

A few, of course, make out:
some mothers are shrewd hiders, some have known
a trooper—the occupied live as they can—
and even a drunken trooper is partly, in secret, a man.

But that evades the question. Being neither drunk
nor presently commanded, having run out
and made it to luck and, possibly, dispassion—what
do we do now? After creative funk?
After picketing flags? After burning the first draft
of everyone's card? After turning right? left?

We are—I believe you—one another's question.
How do we ask ourselves? Half-masted purple
burns from crosses.A genuflection
dips dark, rises golden. The spring-wound people
of Godthank heap flowers
in stone arches. "Come walk green,"
say the bashing bells of Sunday. "This world, ours
shines for you questioner. What will you mean
by what you ask us? What shall we
mean by what we answer? What are we born to be?"

—I am a ghost, and talk vapors. An easy man
tossing a stick for a dog on an Easter lawn,
and talk my own babies, that they grew
chocolate-lucky. Your man, and talk you,
because we were together and got away
without being bashed, and would like to have
        something to say.

Any suggestions?—Well, have a good day.

Censorship

Damn that celibate farm, that cracker-box house
with the bed springs screaming at every stir,
even to breathe. I swear, if one of us
half turned they'd shriek, "He's getting on top of her!"

Her father, but for the marriage certificate,
would have his .30-.30 up my ass.
Her mother, certificate or not, could hate
a hole right through the wall. It was

a banshee's way to primroses that fall
of the first year in that hate-bed wired
like a burglar alarm. If I stood her against the wall,
that would quiver and creak. When we got tired

of the dog-humped floor we sneaked out for a stroll
and tumbled it out under the apple tree
just up from the spring, but the chiggers ate us whole
in that locked conspiracy of chastity

whose belts we both wore all one grated week
while virtue buzzed a blue-fly over that bitch
of a bed hair-triggered to shriek:
"They're going at it! They're doing it right now!"—which

we damned well couldn't, welted over and on
as if we were sunburned. And every night at two
her mother would get up and go to the john,
and the plumbing would howl from Hell, "We're watching you!"

Three A.M. and Then Five

"Do you like your life?"
said the ghost of God-shadow
one wisp of a night blowing.

"You woke me to ask that?"
I growled through the phlegm of sleep.
"What else would wake you?" it said.

I wallowed in that wind forever,
the sheets a hair shirt,
practice praying to no address.

Till my wife said, "Please lie still!"
So I went down into the wind
to where I had left the bourbon.

"No one knows me better," I told it.
"What do you think?"
"I may be too good for you," it said.

But it gentled, glowed, at last
whispered, "Go to sleep now."
I went back, the bed warm with her,

the sheets satin.
"Yes," I said to the ghost
yawningly, "Yes. Yes."

Trying to Feel Something

Someone is always trying to feel something
or feeling something he'd rather not, and maybe
doesn't really—though how can one be sure?

Sylvia, John, and Anne did not entirely
invent what they felt.
                    For a few hundred cash
the shrink my lawyer made me take my son to
as a first fiction toward getting him off probation
came up with "lacunae in the super-ego"
—meaning he lost his temper.
                      So did I
listening to Judge Rocksoff, that illiterate
sac of mediocrity pomposing:
"This is Juvenile Court. I am Judge and Jury.
I say this evidence is incredulous. (sic)
—And you shut up!"
                      But a thousand and some later
my son was a legal adult and was learning to hide
the pot he smoked. And a million ago Sylvia
inhaled her oven. And in another million,
Anne, her exhaust. And John went off the bridge-rail
at plus-or-minus some insolvency looking
for Hart Crane maybe. None of them entirely
invented their feeling, and two of them learned to write—
which can be relevant come time to appeal
the probations imposed upon us by the illiterate,
but does seem possibly a bit fanciful
to what I have just read, over morning coffee,
of a gent in a green Ford who last night,
having driven into the South Bronx by mistake

with the thermometer at almost ninety,
happened to hit and kill a dog, and then
forgot to keep going. He stopped to say he was sorry.

To prove which, some of the boys turned over the Ford
with him inside it, and having nothing to do,
set fire to it, and having nothing to do
and the weather too hot to do it, watched a while,
then watched the firemen come, and dumped some bricks—
not many and with no malice—from the roofs,
having nothing to do, and then it was all over
and only eleven o'clock or a bit after
and too hot for sleep, and what do you do next
but sit and invent the nothing there is to feel
about what wasn't really done in the first place?

—As I sit here in Metuchen and think to invent
something to feel about something I haven't entirely
made up from nothing—except, how does one know?
Isn't the news whatever we choose to notice?
I could have turned to the daily crossword puzzle
with nothing to feel but a generalized small sadness
for the failure of definition—which takes no feeling,
or we're enured to it, which comes to the same

except that my teachers told me and I in turn
told my students that if you want entirely
to learn to write (which can be something to do)
you must first feel something

                                    except, what is there
this side of Anne's exhaust, Sylvia's oven,
John at the rail, Nixon in San Clemente,
Anne Frank and Cinderella at their chimneys,
and my coffee growing cold, which tastes blah,
though I drink it anyway for something to do?

No White Bird Sings

Can white birds sing? An ornithologist
told me once there was a white bell bird
that rang whole tones, though only as separate notes.
"Is that singing?—sound without sequence?"
I said. "No, not exactly," he granted,
"but it is white." I granted him half a case.
This morning I heard a mocking bird again
and claimed my whole case back: no white bird sings.

I know some black poets who have been waiting
for just this image. So there it is, man:
an accident, but accidents are to use.
What else is a poem made of? Well, yes, ghosts.
But ghosts are only what accidents give birth to
once you have learned how to let accidents happen
purposefully enough to beget ghosts.

Bird song is itself an accident,
a code no different from wolf howl, warthog grunt,
porpoise twitter. It is a way of placing
the cardinal in its sconce, of calling its hen,
of warning off others. *That* code. We hear it
and *re*-code it: it sounds to us like something
we might like to try. Who cares how it sounds
to another bird? We take what we need from nature,
not what is there. We can only guess what is there.

Guess then: why does no white bird sing
to our pleasure? Because, I will guess, songsters
nest in green-dapple. There, what is white shines.
What shines is visible. What is most visible
is soonest hunted. What is soonest hunted
becomes extinct. To sing, one must hide in the world
one sings from, colored to its accidents
which are never entirely accidents. Not when one sings.

The Lung Fish

For SPOOF, *The Society for the Preservation of Old Fish, School of Fisheries, University of Washington*

In Africa, when river beds
    crack, the lung fish
squirms into mud deeper than
    the two feet down of wrath, and

sleeps, its tail over its eyes
    to keep them from drying blind, its
snout at a blow-hole blueprinted
    in the egg, too small to read,

but read. No one, the lung fish least,
    knows how long it can wait. If no
creature is immortal, some
    are more stubborn than others.

If all sleep is a miracle, consider
    (through the poking lenses
of unraveling science) what
    miracle this is: The lung fish

digests its own tissues. Its wastes,
    which are normally an ammonia
safely dispersed in water, would,
    in its cocoon, choke it. Therefore

it changes them to urea, which
    it can live with. Lung fish blood
is known to have six different
    hemoglobins—four more

than Moses took to God's desert.
    Like Moses, it has gone to legend
in Africa. It is said to be
    half fish, half croc. It is called

Kamongo there (but does not answer).
    If you cut off its head
(whether in fact or legend, and who
    knows which?) its jaws will snap

two days later. (Which
    we do know, all of us, about
what we cut off.) When
    Dr. Brown, an icthyologist

of Seattle, put Kamongo
    into a mud bottom aquarium
and lowered the water level, as God
    does at whim, this egg-born

instinctus of survival slept
    seventeen months. When it woke
in the reconfluence of time
    and whim, it seized stones with its mouth

and dinged them against the world's walls
    till it was fed—dinged them so hard
the doctor thought the walls might break
    between him and his creature. He drained it

back to sleep for time to build a world
    strong enough to hold both sleep
and waking. If anything can be. If we
    can learn sleep whole and not choke

on what we are while we learn it.

An Apartment with a View

I am in Rome, Vatican bells tolling
a windowful of God and Bernini.
My neighbor, the Pope, has died
and God overnight, has wept
black mantles over the sainted
stone age whose skirted shadows
flit through to the main cave.

I nurse a cold. It must be error
to sniffle in sight of holiness.
"Liquids," the doctor said. He has
no cure, but since I have my choice,
I sip champagne. If I must sit
dropsical to Heaven, let me at least
be ritual to a living water.

In the crypt under the cave
the stone box in its stone row
has been marked for months now.
My neighbor knew where he was going.
I half suspect I, too, know,
and that it is nothing to sneeze at,
but am left to sneeze.

I drink my ritual Moët et Chandon
and wish (my taste being misformed
for the high authentic) I had
a California—a Korbel
or an Almaden. I like it "forward,"
as clerics of such matters say,
not schooled to greatness.

It is loud in Heaven today
and in the great stone school
my neighbor kept.
The alumni procession of saints
is forming for him. Bells
clobber the air with portents.
I sniffle and sneeze,

wad kleenex, and sip champagne,
trying to imagine what it might be
to take part in a greatness,
or even in the illusion
of something-like. The experience
might deepen my character,
though I am already near

the bottom of it, among wads and butts
of what was once idea. And the last swallow.
I do not like the after-taste, if that
is what I am tasting. But this is ritual.
I toast my neighbor: may he
find his glass, and may its after-taste
be all that he was schooled to.

Roman Diary: 1951

A rag woman, half a child,
with a soiled baby, half a bundle of rags,
whined on the Spanish Steps. It takes no words.

I reached into a pocket and found something.
She found words and a tune for them.
Even the flies on the baby rose to drone

Franciscan *deo gratia*. "Hey!" said Coates,
"that was five hundred lira!" Coates had been there
over a month, was an old Roman hand

into everything but his own pocket.
"Don't you know they *rent* the babies?" he said.
"Everything in this crazy town is a racket!"

"We just ate, didn't we?" I said—
he might have forgotten: the check
had slipped his mind—"let them eat."

"Ten suckers an hour like you and she'll take home
sixty-seventy bucks American.
That's damned well more than I can spend in a day!"

He was indignant! Why would he travel that far
to walk that tight for fear
the beggars were getting rich? I started to say—

—It wasn't worth it. Not the eighty cents,
not the big boodle in the poverty racket,
not a fool's fear he'd lose what he didn't have.

"If I go broke," I said, "I'll rent a baby."

Firsts

At forty, home from traveled intention,
I could no longer speak my mother's dialect.

I had been in Italy rinsing my vowels.
She had been in Medford, Massachusetts

thickening her tongue on English crusts.
She had become a patois. What tongue was I?

I understood what I heard her say.
Could say it over and remember—ah, yes—

a taste like cooked wine-lees mushed with snow,
our winter *dolce* once. And how many years

not thought of, not forgotten? A taste
that slipped my tongue. Would I still like it, I doubt?

—•—

At times anywhere someone will say,
"Ah, you're from Boston!" And in Boston,

sooner or later, "Where are you from?"
Who in a last dark ever will call from his loss

as Dante was called, known by his cradle sounds
that spoke him to a birth and sharing?

Something still sits my tongue: that long "a"
down from the Hill, that "r" where no "r" is

I still catch myself sounding, surprised to hear it.
If anything speaks in Hell, it will be, alas,

the English Departments in whose cubicles
of lettered glass I numbered twenty years.

—•—

James Baldwin in back-Switzerland where no black man
had ever been, and they thought he was the devil,

sat a mountain, trapped in a Harvard accent,
and listened for months to Billie Holiday records

learning back Mama's cadence, ashamed to have lost
its glazed mornings, their first light of himself;

learning what had to be learned over. Like going back
to find a chimney in a wildrose thicket.

—·—

I remember losing the rifle my uncle gave me,
a single shot .22 from lathes in Heaven

to my twelfth birthday. I damned a dozen friends
I *knew* had stolen it. Till, ten years later,

Uncle—tired of his own bad wine, and clear
California gallons selling for less than it cost

to make his silty, cleared out the rack of barrels
—and there was the rifle, rusted shut, behind them.

And I put it out on the curb with the trash, and my shame
for what I had done with his gift, once perfect.

Stations

On being scared by a rattler while making a roadside relief stop out
in God's country.

An organization of clear purposes
braided hard as an Indian quirt,
the rattler coils and rings, instant
to the instant it lives.

It does not strike. Does it sense
my trembling recoil? I am nothing
to it. Not its food nor road-runner.
It warns and lets be. There's that

much mercy, thank you. What else
is it braided to? Escapes,
I suppose. The means of grace
food is to hunters. Burnt sand.

Hell must be full of rattlers, though
in a moral geography that interests us,
not them. (I am back in the car now
and can philosophize, air-conditioned

and manly in steel, glass, leather.
Next time, I think, shifting
to moral instruction, wait
for a gas station.) Meanwhile

if only to belittle fear, I ask
what God might have intended
when we imagine Him imagining
His patterns braided to venom.

Had I believed earlier and enough
I should have come in faith
and fearless to these ledges,
my hand open to the whip to prove

nothing harms saints
where all is an illuminated Godwork
of clear purposes braided hard.
What could such fangs be then

but witness to the intensity of God
shimmering through His own heat waves?
The pious beast at my feet
would have bitten its tail to omen

unending unbegun, its ornaments lavished
for the pastime joy of the making,
the Weaver's mood forever changing
on the constancy of His thread.

And having come so saint-braced
with the code of final intentions,
I need not have startled, and not run
to fantasize now a deadeye hipshot

I cannot make, leaving it headless
to thrash a ripple that washes out
under a spooked horse I, a tenderfoot,
could not have ridden to begin with.

Yet am I moralized as firmly as any
bestiary schools the pious: we are the beast
that must go when it must, but in God's
country keep to the stations.

For Miller Williams

Though Miller lives in Arkansas,
and though his back is bent,
the bush of beard that hides his jaw
like the Old Testament

is all his crop (and all his face).
When Miller parts that beard
the words come out and fall in place.
Were Miller to be sheared

there'd be a bag of wool for all.
And still the barefaced words
would find the thicket of man's fall
and settle it like birds.

There is a place in Miller's head
above, behind his bush,
where some of everything gets said
and nothing needs to push.

For everything comes out as whole
as once to Abraham,
as he was offering his son's soul
to God, there came the ram.

His father was a preacher,
a hilltop Methodist.
Miller is his own creature
but he has his father's gist

of hammering at God and man
remindfully. I doubt
he has his father's faith more than
as diction, but the words come out,

and every father, could he hear,
would do well to sit still
and listen and let down a tear,
as would have been God's will,

when God's will seemed to be a law
between the grave and shack
where holy mule-drawn Arkansas
pushed the ram's thicket back

and built a school and sent a son
who learned what he must say
of what is seen and felt and done
down to the roots of hay,

down to the pine-dark edge of sight,
down to the underbreath
that sugars sorghum and turns white
the chicken-shit of death.

For Myra out of the Album

I changed the baby, fed it, dithered
and got dithered at, with a grin added
and arms and legs pumping,
which means "Hug me!" So I hugged
small as anything is done soft.

There was that hour once in a cone of light.

Outside the cone, the dithering universe.

I have been here, and some of it was love.

Note: The original publication in For Instance *mistakenly titled the poem "For Jonnel out of the Album." The title "For Myra out of the Album" follows the corrected version in* Selected Poems.

Donne ch'avete intellètto d'amore

An elegy for the American School System

Mary and I were having an emotion.
"Thank you for having this emotion with me,"
Mary said, "I needed a reinforcement
of my identity through an interaction.
Have you accomplished a viable realization?"

"I know it was a formative experience,"
I said to Mary, "and yet, as I critique it
at my own level, I still feel under-achieved."

Mary touched me thoughtfully—reassurance
through personal contact. "Yes," she said, "I see."

"Is that susceptible of remediation?"
I said to Mary. Mary looked at the clock.
"I have a class to teach in an hour," she said,
"Do you feel you can wait?"—"Of course," I said,
        "if I must.
But frustration is always negative. May I suggest
a release-therapy impromptu now,
and a more fully structured enactment later?"

"All right," said Mary. We had a quick emotion.
"Was that an acceptable quick emotion?" I said.
"I do not wish to seem non-supportive," said Mary,
"but since you ask, permit me to stress the point
that an optimal interpersonal encounter
should emphasize mutuality.—Where are my pants?"

"Shall I drive you to class," I said as she was dressing.
"A truly empathetic response," said Mary,
"and approval is to be strongly indicated

as tendency re-inforcement in trait-development.
But might it not be even more constructive
for you to sit here and to introspect
a clarification of your personal goals?"

"It will also give me a chance to shower," I said.

"Mens sana in corpore sano," she said at the door.
"I shall be looking forward to relating fully
To your raised consciousness." And she smiled and left.

O intellect of love, may I prove worthy!

Saturday, March 6

One morning you step out, still in pajamas
to get your *Times* from the lawn where it lies folded
to the British pound, which has dropped below $2.00
for the first time since the sun stopped never
setting on it, and you pick it up—
the paper, that is—because it might mean something,
in which case someone ought to know about it
(a free and enlightened citizenry, for instance)
and there, just under it—white, purple, yellow—
are the first three crocuses half open, one
sheared off where the day hit it, and you pick it up,
and put it in water, and when your wife comes down
it's on the table. And that's what day it is.

A Crate of Sterling Loving Cups

I had gone to a freightyard auction of sealed crates.
Like parenthood, you bid, then see what you've got.
Mine opened to an idea: I was sure I knew
enough beautiful people to give them out to.

The engraving couldn't cost much: *This cup is presented*
to X-X-X from our shared transience
in recognition of at least one moment
in which the donor thought YOU ARE BEAUTIFUL.

I had the first in mind for Archie MacLeish.
I'd have to come down a notch to find a second,
but the precedent would be set. To qualify
one would have, by God, to qualify. What are we

if we can't choose example?—A local fool
printed the story with application forms.
As if one could apply to be beautiful.
In a sense, I suppose, one must, but supporting letters,

especially from one's mother, do not count.
Nor fair employment practices. Nor guide-lines
from the grinning presidency. Nor minority pickets
blatting definition from a bullhorn.

I have nothing to say to this mindless generation
that thinks to be chosen rare by filling blanks
in my fool neighbor's forms. This mail is his.
I dump the daily basketful at his door

and burn what he returns to me. Soon now
I shall be leaving for Key West for the winter.
My house there is un-numbered, my phone unlisted.
It will do no good to try me as OCCUPANT:

you won't have found me till I answer, and I
shall be busy reading. The contest is called off.
(I'm sorry, Archie. New postal regulations
forbid the mailing of anything real and accurate.)

When I get back I shall have them melted down—
or hammered, or whatever it is one does—
into something useful. I'd like a large tureen
with a matching ladle. I do make a good soup.

What's left could make bowls enough and spoons enough
to set a table for a trial guest list.
Or even for a more-or-less open house.
Soup is a good that doesn't invite ambition.

The Birds of Pompeii

—·—

(1985)

Happiness

Whenever I waken and this animal,
in glandular reprieve, curls to the sun
as glad as trout are wet, as slugs crawl,
as fledglings nest in stink, each in its own
lack of confusion outright to a success
that does what it does because it does it because

it knows no other and what works is joy
in the habit of the fitted habitat—
then I am no man but indigenous boy
bright running fields across, until the fat
and failing man after the boy stirs wheezy,
his body a separate mind, his mind uneasy.

What am I doing dabbling here in bliss
as if with a child whore who pouts for more
when I am dead? I am too old for this.
Yet, like an Easter in a candy store,
wafts of spiced angels shimmer and invite
all greed to gorge, and give it appetite.

Inanely happy, humanly out of place,
I sip black coffee and the morning news,
the collected daily rages of the race,
till everything is as bad as it always was.
And I grow serene. I have not lost my mind.
I recognize our disastrous humankind

and am in control of my own wits again
to live and die in accurately. Amen.

The Glory

If it does not return, as seems likely now,
and Heaven is a broken appointment, yet
I have attended it with all I know
of protocol. And attend. And will not forget.

My wife said, "There's an angel at the door!"
Something certainly had taken the air.
A suffusion like mountain mist with sun at its core,
its arrows drawn and blazing. So the rare

subsumes the usual. She herself had never
appeared more radiant. Our best glasses
burst in high C haloes. May I ever
be open to seizure. As a life amasses

the power of its choices. As no part of Heaven
can be intrusive. Yet I had nothing on
but a frayed robe, hadn't shaved, hadn't even
finger-combed my hair. What could I have done

to receive magnificence? With so many means
to annunciation why would the messenger come
in a sunburst before breakfast? before a man's
dentures had warmed? "Please say I am not at home,"

I begged. "If he/she/it—whatever they
turn out to be in essence—is free at ten,
I shall make it an homage to rearrange my day
to the convenience of Heaven."

                                    Since then
I have shaved, showered, dressed, and waited till the sky
clotted the trees. I have sat here needled numb
by congested hope, my shoes shined holy, my tie
precise as a Credo. Let the Glory come

if I am fit to receive it in the dress
and form that is its due. My wife and son
wait with me in their observant best. Unless
the Glory is met in ritual, there is none.

Memoir of a One-Armed Harp Teacher

Of my three certainly most impassioned students,
one lived over a disco and could not practice,
one split her calluses red and was admonished
by dermatologists, one married a psychic
and took to listening. There are always available
good, or good enough, reasons for putting by
the incompatible, the painful, the unserviceable.
One decides what is important by what one does.

But the most demanding instrument forgives least.
I, who have been the teacher of many failures,
do not blame everything on the student body.
I could have done better with both hands. Perhaps
with an unamputated mind and the heart for it.
Passion is a crippling hobby, a killing trade.

True or False

Real emeralds are worth more than synthetics
but the only way to tell one from the other
is to heat them to a stated temperature,
then tap. When it's done properly
the real one shatters.

                I have no emeralds.
I was told this about them by a woman
who said someone had told her. True or false,
I have held my own palmful of bright breakage
from a truth too late. I know the principle.

Quirks

I. Breakfast on the Patio

Not much but something. Before the morning glories
closed on the patio and my coffee went cold
whole wafts of monarchs blew from histories
that happened only to be told and retold
by marshmallow bushes in the gingerbread glade
where Snow White sleeps, half holy and half mad.

Well, one or two at a time, but over and over
surfed the last white edges as they shrank.
Fluffs so slight they do not fly but hover.
Yet I had read—in the *Geographic,* I think—
they breed mostly in Mexico, and some
in Monterey. How far so little can come!

Someone statistical has found a way
to mark them weightlessly, and has traced their skim
as far as Nova Scotia. But one that day

paid off the wind. It fell into my cream
and twitched off the last dust of its last tatter.
I forked it out to sun on my bread platter,

but it had frayed forever, having left
a whorl from some lost fingerprint in the bowl.
I spooned it for Hansel and Gretel and drank a draught
from their first Sabbath. Tasteless. But all in all
a kiss to change a frog. Then the last flower shut.
The phone rang. And the day trekked on and out.

II. That Afternoon I Remembered

There is a photo of Walt Whitman posed
with a butterfly aflutter on one finger.
The Bard as the Olympian *quelque chose*
of his own fairy tale. I, the humdinger
who breakfasted on butterfly dust with Zeus,
or Jack and Jill, cite Walt as my excuse

for letting my impulse flicker grandiose.
In meager fact, Charles Feinberg bought a trunk
that had been Whitman's, and among old clothes,
the boots Puss wore, and miscellaneous junk,
found folded flat the paper butterfly
from the finger Walt had poked into God's eye.

That's more than I had pretended. I was still
halfway into and halfway out of sleep
when I spooned up the last dust of what fell
ex machina—a notion that wouldn't keep
to be collected, a least creature touch
back through drowsy nowhere to nothing much.

Two Dry Poems

Drought

Will prayer temper the wind to the shorn lamb?
Lambs are not for shearing. Nor the wind sent.
The ewe grieves. Or it sounds like grief. The ram
hugs a small dune to windward, its cusp rent
by the jut of one stiff leg. The ripple lifts
a feather from the fleece. The dust drifts
over the dead creature where it fell.
My tongue cracks when I call thee, Israel.

Praying for Rain in a Cracked Field

Few get wet by it. Nevertheless, the fact
of declaring hope in the best words one can find
has been known to help congregations adjust to the act

of remaining dry. Nothing speaks to the wind.
The words are spoken from and for and to
the congregation. As hope is dew to the mind.

As religion is above all something to do
when there is nothing to be done. As a poem
is also a something-nothing going through

the motions of saying itself to rest, to some
knowledge of what species dreams a kingdom
and, while the words lift, has its kingdom come.

Poetry

Death is everywhere in it. Yet
it may be the most act of not-
dying. Listen when there is time.
Make time till it is still enough
to hear across water and time
the tilting band of the *Titanic.*
Nearer my Oom to Pah! The tuba
pumping behind prayer over
and over. The North Atlantic
already in their shoes. But one more
time long as there is time over
and over, the music holding
to itself, holding everything
not long, but for its while,
forever. The cornets throwing
their lifeline high and clear
over the cold bald misted curve
nowhere, the tuba pumping
the prayer behind the prayer,
an echo off the ice.

Oompah!

Going to the Dogs

The head of the German Shepherd I have now
is bigger than all the pup I started with.

He looks dangerous, and used to be. A wolf
and territorial. All the lock we needed.

It hurts to see him age and gentle creaky.
He follows from room to room to grunt, and sprawl

three feet away. Dependency needn't touch.
Even the puppy used to fight off my lap.

It wanted its own four feet on its own ground.
So we came to an understanding I have respected:

We are on one another's side but never
one another. Let be and let be.

He does grovel for food. I can remember
what cockroach jobs I stank through once for bread,

saying yessir to the mongrel bloats that paid me.
I know dependency, not to like it. It's his

—it's anyone's—universe as much as mine
by an equal ranking so long disarranged

it won't dress right again. It's my turn now
to pay, and I pay, and he takes. That's in our contract.

It will be over soon. I'll probably live
to bury him; but not whole campaigns longer.

I have grown to need him sprawled there on the floor
of every room I come to. The sound of his breathing

keeps keeping time for me. When I think I need
his love, or obedience, or whatever response

I think I need, I am happy to be shameless.
I reach for the dog biscuits I keep cached

all over the house, and he is utterly mine.
Movies and most of the women's magazines

my wife subscribes to, argue for more. But why?
We want one another for what each needs from each.

What's wrong with bribery? I'm a democrat:
I want no special privilege for myself

that can't be had, at need, by anyone else
for the same bribe, *pro rata*. I need. He needs.

Amo, amas, amat.—I have never tried
nibbling dog biscuit. It could come to that.

Right now it would be too much like eating money,
and that I have to save for my last whore

or be left to the unanswerable unanswered,
even by a gut that pretends love.

Barmecide Feast

I have been told, and have been glad to hear,
of the resonance and radiance of God's intention
arching the canopy over wakening man,
bending the branches with fruiting, frothing
first waters with pearl fishes, gilding the wheat spikes
of the bee-hymned land, uncoiling
the goose from the font of the egg, the spline
of the onion from its sheath, and welling
mint springs from deep earth, all
in a single happening more than occurrence, done
round to its doing as a wheel
spins wheels that spin wheels till all plenty
is motion from one center.

                  I spoke of this
to priests and rabbis who had understood
the feast of intention, who could quote
more calories than I could eat, and touch
the water of the wedding to wine,
the germ of birth to the risen bread of angels.

They sat me in the vortex of His bounty.
Their servants brought gold dishes beaten weightless
and steaming like censers with miraculous nothing.
They brought me goblets carved from a single topaz
brimming with radiant vapors. Seven poets

blinded by God served me described fish.
And while their lutes shook out the bleeding seeds
of conceived pomegranates, I starved supposing
my animal could range on feasted assumptions.

Diary Entry

I was in a mood for disaster
but couldn't afford much.
At the God store I counted out
my last three worn *perversos*
and ordered an ounce of avalanche.
His thumb on the scale,
it came to one grain of sand
which He blew in my eye,
perhaps to teach me something.

Which He did. A rule of thumb:
all else being equal,
I'll not be caught, not soon again,
trying to do business on His scale.

Elegy for a Sweet Sharpy

When everyone else dropped in a handful of dirt,
I dropped a Preciso pocket calculator
with Sure-Seal Everlast Batteries. Chances are
not even you will figure a way out,
but how could I not give you a chance to try?

It can't be any harder than smelling the lilies.
And I still half expect—enough to dream it—
the ground will open a crack and you'll sneak through
spinning the angles of one more everyone-wins
razzle-dazzle. Give it your sneakiest shot!

Who would not welcome proof the spirit lives?
I've put down thirty-nine ninety-nine plus tax
you'll come up Easter yet. On anyone else
that goes as a sucker bet. But win or lose,
it is longer than lilies to be remembered in kind.

An Interruption

Aphrodite phoned. Could I come over?
I was, at that moment, writing a poem about her
and how I "yearned"—that was the word—to be with her.
Could I interrupt the writing? I begged off.

She hung up in a huff. I cannot believe
she will be calling soon again. So be it.
There comes a season for saying only what's possible.
I ask nothing but to say it right, if I can.

It is when nothing comes to mind that "yearning"
gets sucked into the vacuum. I knew
all the void next day of bone revision
it is a vacuum, and that nothing fills it.

It is madness to say no to her for a word's sake.
Madness to scrub for the word and not find it.
She, too, is mad, but if I do not sit
and "yearn" to say her—always that word again—

she may find she is not there when she thinks to call.
She probably will not think to. I will wait.
She will learn in her own vacuum, if I tire,
how Goddesses, above all, must be said.

Domestic Sonnet

The cat gave birth to an adder. The dog died
of roughing up the unknown. The mynah bird
denaturalized him in three undeleted
expletives. The mice, if any heard,
stayed in the walls of instinct. Something
must speak for nature when everything else here
bends off its genes.—The last Easter duckling,
for instance (the other five died), that drinks beer
and quacks for pretzel bits while Father Dust Pan
follows it brushing up the dotted lines
across everything. (Splatterfamilial man
in his turd-stippled castle of dotty scions,
as much changelings as brood.) But what the hell,
it works somehow, never entirely well.

Socializing with a Creature

"Creature," I said to the blue jay nesting
in the ilex bush at my window,
"why so visibly? You are more than welcome,
but do you suppose our midnight skunk,
our garbage can raccoon, and our ghost possum
are blind, earless, noseless, and hate eggs?"

She sat to her doing. I was under glass
in another continuum. When her cock came,
a twitching snarl in his beak, I still
did not exist. She flicked and the tangle
straightened down a surviving reflex.
And he left and came. And she sat.

l think I have seen two eggs. I have not trimmed.
The nest has blurred into new growth, not enough.
Do they really know what they are doing?
They could at least have started
a foot down into the thick of it,
or higher, in some crotch of better instinct.

"Creature," I said to unnatural foolishness,
"some forty or fifty thousand years ago—
whatever years are—my egg-sucking parents
gave up instinct to take a chance on reason
and lost their balance forever. You, I had thought,
are still spun on the original gyroscope.

"Or are you, too, tip-tilted? Is the tilt
something we knocked? Have you, creature,
taken example from us? I can believe
in an idiot presidency. But a stupid nesting?—
Ronald Reagan could have done it better.
I'll lay you grubs to turds you're hatching candy

"for my wife's denatured cat. And be glad to lose.
Or even to hope you'll make it through the night
if I can heap our garbage in your favor.
Do you think there are make-up courses in evolution?
If birds no longer know about being birds,
why not nest on the hardtop and be done?"

Corpus Christi

Once a year in some self-secreting Lent
or Carnival, Gulf lobsters form in chains
and move in ritual. Divers who saw that pageant
went down with cameras and lights. But what explains
the unknown to itself? In a slow, dim,
endless sequence from a Fellini film

I lockstep a last bottom beyond sleep
behind my father moving behind his father.
No way to make a living. But we keep
an appointment with ourselves. If we do not scatter,
sooner or later a shrimper's drag will find
our line of march. It may come from behind,

ahead, or across our linkage, but it comes.
Sometimes it misses. Sometimes it gathers us in
to the feast of something else. A thousand domes
on a thousand roads to a crab-clawed Vatican
are its told buoys. We move under and through
the dark and drift of whatever it is we do.

An Apology for a Lost Classicism

I was writing a *trentesei* for the boat-people
when I ran out of chocolate mints and lost rhyme.
There is no conspiracy against creativity.
One yet notes art must be a precise encounter.
It is possible only at the fullest confluence
within the circumstance of concept and creature.

When I ran out of chocolate mints and lost rhyme
I was alone in grieving for my failure.
The boat-people, adrift in their killing freedom,

cared nothing that the demands of art are total.
They were too busy bailing, and thirst lacks style.
I was alone in grieving for my failure.

There is no conspiracy against creativity.
It is the conceiving creature, not the concept,
falls belittled by its creature-craving.
And also that one's subjects, caught in their agon,
refuse to see that they matter only as instance,
dismissible witnesses to perdurable form.

One yet notes art must be a precise encounter.
I had been nagged from an epic sympathy
by nothing more than the teasing of my sweet tooth.
A stupid insistence. Yet concept must not be riled.
Can be shaped only by undistracted energy
freed of all need to provision its own survival.

It is possible only at the fullest confluence
of analogy and order, whose traditions
testify to us that ideal Greece herself,
our cradle of concept, was raised to the noumenal
on the bones of slaves, whose otherwise pointless *soma*
subtended the *neuros* of the master encounter.

Within the circumstance of concept and creature
I tried to make do with Oreos. But there are
no substitutes for essence. Perhaps tomorrow,
when I buy another paper and infinite mints,
I shall fix these drownings from *incidence* to *summa*,
and need not grieve alone for the boat-people.

Leaving Longboat Key

In memory of William Sloane, III

The drawbridge blinks red, yawns. The airport limo
gnashes its teeth and waits. A blown gray scarf
of pelicans flutters high across the water,
then wavers over the edge. A white convertible,
top-down in the glare outside our air-sealed windows
bursts chrome grenades in the heat shimmer. I look,

then look again, having glanced once and by.
—It's true! An instant can be! You are tanned,
a cultivation of tan. What a basking grave
you must have drawn at the lottery! I know
I mustn't speak. That there are rules. But thank you
for what still visits.

                    —The bridge rings and swings shut.
Half-naked fools in a white sloop wave beer cans,
two egrets almost hand in hand above them.
We groan and glide. The light, and everything, changes.
A spangled man in a programmed tan turns right
on a white coral road into the sun.
I touch my inside pocket and feel my ticket.

At Least with Good Whiskey

She gave me a drink and told me she had tried
to read my book but had had to put it down
because it depressed her. Why, she wanted to know,
couldn't I turn my talent (I raised my glass)
to happier things? Did I suppose it was smart
to be forever dying? Not forever,
I told her, sipping: by actuarial tables

ten years should about do it. See what I mean?
she hurried to say—always that terrible sadness.
Well, maybe, I said. (This is good whiskey, I said.)
But ten years, plus or minus, is not much time
for getting it said—do you see what I mean?—which leaves me
too busy to make a hobby of being sad.

A Damnation of Doves

Where did doves perch before there were telephone wires?
I think they evolved in cemeteries. The dead
might tolerate them. They don't have to hear
that eternal cooing. Yes, Mohammed said
Noah's dove is in Heaven, one of the ten
creature-saints so honored in the Koran

for having done God's will. But tell me how
it managed to break that branch from the olive tree.
What did it use for pruning shears? I know
it was miracle time back there in deep B.C.,
but who would have been offended had a hawk
with a proper cutting beak been assigned the work?

Were there a hawk in Heaven, I'd pray it down
to prune these flocks. That wouldn't interfere
with the balance of nature. And once the work was done
I might manage to rinse this cooing from my ears
by singing hymns, or kneeling to TV,
or whatever does for ritual in A.D.

Apprehendee Then Exited Vee-hicle

"Sorry," said the cop who had shot me,
"you know how it is with mistaken identity."

I knew. I have never really liked my looks.
I have never really looked as I really am.

Not as I know I'd look if I turned real.
"We all have something to regret," I said.

"Please inform my estate that my last thoughts
were all of her—and, of course, Internal Revenue."

"Hold on," said the sergeant, "there is still the matter
of six expended bullets to be accounted.

You know the regulation shooting form."
"Only four hit," said the cop, "and he's not the man."

"The form is the form. Six fired is six expended.
You will report accordingly. Now to the charges:

He led you to think he was someone else—what's that
but impersonating intent, obstruction of justice

by misleading an officer, and accessory
to damn poor shooting? Read him his rights and book him."

"You have the right," said the cop, "to remain silent . . ."
"Thank you," I told him, "I feel it coming on."

Mutterings

I may have no more to say to my left arm.
We used to be friends till it took to hanging out
with a cervical pinch. Now it sleeps all day
or wakens to needle me. When I try to sleep

it raises foolish questions. I do not care
to be interrogated by my components.
Especially when I am trying to sleep.
I don't mind honest questions—what have I to hide?

(Forgive me: strike that question. It took this race
billions of lives to code me devious.
I will not dishonor my making by pretending
not to know father and mother. I meant to say:)

What can I have to hide from my left arm?
Except what my right is doing? And it is blameless.
It is helping me write this poem. For better or worse,
a poem is exactly where the devious ends.

(Forgive me again: by the split tongues of my people,
there is no point past lying. All saying's bent
to its own forked words, our own, not of our making.
. . . And yet to lie some halfway to a truth! . . .)

But on with it. When my sacro-iliac
blathered me off my legs a neurosurgeon
harangued them back to me. There can at times
be a winning argument, if only a jargon.

Another logician hanged me from a door
in a slip-on gibbet: a noose from chin to crown,
a counterweight dangling like a corpse from a pulley.
He called it traction. I sat and discussed it with Plato,

stretching myself to noumena till I retched.
I am tired of the mutterings of my own sub-surfs.
I howled them down, a pink pill under my tongue.
But my speech perfected, I had nothing to say.

And what now? Sometimes I look down at my knuckles.
Are they thinking to pop a question? I'm bone-weary
of being nagged to death from inside. And still
the questions come, and one of them is the answer.

The Limits of Friendship

For Joe, the sullen bastard

Dinner was duckling with tangerine sauce
and celery remoulade. He would not eat.
The wine was a classic Chablis from Wenty Bros.
He would not drink. Nor did he care to meet
the girls in the hospitality suite. "If you're flat . . ."
I offered, wallet in hand. He just sat.

Soon he began to stink. That made me nervous.
There are limits even to friendship. "That's dead enough,"
I said to the Armagnac and called Room Service
for a body bag and deodorant sprays. It's tough
to lose a friend, but pointless to hold on
after everything possible has been said and done.

Friends

A man from a house not far who rode the train
I used to take to New York till I stopped going,
though we still nodded, and later I learned his name
when my wife met his, and once when we were throwing
an even-up munch-and-swozzle open house
they came, and a month later invited us

to his country club, so later we asked them to mine
and were next-to-last one year in the member-guest,
and became, as you might say, friends, or from time to time
had drinks, or when we were out with someone else,
and they were, we bought their table drinks around,
and they waved and came over, and once, having eaten, we found

he had picked up our check, so we sent champagne,
a magnum, and stopped for a glass with them because
we were doing well, or at least feeling no pain,
which led us to think we were friends, and there certainly was
no reason not to, and none whatever to know
more about him except as a good Joe,

—died, omitting flowers for the cancer fund,
so we sent a donation card and went to the viewing,
and Tuesday morning to Woodlawn, and stood around,
and a decent later we phoned her to say we were doing
nothing much and how about dinner, but she
had been disconnected, had moved to Marathon Key

we were told by the agent who had sold the house
and sent her the check. So on our way to Key West
my wife tried to phone, but couldn't, and had to guess
she had maybe remarried, so we drove the rest
of the way to our condo and said a big hello
to all the people there we think we know.

Audit at Key West

You could put silver dollars on my eyes
and say I died of inflation. Strictly speaking
this isn't expense but unexpendability.

Like being a crooked cop: I was last night
on late TV, but woke here unnegotiable.
How am I to sell out when no one's buying?

Somewhere a naked boy without bus fare,
and with nowhere to go, is bending over the bed
of a girl about to inherit her own body.

There are always investment opportunities.
But who breaks even? I might have been born rich
but couldn't afford the taxes. Perry was.

He died with a silver dogtag in his mouth.
In the cleft of his teeth. Everyone, Doc said, has one.
Eddie could spit like a B.B. gun through his.

But I don't want to start over. Suppose I could
spit bullets—what's a target? Last month in Frankford
we took flowers to the graveyard. A hundred names

spoke from their stones but we knew no one in town.
The house had been sold to strangers. The world is divided
into those who managed to buy in time, and their children

who can no longer afford to and must wait
for their parents to die. I'm willing in no hurry.
I have a book to finish. I'll put the contract

in the childrens' names. If there are royalties
—sometimes there are—at least I'll die a tax cheat
thumbing my clogged skull at the sons of bitches.

I carry a donor's card for what's left over
that could be any good to anyone.
If anything is. I doubt there is much left,

but the eyes aren't bad. Someone might still see something.
I'll leave a picture in them.—There, my Cuban
neighbor's fighting cock posed on the roof ridge,

a bomb of lit red fuses sputtering day.

At O'Hare

"You!" we chanted together. "How long has it been?"
"Twenty-five years," I counted. "A long time,"
he said, edging toward definition.
We stopped at a bar and edged closer.

But he was flying to Bozeman; I,
to Tallahassee. You can edge as close
as a second drink, a third. Sooner or later
it is time to start another twenty-five years.

Longer now. This time forever.

January 1, 1973

If calendars are made of square holes, something
slipped a round-peg late March morning
into this opening. The dog and I
sniff wet-loam stirrings. I look for crocuses,
glad not to find: we're wrong enough already.

By way of omen, we're one second late.
Astronomers ticked it on to the last minute
of the dead year in their fussbudget accounting
of our eccentric orbit. As if one tick
could reason us to time. And yet in time—

in time enough—all seasons would drift loose
but for such finicals; as they did once
in Julian time, the Vernal Equinox
precessing through the centuries toward July.
We can learn to be more accurate than we have been.

Even corrected, we're wrong. If that tick's true,
morning rings false to feeling. A New Year's Day
smelling of wet roots? Let the dog run it
as if gifts were free. I thumb a forsythia bud:
is it too soft for this side of sun-shadow?

I mean to know. I get the pruning shears
and cut a stem to see if it will force.
Indoors again, I put it in a vase
and the vase on the mantel still decked out with holly,
the last dry scratch of Christmas. If this starts,

let the dog shed.—I may myself go bald
on gullied lawns—and leather apples shrivel
in the stubble of all season gone to random.
Just as it felt inside that astronomer's tick
between the year and the year, where Zero is.

Starlet

Tilda Trimpett and her seventh stage name,
having substarred and been left unconstellated,
OD'd on heroin purer than her habit
and died on her bed in a locked cube of mirrors.

When they found her twelve days later her toy poodles
had eaten a breast and part of a bicep to bone,
the exact details confused by liquefaction.
"Ah, Jesus, a sorry sight," said the cop the landlord

had called to turn the key for his lost rent.
The studio vouchered fifty-two dollars (exactly)
to get those damned let's-hear-no-more-about-it
poodles veterinized to their toy rest.

Secondhand Charley, in return for the mirrors
and the advertised bed, incinerated the mattress
and made a deal with Mendelsohn Morticians
for what they billed as "disposal cremation service."

Now and then on the Late-Late Milkman's Re-run
Tilda still smirks through portiers in Macao,
or sidewinds through tramp crews and sotted skippers
in the inscrutable haze of Singapore Sadie's.

Is there point in telling a ghost she couldn't have made it
in a thousand slinky crossings? She was not more tinny
than Harlow, say, or Grable, or Joan Crawford.
Tilda died knowing it's all in who you know

but made a wrong connection and went to the dogs.

January 2, 1978

My neighbor and his children are shoveling snow.
Or he is shoveling and they are rolling snowmen.
There is barely enough snow for shovel or play
and the sun will melt it, but for some, ambition
is an isometric and autotelic flexure.

Possibly, the sun will not melt the snow,
though my clogged gutters are already pelting
a rain on the back steps. If tonight turns cold,
my driveway may slick dangerous. Let it.
I shall be off to Key West in the morning

with nothing to care about anything until April.
If the house is here when I get back, I'll try it
for one more year. But it belongs to me,
not I to it, and I'm tired of working for it.
With any luck, a generalized inattention

should hold it together about as long as I
will hold together, after which someone else
can do as he likes with what I leave unshoveled.
I don't imply my neighbor is wholly an ass.
He is only young enough to want to do something

even when there is nothing. I sympathize
with most mistakes. One reason for Key West
is that doing nothing is an art form there.
And the fishing is good—precisely, I think, because
I don't much like fish, and don't care what I catch.

Obsolescence

My wife, because she daydreams catalogues
and never knows what to give me (though, ah, she does!)
ordered for my birthday from Future-Now
an Omni-Function Digital Synchro-Mesh
Alarm-Chime wrist watch that beeps *Caro nome*,
(also available with *Vissi d' arte)*
though when I set it A.M., it beeps P.M.

I showed pleasure in her pleasure, and because
I have always accepted her choices, but when our son
seemed avid to borrow it, I let him keep it.
I know time only as a circle. Star time.
Rotation and orbit time. Dark and lit as tides.
He reckons it as a series of linear blinks.
He may be inventing a new code of perception.

Because I am obsolete, I cannot read it.
Or do not care to. Why should the old hound
stop sniffing and sprout wings? What is the scent
of the upper-air? I am rooted nose to ground,
circling and tracking memories of deep earth.
I nuzzle day and night on a dirt dial,
glad to die thoughtfully, in no hurry.

And to will him the many-tabbed side functions:
push for day, date, month, horoscope sign,
omen-computer, saint's day, point in orbit,
life expectancy, gross national product.
It could set its own alarm. By sonar scan
it could activate a robot whose eyes blink
the identity code of the successor species.

It could set itself to say: "At the sound of the chime
all circuits will be charged with induced Hebrew
in time to hear God announce the next illusion."

—I look out the window far as my father went
beyond the bird-limed sundial, and hear my son
—or something—ping in a solid state cathedral
programmed to project a 4-D God.

Credo

I asked the doctor who had pronounced me dead
to check his instruments. He owed me that much,
if only to escape my second opinion.
"What are you?" he said, "an enemy of the state?
My instruments have been federally certified."

I assured him I did not seek the overthrow
of force and violence. "I am a combat veteran,"
I said by heart. "I have received the vision
of the rose that blooms in bombsights. Yet I am pledged
to go on matching systole to diastole

more or less one to one. In sacrament.
By the power of which I beg to ask in doctrine
with the First, Fourth, and other revealed Amendments:
Can what you are trying to measure be measured by
what you are measuring with?"

                              —"Please spell your name
as you wish it to appear in the statistics,"
he said, gold pen in hand above a scroll
engraved CASE CLOSED. I spelled. "There is," he said,
"an optional blank marked *Comments.*"—"I fantasize,
therefore, I am a fantasy," I avowed.

Even reading upside down, I recognized
he wrote an elegant hand. I will not argue
with elegance. Too rarely are we offered
that opulence more than wealth. "Amen," I said,
assured that every error must yield to style.

Useless Knowledge

To trap a chipmunk put a bait of nuts
in a glass milk bottle and lay it on its side
by a bush or a stone wall you have seen it favor.

The chipmunk will pop through the bottle neck,
fill its cheek pouches as if with Heaven's bounty,
and find there is no escape from the gifts of God.

By creature law, the chipmunk is forbidden
to spit from its mouth the nuts of life, once given,
until they have been brought to holy storage

in the ark of the winter covenant, and rather
than break commandment, this fluff of life will starve
with its pouches full and more food in the bottle.

A Vermonter from the bone-scraped ridges told me
that one starved winter's end he bottled a chipmunk
and filled the bottle with water to force it out,

but the thing drowned. He had to smash the bottle
to boil that ounce. He had no other bottle.
He said he starved through mud-time sick on roots

and curls of fiddler fern. He could have been lying.
Or stretching. But only God knows all His saints.
Something is always fevered by hard intention

for less than the wholly edible. These are notes
for a sermon on the sanctity of survival
to teach that life is not worth dying for.

But have we a choice? I have flown my hot missions
in a flammable bottle when I could have been grounded
on permanent garbage detail.* What's wrong with garbage?

544

those fragrant, bursting calories of revulsion
yardbirds can fatten on?—and damn the stripes
that jammed us lockjawed in the bottleneck!

All this may be as relevant as sainthood
inside a cyclotron. I haven't seen
a glass milk bottle since home delivery stopped.

If I could find one in an antique shop,
I could trap a chipmunk I would have no use for
and wouldn't know how to free without some danger

of killing or maiming it when I smashed the bottle.
This feels like something I know too well already.
It is useless knowledge, but what other is there?

*In the 73rd Bomb Wing aircrewmen who lost their nerve were no good to their
crews and were allowed to ground themselves, the enlisted men losing their stripes and being
put on permanent garbage detail. In my ten months on Saipan, only two gunners in my
squadron chose to go on the garbage truck. I never knew anyone to mock them. There were
times, in fact, when I envied them the certainty of their stinking survival.

Finally That Blue Receding Sphere

It is only after
you have hesitated too long
that the angel comes.

"No more time?" you say.
You are determined not to whimper,
but is this fair?

The angel shrugs.
"I am not exactly news," he says.
How drab he is!

"But why now?"
you insist. No whimper.
You are indignant with reason.

"Don't," he says,
"be tiresome." Yes, he is right.
You still wish

You had not hesitated.
"I love you! I love you! I love you!"
you cry back,

but the world
is receding faster than anything
can answer.

Where have you seen
this dwindling, blue-misty bubble before?
—TV, of course!

Among infinite rubbish.
What else makes him so drab?
At least you have said it.

Poems
of Love
and Marriage

—·—

(1988)

For Judith

Waiting
Seems to be most of everything.
It keeps growing. It can stretch
past seeing and being and still
be only starting to start.

It ends where you begin.

Morning

A morning of the life there is
in the house beginning again
its clutters in the sun

babbles and sways and tells
time from its sailing cribs. Enter
three pirate energies to murder sleep:

the bed rocks with their boarding:
a fusilade of blather
sweeps the white decks. We're taken!

—Good morning, sweet with chains.
We win all but the fight.
Do as they say—I'll meet you here tonight.

I Was Not Sleeping nor Awake

I was not sleeping nor awake. It was
that hour that beaches from the change of sleep:
a touch first, then a shove, and then the wash
of a tide's leaving. Flotsam, still half deep
in the sucked edge that is half sea, half land,
I lay, still blinded, and put out my hand.

It was my hand awoke me. It reached out
and touched where you should be and you were gone.
I sat up, still half nightmared by some thought
the sea had not washed back, half man again
and half a creature still—and you were there
before your mirror, doing up your hair.

I sat back and, a chuckle in my head
the sea has never heard, thought how a priest
might die and, being certain he was dead,
wake to start heaven, and find himself at rest
on nothing, and unwitnessed to that deep.
—Had I been lying out there in my sleep?

my collar turned? my sermon on my cuff?
and all my service canceled to a truth?
Who knows what sleep connects? I'd had enough
of floating edges and the idiot froth
that bubbles out of sleep. I had arrived
back to some manhood. Back to where we lived.

It was a morning of a house in time.
My hand lay empty, but the fact is full
as any made our room as bright a tomb
as heaven is preached. And if its preachers fall
to nothing, why that's nothing. Not to us.
When I woke, all I thought would be there, was.

Darling

Some have meant only, though curiously,
to believe on evidence. Othello for one,
I suppose he took himself too seriously.
He certainly hadn't much talent for having fun.

No one sets out with intent to become ridiculous.
I used to do push-ups, shower,
read into the lives of the great victorious
and of significant losers. I was sure

something was sure. That there was continuity.
Start with a stone: chip away
whatever is not Apollo—the perpetuity
of Apollo, the locked interplay

of thing and idea— and there you are.
Like Venus from foam, David from a slab
of impossibly cracked Carrara,
soul and its given name even from this flab.

In some sense Commandants
drill time to, this tumescence
of bags and flaps doubling over my pants
is my own doing. But are intentions

nothing? It was done while I wasn't looking,
or looking at something else—at a stone
from which I imagined I was chipping
all that wasn't idea. And down

to gravel too small for anything but bangles,
and too dull for that. I grow, alas,
even tempered. It is ambition jangles.
We have given and taken mercy. Was

a god locked in the ruined stone? I have come
to a continuity of feeling. It is like leaving
a hung jury and coming home
not guilty, not acquitted, not quite believing

there is a possible verdict, but gladly free.
It is true I made a mess of it. I meant
a shape that eluded me.
I could say I half repent

but that's a dramatic luxury beyond my means,
a handkerchief for Othello. Let us
stay bloodless in love, and not in separate scenes
but in one slow thought gentling to forgiveness.

The Aging Lovers

Why would they want one another,
those two old crocks of habit
up heavy from the stale bed?

Because we are not visible where we dance,
though a word none hears can call us
to the persuasion of kindness, and there sing.

A Love Poem

I have labored for her love.
I could not hide my failure.
Nothing could hide my need.

I believe she is grateful.
I bribed her with dances.
A joy still skims.

It makes no difference
except to me. Except
as she is moved to be kind.

I think she is so moved.
We have taken habit of one another.
I can imagine no other mercy.

It is too late for flying lessons.
The bifocal clouds blur.
I am too heavy to skim

what swims before my eyes.
Darling, forgive me,
I can no longer beat time.

One Easter Not on the Calendar I Woke

One Easter not on the calendar I woke
    and found I had survived ambition.
There was nothing I wanted more of. Time, yes,
    if it was given. An unfinished thought
to add a page to, not for the thought's sake,
    but for the pleasure of writing the page well,
if I could write it well. Or if not, for the trying.

My dog, having already outlived averages,
    sprawled at my feet, happy enough to breathe;
sometimes to raise a rabbit ten years dead
    and give chase, but wake foolish. When it happens
I give him a dog biscuit. There should be something
    after such dreaming. We sit and discuss
how fiercely the world ran the first of us. He knows
    there is always a second biscuit, waits for it,

then groans back to his rug and tries again
    for what can be raised from sleep. His habit is rabbits,
mine is pages. All night in the tomb
    the ghosts of pages walk—white revelations—
but when I wake still clutching the one I caught,
    it is always blank. I roll the stone away
and try to remember, and cannot, never enough.

But it is enough not to be back in the tomb.
    Come Easter one may try for no reason,
for the sake of trying. Because it is Easter.
    Because the sound of the old dog grinding biscuits
calls women singing to the well, and camels
    from the unspeakable sands, heavy with bales,
And bit by bit the page begins to fill.

A Man and a Woman
Might at This Moment

A man and a woman might at this moment,
in the complexities of rut, be begetting
a child, who in the gradual unevent
of journalistic history, by bed wetting

to patient training and a loving, slow instruction,
may some day read a poem and be changed
into himself in ways he could not have known
by reading the papers. This has been arranged

since the first glyph became an ancestral letter
and started to say a word. Or it took place
without arrangement, if random will do better
than the inevitable. In any case,

what that child does raising words from a page
to cadence and reverberation blows out
ministers, generals, and all the rage of passion
to waken a resonant place at the core of things.

Done for the Doing

Ape-handed, too bungle-knuckled
to hold a brush true
to the eye, and the image beyond it—

ham-fisted stumblier than any
instrument will sound
imagination from, or even feeling—

I am driven to scrawl words,
leaving printers to set
the spilled worms of my hand.

Sometimes I read what the printer did
and dare think, "yes," but don't
care. It's over by then.

This is for the doing. Done,
it's dead as the Chopin
my wife played years ago

and never went back to, though
a presence once. Like being.
And then, having been.

Love Sonnet: Believing Part of Almost All I Say

It was a day that licked envelope flaps.
My hundred-roll of stamps solidified.
So much for communication. Is there perhaps
a self-improving technology? I tried
storing my writing things in the freezer (a tip
from the Anxiety Editor). All stuck
in a half-twist endless plane, a Moebius strip
flypaper logo of perpetual guck.
Since I was glued to my desk, I tried to write.
What might it not be like to have something to say?
In another continuum I stayed up all night
inventing a language I cannot read today.
But is time legible? I think of you.
No message. No medium. But still something to do.

Poetry

All poetry up to the present time
Has been a tribesman's venture into rhyme.

A praise of home, yes, but at heart a boast.
The animals of one valley, of one coast,

Of one belief—one people chosen right
To shine alone among the sons of might.

And if the tribesman wandered in exile,
That was his expiation, for a while.

A soul among the soulless, he was still
The braggart of one village on one hill

Unmatched by any Alp; and of one pond
Deeper than any seas that lay beyond

The call of fishermen in his one tongue.
However many lands he moved among

Odysseus lived at home, and Homer sang
To homefolks the glory of that gang

Of raiding roughies, and every clanging strophe
Meant only, "Folks, our boys have won the trophy!"

Freshman Sonnet: Success

Success in life is when one has a goal
and makes it. If, naturally, the goal is a good one.
Money is useful, but no man would alone
be successful just financially. Man has, also, a soul.
Therefore he should plan his life for more

than possessions, though they are a very fine thing.
To succeed, you should help the other fellow, and bring
a ray of cheer sometimes, and know what you stand for.
Success is to God, to country, and to community.
It is finding pleasure in giving pleasure.
It should also have diversity as well as unity.
Success is not one thing but it runs through life.
Success in marriage, for example, in large measure,
depends, of course, on getting along with your wife.

Dear Sir

Dear Sir: We haven't met but my father knew you
and spoke of you often, implying an intimacy
on which I perhaps presume. Soon now I too
must make a more formal visit, just as he

knocked, seemingly sure of being received.
I enclose a book I have written. It's mostly questions
he, perhaps, could answer. He once believed
we might communicate. Are there provisions?

If so, would you pass it on to him? If not,
I beg you to forgive the intrusion. We
are uncertain of the protocol. The thought,
whatever the form, is all of courtesy,
and in the hope of hearing from him again.
Till which, with your permission, I remain

etc., and for a while his son
and in some sense I suppose yours also—

John.

Late Peaches

Whatever this is of nature, the peach tree
is in three parts: the trunk and limbs
are a nerve-form in black jade; inside that form,
curled shavings of burnt metal hang in balance,

and among those irid balances the peaches
are a red-buff marzipan. I do not know
what form this is which is equally
sculpture, metal lathe-waste, and boiled sugar,

but these mornings I look out at the peach tree,
and when the mist has dried to diamond points
I see my mother, dried to starch and parchment,
drift from the day like milkweed, pause,

and there, as if she meant to light a candle
inside each peach, stand by the tree and be.

Back

On the mountain after Vesuvius
in what I have left
of the dialect I started from,
I sit with unknown cousins.

Except for the Alfa Romeo
nosing the mayor's house,
a fluorescence of TV reflected
in the glass of an open door,
and the monument to the war dead,
we could choose at a whim
what century we sit to.

We have red wine, bread, *peccorino*,
fave, and garlicky olives before us.
A table set in Pompeii.

Below, at the cliff of San Barbato,
the bearded saint, is the stump
of the Lombard tower my name
came here to in the tenth century,
having crossed the Alps with Alboin
four hundred years earlier
as Gerhardt.

       I explain
what I have read. They nod respect
that I have read a book.

How he came clanging in 568
allied with Saxons, the conquered
Gedidae sworn to him. Rosamund,
daughter of their murdered king,
his slave queen till 572, when—
all of high Italy under his axe—
she cut his throat to vengeance
for having had a wine bowl
made from her father's skull
and forcing her to drink.

. . . They know the blood of history.
They drink it to fable
and fill the glass again.

A cousin asks, "Was there
a son of that marriage
and was he king after?"

"No. Cleph succeeded.
A chief of another line."

He sips. "It is better so.
But who was Gerhardt?"

. . . An unknown axe-clanger,
the name changed to Gherardi
on his sons' new tongue,
and that to Cerardi
by the time it reached here
some Lombard lordling later,
and again to Ciardi
as, round the mountain
at San Potito Ultra, my fathers
spoke it eight hundred years
till its last sound there
moved to Dover, New Jersey.

They nod. They, too, have names
from these same marches.
Though not my mother—none
she could follow. De Benedictis—
"Of the Blessed"—a church gift
to a foundling at old doors,
its shadow mother
gone to forgotten sorrows, the name
already a thousand year line
in the one furrow it lived from.

On father stones we sit drinking.
The men have bad teeth and loud voices.
Their hands are knobbed
as if by broken knuckles. Haft hands
axed from harder wood than grows here.
The women stand behind us
where the Greeks left them.
When the bottle is empty
they bring another.

We talk.
Enough of history. It has been said.
We say nothing. Nothing is necessary.
The wine, the food, the sitting to it
is what there is to say. We say
the wine is good. *The peccorino*
is good. And what olives! Here,
taste this spumanti that I made
myself. Could you buy
a wine like that? Could you?

I am fat, soft-handed,
and have tickets in my pocket—
a choice of oceans.
I am from the miracle
great-uncles left for a century back
leaving them what land there was
to break the knobs of their hands on.

I am of my wristwatch
as they are of sun-up.
                    We talk.
The women the Greeks left
bring us wine and twilight.
Indoors the children watch TV
and the image shimmers
on the glass of an open door.
The mayor's son waves and goes by.
It grows dark.
We sit in whatever century we are left in.
The wine is good. The *peccorino*
is good. The *fave* and the olives
are good.

Echoes

Mother and father knew God and were glad to explain.
I was happy to listen. Love is a conversation.
When I said yes, they agreed, and I agreed.

They touched me when they said. I understood
the touch before the words. There is nothing to argue
in being held closest. Had God been a lion,

I would have done my best to grow a mane,
and to catch lambs to leave dead on His doorstep.
I could catch nothing. I was left to believe.

Love echoes love. I said what I was told
for my pleasure in who told it, for my need
to be held in the telling, apart from true and false.

The conversation is over. Given a choice
between Dante and a stone over two graves,
what shall I read? I have no mother and father.

They have no God unless I remember one
as part of a conversation I forget
except that it pleased me to be touched in the telling.

For Myra, John L., and Benn

If poets are evidence, let's begin with the fact
that most of ours have been father-bent-and-bound.
If you run to poetic form, I have some contract
to haunt you forty or fifty years beyond
all I can care. But it's you will have to worry
how I behave when I'm out of attention. Sorry.

I hope I don't go boo when you open doors
to closets I'm not in. Not that I'd care,

but I'm moved to now for then. I remember floors
we romped on giggling. You got up from there
lighter, faster, freer. But how can I tell
what you will choose to remember? I know too well

we are already strangers. I am an old
doddering sad-sack with his head in a book
till the book closes on it to all-told
nothing-much. Poor stuff for a real spook,
though you can always sniff the bourbon jug
to summon up a glimpse of the old boy's mug.

If ever I was impressive in your eyes,
and for every time I shouted *no dammit!*
in the finals of self-defense, I apologize.
I hope to slip out the door and not slam it.
I hope I will not rap back with more to say.
I hope I was never too much in your way.

Midnight

He runs in his sleep, snaps, leaps up, without
the rabbit, slipped out of his mouth again. He stands
foolish to the fact. *Where is it?* He lays his snout
across my knee. I show him my spread hands.
I haven't got it. Some of them get away.
He whines—that killer beast. And since I am
God and benevolent, I pay him back
with the last cracker and the bit of ham
left on the plate. Not prey, but at least a snack.
He understands enough theology
to gulp it and curl back to hunt his sleep.
If there are rabbits, that's where they will be.
Who knows? His next kill may be his to keep.

It Is for the Waking Man
to Tell His Dreams

sommum

narrare vigiliantis est.

—*Seneca*

In the stupors before sleep
I used to hear in my head
poems at which God might weep,
each line an angel's bread.

They died awake, their myth
like the gold plates, God-bright,
Moroni brought to Smith
and then took back each night.

I wired my bed and taped
those oracles. Come day,
I heard: "The cat escaped
when Jesus ran away

with Mary's lamb, no doubt."
—And then a snore,
until the tape ran out,
the dog scratched at the door,

hearing its master's voice.
It is a dog's mistake
to wagtail and rejoice
because the fool's awake.

Sounds

Sin for my Master's sake
whispers the Snake.

Carve me erect on Zion
roars the black Lion.

Repent for what I am
quavers the bloody Lamb.

I am for love, for love,
mourns the soft Dove.

Mankind will keep me fat
chitters the sitting Rat.

I'll always be around
whimpers the Hound.

Not if my tusks can gore
grunts the sharp Boar.

(I had a dream I can
hardly explain, says Man.)

This Moving Meaninglessness

It is, I think, a robin tinkling away
in the hemlock shade of noon heat.
It is not much song. Listless as the day
it slurs three, and repeat, three and repeat.

The grass needs cutting. The day lies flung in a shade,
half into the ground. The tinkling skips a beat
then stops. Has all of it been played?
It was not much song but may it repeat and repeat.

A Trenta-Sei of the Pleasure We Take in the Early Death of Keats

It is old school custom to pretend to be sad
when we think about the early death of Keats.
The species-truth of the matter is we are glad.
Psilanthropic* among exegetes,
I am so moved that when the plate comes by
I almost think to pay the god—but why?

When we think about the early death of Keats
we are glad to be spared the bother of dying ourselves.
His poems are a candy store of bitter-sweets.
We munch whole flights of angels from his shelves
drooling a sticky glut, almost enough
to sicken us. But what delicious stuff!

The species-truth of the matter is we are glad
to have a death to munch on. Truth to tell,
we are also glad to pretend it makes us sad.
When it comes to dying, Keats did it so well
we thrill to the performance. Safely here,
this side of the fallen curtain, we stand and cheer.

Psilanthropic among the exegetes,
as once in a miles-high turret spitting flame,
I watched boys flower through orange winding sheets
and shammed a mourning because it put a name
to a death I might have taken—which in a way
made me immortal for another day—

I was so moved that when the plate came by
I had my dollar in hand to give to death
but changed to a penny—enough for the old guy,
and almost enough saved to sweeten my breath
with a toast I will pledge to the Ape of the Divine
in thanks for every death that spares me mine.

I almost thought of paying the god—but why?
Had the boy lived, he might have grown as dull
as Tennyson. Far better, I say, to die
and leave us a formed feeling. O beautiful,
pale, dying poet, fading as soft as rhyme,
the saddest music keeps the sweetest time.

An invention meaning "merely human," from the Greek psilos *(mere)
and* anthropos *(man).*

Obit

After he retired, for something to do
he took up high-stakes gin, an exercise
in pure chance where always the same few
winners chance in and out. The surprise
is he didn't break sooner. At sixty-nine
he started a new business, an end-of-the-line,

make-it-or-go-on welfare venture. But there
he knew what he was doing. At seventy-four
he sold out to Conglomerate Money to Spare
for seven million and stock and once more
was looking for something to do and tried
collecting stamps but it bored him and he died.

His children were grateful. His widow, who had feared
they would have to sell the house and take a flat,
memorialized him with a tomb they shared
after twenty-three years of finding out
it doesn't matter how much you get through
day after day when there is nothing to do.

An Overthrow

Under the cottonwoods
by the iron bridge
the dead man lay to summer,
his mouth
a bomb of flies,
his eyes the color of meat
in a face faintly iris
through a film
dust-gray as pigeon wings.

Fred Armbuster was with me.
"Ned Forey!" he said.
"We'll have to remember exactly
how we found him
and how he looked
and we'd best touch nothing
till the sheriff comes."
And because it was necessary
I remembered exactly.
But the coroner
certified natural causes
and I was not asked.
It was no longer
exactly necessary.

But when I was twenty-three
on this same grass
under the cottonwoods
Ned Forey's Ava and I
rolled naked as fish
one summer night.
I remember her
taken and warm, her thighs,
like a nest for moonlight.

I forget her eyes.
I could not see her eyes.
But her flesh went down
from breast to ribs to belly
in three falls
the color of moon and honey.

And for these reasons
I know this place exactly.
Ned's gone from it, and Ava
is married in San Diego, and I
walk past it with my daughter,
wishing her moonlight.

God

I used to be good friends with God, but He
kept playing practical jokes—above all,
when I was sleeping. It is hard to be
easy as friends with someone who can call
Huns from wallpaper roses, or set fire
to brick sidewalks, or leave you without pants
at graduation. Talent is to admire,
but uneasily. You feel you're taking a chance
just saying hello. Well, it's been years now
since we had much to say to one another
and I sleep easier. I don't even know
these nights what my dreams are doing. My mother
used to ask, Do you see Him? And I'd say, I do.
But she's dead. And who is left to lie to?

Matins

It froze in Paris last night and a rag doll
that had been a woman too tattered-old to notice
turned up stiff on a bench. So the police,
who spend least on the living, paid to haul
nothing to nothing. She could have lived for a week
on what the bureau will spend on paper work;

for a year in the sun on the autopsy fees,
filing, storage, crating, and putting down.
What keeps us wrong? Dolls cannot walk around
all night on shredded legs. And in a freeze
everyone else walks faster. Dolls need to rest,
then can't get up again. It may be best

when there's nowhere to go, to fall asleep and be there.
I have only the *Times* item of squeezed prose.
It was a cable in by night-rate, I suppose,
when everything's cheapest and easiest to bear
deepest under and a sea across
to my breakfast table, still anonymous.

But told. And not to nothing. Every child
risked from love and held must be put down
to walk itself away, and turn by turn
become another. This dirty doll unheld
by any arm is the one altar piece
from which mad Francis learned to be a priest.

Elegy for a Cave Full of Bones*

—Saipan: Dec. 16, '44

Tibia, tarsal, skull, and shin:
Bones come out where the guns go in.
Hermit crabs like fleas in armor
Crawl the coral-pock, a tremor
Moves the sea, and surf falls cold
On caves where glutton rats grow bold.
In the brine of sea and weather
Shredded flesh transforms to leather,
And the wind and sea invade
The rock-smudge that the flame throwers made.

Death is lastly a debris
Folding on the folding sea:
Blankets, boxes, belts, and bones,
And a jelly on the stones.
What the body taught the mind
Flies explore and do not find.
Here the certain stood to die
Passionately to prove a lie.
At the end a covenant's pall
Of stones made solid, palpable,
Moves the victory to the sea,
And the wind indifferently.
Hate is nothing, pity less.
Angers lead us to digress:
I shall murder if I can,
Spill the jellies of a man.
Or be luckless and be spilled
In the wreck of those killed.

Nothing modifies our end:
Nothing in the ruin will mend.
If I moralize, forgive:
Error is the day we live.
In the ammoniac caves of death

I am choked for living breath.
I am tired of thinking guns,
Knowing where the bullet runs.
I am dreaming of a kiss
And a flesh more whole than this.
I am pondering a root
To destroy the cave-rat's loot.
I am measuring a place
For the living's living grace.
I am running from the breath
Of the vaporing caves of death.
I have seen our failure in
Tibia, tarsal, skull, and shin.

Mistakenly published in Echoes as "Elegy for a Cove Full of Bones."

A Traffic Victim Sends a Sonnet of Confused Thanks to God As the Sovereign Host

Please do not think of me as a surly guest.
I ate, drank, read, roamed, romped in a few
of your lavish oceans. I suspect you knew
I was bouncing your daughters—may they be ever blest!
Then, suddenly, crossing the street, I was under arrest!
I can hardly believe it. Nor can I get through:
not one phone call. I have tried to thank you;
my prayers keep coming back to me misaddressed.
I feel my case has been blown out of all proportion.
Tomorrow I am being taken to death row.
For jaywalking! Law is its own contortion.
It insists on holding me incommunicado.
But I'm still free to scratch a thanks on the wall
To say you host a sweet world, all in all.

Thinking about Girls

All day I have been thinking about girls.
All the girls I have really thought about,
my daughter excepted, are grandmothers now.

This morning at half-past-nothing on Delauncy
I met a grandmother I had thought about once
as something else—because she was something else.

We said our surprises and had a cup of espresso.
She asked for Sanka but they didn't have it.
"It will keep me awake forever," she said. Some cups

do that, but must be drunk. We sat and drank.
I stared at her wrinkles that had wrinkles in them.
She stared at my flab as if to find me in it.

We kept trying to remember. Then looked again
with no cause to remember, but only to see
there was more ruin than there had been Rome.

The stones multiply in dividing to nothing.
I sat in the enlarged city and watched the young
dance by us on Delauncy in plate-glass time.

A single blink froze us a millennium dead.
I studied us one instant from my own death.
Then left some money, kissed a ghost we know,

a dryest peck, then blinked it off in a taxi
to a street below two temples one on the other.
Then back to today in which I thought about girls.
Which came to nothing really. Where it began.

An Old Man Confesses

I have no cause, and God has not confessed
what purpose time serves. I am bored by death.
I have its cave-damp glowing in my chest.
I have its stone-dust muddied on my breath.

Carrion. Age is carrion. I disgust
even the flesh I am. And where's the priest
so clean of bloat, so justified and just
he could strip back such skins and find a feast?

Get him away, half-woman as he is
and smelling of old cupboards. I am gone
into a mud deeper than the abyss
down which his adolescent angels shone

like energies. Ah, what a world that was!
I could have leaped to Heaven on my own legs!
Now bats hang from the rafters of the house
and blow-flies bore my flaps to lay their eggs.

Only my tongue stays fast. Rattle and clatter.
As if it signified to say and say.
Maybe saying it is the heart of the matter.
Or just that it costs so little to prattle away.

Say the old fool went prattling to the end.
All words taste better than the gas I sigh.
And while words last me, I can still pretend
that I may phrase some reason not to die.

I doubt it. Let these words do: "The old sot
lay at his last gasp in a rotten hide
and ran words like a leakage, till the rot
inside the fact had drained. And then he died."

A Successful Species

Horseshoe crabs, which are not crabs at all
but hardshell salt-marsh spiders, made their way
under the froth-edge of the littoral
and back to the marsh precisely on the day
and night and noon of the animal flood tide.
The females puddle their eggs and males ride

over the pools in clouds of sperm. They are
a successful species. In part, perhaps, because
they are food for nothing in particular.
For nothing, in fact, till they die and decompose
into the generalized stock of the salt broth
fans and tendrils reach for under the froth.

Success of species, as it is understood
by species watchers, is measured by how long
they manage to come ashore timed to the flood
of their breeding stew. The flight continues; the wrong
leak back into the salt soup, whereat
they fail their tidal appointment and that's that.

Our colonial founders, who may have seen straighter,
called it the horsefoot crab but could not explain
its boney tail which, as discovered later,
is mostly for turning upright once again
when a gust of surf flips it half-defenseless
onto its back. Nothing in nature is senseless.

Except perhaps what thinks to scriptualize
what it has lost adaption to; for instance,
this creature's infallible timer. We surmise.
It is. And seems prepared to go the distance.
To nowhere in particular, to be sure.
But the one success of species is to endure.

Sea-Birds

Sea-birds on a windy carousel
spun spinning holidays offshore
one of the days the world went well.

The battleship *Potemkin* wore
a flag of weather at its top.
It passed those birds and passed no more.

The *Big Mo* had no time to stop.
It pushed the weather to the East
and there its shells began to drop.

The wolfpack's commodore had at least
his own skin to think about
and once torpedoes were released

he dove and could not look out
to see the sea-birds' holiday.
Given the facts, there's room to doubt

he would have seen them, anyway.
And when the depth charge made a mess
of all the tricks in which he lay

the sea-birds, full of this success
at being happy in the blow,
beyond perfection or distress
never saw the navies go.

In the Audience

A sparrow lights on wisteria,
jitters like a wind-up toy,
spins feathery propellers,
blurs off.
        Last night June bugs
flew bomber missions, crashing
against the porch screens
as I sat reading.
        This morning
I went crabbing, and one
that fell out of the pail
crossed the sand like a dismembered
magician's hand limbering.
I could have caught it back
but there was more to see
than have. It closed its fist
on sea-lace and disappeared. What
a good act!
        There is this
world I go to. Everything's
in it. I watch changes,
waiting for what things
turn out to be, not always
good, but there, and always
changing.
        I shall be sorry
when the show is over.

December 13, 1979

Three squirrels wound and sprung to this remitted
December day chase tumble tails on the lawn.
They must be winter-sure in the elm, permitted
by a plenty in its boles. There's not one acorn
on or under the oak. They go to go.
But why this lawn party? I think they know

the dog is old and stiff, his monster slacked.
His ears tense toward them but it takes four
deliberate heaves to get his hind legs cocked
as if to spring. And what shall he spring for?
There is no energy after energy.
He quivers feral, but then looks at me

as if I might serve them to him in a dish
like Greeks godsent to the ogre. Of my guilt
that I have uncreatured a world to this mish-mash
whine and quiver half-down in the silt
of a sludged instinct, I toss him a soy bone.
He settles for my bogus and settles down.

And the squirrels spin, almost as if they flew,
to the top of the split shake fence, into the spruce,
across it over the roof, over the yew
and into the hemlock thicket, fast and loose,
as fast as easy, around and around again
in the feast of being able to. Amen.

Stations
of the Air

—·—

(1993)

And Thy Mother

In my first dark before the world began
God said: "John, John, nothing but tears are true.
Kneel, beat your breast and weep to be a man.
I have your father and I'm watching you."

My mother, deviled soul, wept on His side.
And I, who found myself with three to please,
Lowered my head and beat my breast and cried
To be God's pink-eyed sheep with calloused knees.

Let sons honor their mothers. Mine was mad
as a Sicilian passion. Wolf and lamb,
she ripped with her own teeth what flesh she had
and fed it, poisoned, to her young. I am

The son of deaths to honor. She meant well,
and died for that—for God, her man, and me.
I housed her death in my first tear that fell
Sweetly for someone else. Then, washed and free,

I smiled and the world began. What a long case
Follows forgiving! What *was* that dark about?
Those voices?—I can listen long as trees
And nothing happens but the world whirled out.

Storm

The morning after moonsnow, the bone dunes,
like a mathematician's imagination strewn,
lay saltdead in the sun; their worldless crescents
an invasion of ultimate functions; not sent—
a man could swear to that at a glance—but blown
from the unresembling sense of a last unknown.

Then bit by bit as the sun waxed back toward man—
toward what we think the world is—one by one
that many-faced enforcement of anarchy
began to sweat. It was possible to see
the ultimate changing back to continuum.
It was possible to think of being at home

on whatever world it is. It was possible
to think in similes that would do, or all
but do. So a snow face at the window
began to look like an apple broken in two,
the tears of juice clinging to the quartz flakes
of the split halves, that being how apples break.

And how the impossible mends—which is to say,
how it grows back to resemblance in a day.

Food Notes

Asparagus is back in all its glory.
Cut on the bias to two inch lengths, quick fried
(with salt) in a wok by Amy Nugatory,
then parboiled (still in the wok) then set aside
(or on low-low) and covered till the steam
of art and mystery have fulfilled the dream

God sent to Amy of his green thumb plumbing
the stirred and watered day of his first making
to steaming essence. Such is the told coming
of the glory of asparagus. She, partaking,
gives forth the glory. The first ecstasies
of sibyls tranced in visions, prophecies,

and exaltations of soul-swelling praise
exult from Amy's rapture and God-gloss.
I, too, taste. Hm, not bad. I raise
an almost good chablis by Wendy Bros.
and drink to the body and blood of holy prose.
Any glory is something, Heaven knows.

And the glory follows. Driving, the windows down,
where Newburgh spills untreated essence
into God's Hudson, I sniff. One waft makes known
it is the promised season. Pure, intense,
as the soured manger hay breathed forth His story,
asparagus is here in all its glory.

This Morning

This morning in installment property
I rose at five, shaved, showered,
had orange juice, decaffeinated coffee,
and dry toast. When the cat meowered
I opened a can of hashed guts and fed it.
When the *Times* arrived in a cellophane bag I read it

more or less glancingly to no conclusion,
folded it back in order for my wife,
rinsed the breakfast things in some illusion
that there is a proper order to a life,
and sat to the sunrise in the breakfast nook
with a stack of monthly statements and the check book.

By seven I was paid up. Had an angel come,
he (he? she? it?) would have found me blameless,
still slightly scented, and precisely at home
with the lawn maintenance men at work in the green seamless
vista and to the well-kept property line
to the unannounced angel. Till, at half-past nine

my wife comes down. I pour her coffee and juice
and explain the checks are written and ready to mail.
She turns time's pages. There can be no excuse
for ignoring the details of how badly we fail.
Having finished she says, "What will you do today?"

and I do not flee the question but turn away.
I go to my desk and arrange clean paper, pen,
neatly next to nothing whatever. Well,
there's the crossword puzzle. But I finish at ten,
and still no angel. There is the mailman's bell:
perhaps he will bring me word. But I sort through
his strew of announcements, and back to nothing to do.

Christmas Alone in Key West

That Christmas alone in no difference really
in the sun I needed, I strolled by the tree
and picked a star-fruit, but it was dry, mealy,
and puckered the tongue. Nothing is free.
Certainly not freedom. Selkirk, demented,
insisted on being left. He, of course, repented

when the ship was making ready to haul anchor.
He begged to change his mind, but captain and crew
had bloody well had enough of his cantanker.
Some ship would water there in a year or two;
or if not two, five, and if not five, ten.
And maybe his manners would have improved by then.

Mine have already. Yes I could take a plane
and dodder kindly, while everyone is busy
wrapping and running around and wrapping again
while I sit stranded in bliss watching TV
or I can watch it here without catching a cold.
The barest desert island is growing old.

And that one you have to take whenever you go,
with nothing to do and nothing to retell.
I'm not inclined to wait around for DeFoe
to pretty up the story. He spins it well
but Crusoe is marzipan. What I have to say
is there's no reason to go and less to stay.

An Elegy for Moral Self-Assurance and Country Virtue

I could have plowed the slim forty and back eighty,
had I been taught, and sweaty proud come in
to strip on the well-rock while Katie,
happily scrubbing my back, turned woman,
delaying supper, since she, too, had to wash,
while I slopped the sow and gave the layers mash.

I could have learned to like it, I suppose,
and to teach the kids their likewise aforesaid.
We'd have had to be careful about shucking our clothes
once they popped in, but we still could whisper in bed.
I could have stood a man on my own land.
There's legend for it. I think I understand

What the gaffers are saying forever and again,
watching haircuts at Roy's starting at seven
till the last head's done. It has been made plain.
The good life has grass roots. I guess I could even
have walked old Betsy wide and staked a spread
and gone to Jesus in a mail-order bed,

honored the community, decently planted
by my professional sons mouthing a hymn,
their Avis doors ajar for the enchanted
airport to better mousetraps, with the slim
forty and back eighty, the whole spread,
on shares to Jimmy Lee Shaw and his boy Fred.

The Logician's Nocturne

The fundamental characteristic of matter
is its existence. Nothing can exist
apart from its particular properties.
Properties, in existing, interact.
In interaction, particles form cells.
Already creatures, these particular cells
colonize their properties and evolve
to a reflexive cognition. Reflexive cognition
characteristically recognizes matter
in the forms of what perceives it. So perceived,
we are the assumptions of our means of perception
insistently reflecting our reflexes.
And why strain to see through them? At such ease
as creatures shape to in their shaping nests,
I tend the environment of your undressing
to rondures from whose eloquences I learn
reason is prattle till you come to bed.

A Sleep (by Rousseau)

The deer stand black by water, the Lion's head
    comes golden from its cave, the snake goes down
like a brook through ferns. A man who may be dead
    lies face up in the puddle of the moon.

Night is the dream about him. Burning birds
    brush at the breasts of cloud, their colors gone
to black and gold. The trees come down like herds
    to drink beside his sleep. Later the lion

sniffs him and leaves, the deer go trembling by,
    the snake spills past. Out of a cloud, Orion
opens and closes on a chalky sky.
    The trees fall back and back into the dawn.

Loving You Is Something to Do

Imagine having forever nowhere to go.
Or having all the tickets to everywhere
with no good reason for either going or staying.

Isn't that how to be dead in no easy lessons?
Loving you—do you see?—is something to do.
It makes everything else an inactivity.

Time on my hands is dead weight. It slips through,
and I am left emptied by another death,
until you smile and make me busy being.

Call It a Day

On a day I long since started
to remember from my death
(which may be forgetful),
we drove to Vermont, the kids
a back-seat nest of shrills,
or shouting cow-counts, Judith
a pearl-flesh glow beside me.
We stopped for every ice-cream
and, on Bread Loaf mountain,
at the Homer Noble Farm
with schnauzers, horses,
flowers to the end of the world,
and Robert Frost signing their books
"from a friend." And after dinner
with him and with Ted and Kay,
on the long lane back to the road
to our house, just at sunset,
Benn said, "Oh, look!"

and there stood a doe in the rut,
as nervous-still as dapple,
and we sat and watched,
and it stood and quivered,
then disappeared. And we drove
across the shadow of everything,
carried stuff into the house,
started a fire, and Jonnel said
from a face fire-dappled as our doe,
"What an all-over day!" And Myra:
"I am going to remember everything
forever." And Judith smiled.
And I did. And we started to.

Lines for Myra to Grow To

A line drawn straight from my heart to your heart
where you lie sleeping and I sit idle from you
would pass from tissue to a rubber kitten,
on through an oilskin dog, into the wall,
the dry pauses of plaster, then out through my bureau
just missing the .38 among the socks
in their turn-back rolls, like buns, then over the bed,
through the O.E.D., on through another wall,
and back to tissue again.
                              There is no moral
but to place objects in their true disjunction.
—But see, I have said "true."—So there is a moral.

Carving the Turkey

Meleager, one of Jason's heroes, died
in an average hero-storm of blood and guts.
His sisters, being abnormally raucous, cried
so loud so long Apollo changed the sluts
into guinea hens. *Pot-rak!* In that death of song
even the name of what they became went wrong.

Meleagris gallopavo ought to have meant
"Meleager's peacock," which will hardly do
for guinea fowl, and which, in bastard descent,
came down to the turkey, though no one, to start with, knew
it was going to be discovered in a place
called Massachusetts. Once you start to chase

hysteria round itself, what have you got
but that bird that squawks around in ever-decreasing
concentric circles to vanish into its butt
with a sound like *pot-rak?* Do not look for reason
in the language-gnomes who in *hystera,* the womb,
found the organ of *hysteria.* This Tom

is the misnamed loser at everyone else's feast.
It was Carolus Linnaeus, I think, who chose
his slant and noisy name. The bird at least
keeps a glazed silence from crop to pope's nose.
So peace and plenty may come even from din
if only by error. Is everyone served?—Dig in.

Mr. & Mrs.

It came bone-time. The metric of ten thousand
alarm clocks striking them from sleep
brought them a tired end from love. A brook of mist
poured from a steaming spring. Crows tore open
the stiff film of the sky. Pines and the stumps of pine
watched them from ages they had forgotten. The grass
was full of entrances to be avoided.

They sat stiffly and said little. Strolled sometimes
as far as the road and back but their feet maundered.
They limped back to the porch chairs and sat again.
Everything shook when they touched it. They learned
to touch little and to be reminded of less.
It was sure soon and no matter. Their dread was only
which would be first, and each prayed for himself.

Statement

Our fathers, whose art was Heaven,
honored be your names. Our kinship shown,
your need be known on earth
as it were in Heaven. Show us this way
our doubtful breed, and forgive us
our truth's passing as we forgive those
whose truths pass against us.
And example us from evil.
For yours is the kindling, and the pyre, and the storied
endeavor.
                    —A man.

The Rite

I wrote the president
a letter never sent
of which he took no note.
So in the booth today
I stood alone to pray
as if I had a vote.
As if the government
keeping the covenant
would count it and rejoice
that one man kept the law
and, bowed in holy awe,
surrendered to no choice.
Arrayed like candle flames
the levers with no names
glowed there under my thumb.
I pondered yes and no
the same, then turned to go
with no viaticum.

A Gray Spring Morning

I can just see from the attic window
how the jay in the dripping hemlock
rises from her nest
to shake off the weather,
then settles back upon her eggs
the tropic of her breast.

How many small lives there are
at a roof edge! In the pin oak
a gray squirrel nibbles the buds

that were not there yesterday.
A grackle one branch away
sits by, looking and not looking.
Wary, but sure of himself.

The hemlock is nearly solid
against the sky. The pin oak,
barely open, barely traces itself
against the total gray.
Below me, under the pin oak, lilac
raises a green cloudhead,
wet and abundant.

Under the lilac,
in red and yellow rain-hats,
children raise their faces
and shake rain
into their laughter.

If God is leaning
from any sill of Heaven
he could ring himself a praise
to out-echo all arches
by looking here.

Last Rites

A jay slants into a dogwood cloud, then out,
a dart through the many-tiered banks of blossoming light.
I invite it and the sun to my funeral
to be my last thoughts down as I mean to think them,
now for then, at these stations of the air.

Title Index

First Line Index